I0810270

IMAGES of America

PAWTUXET
RHODE ISLAND

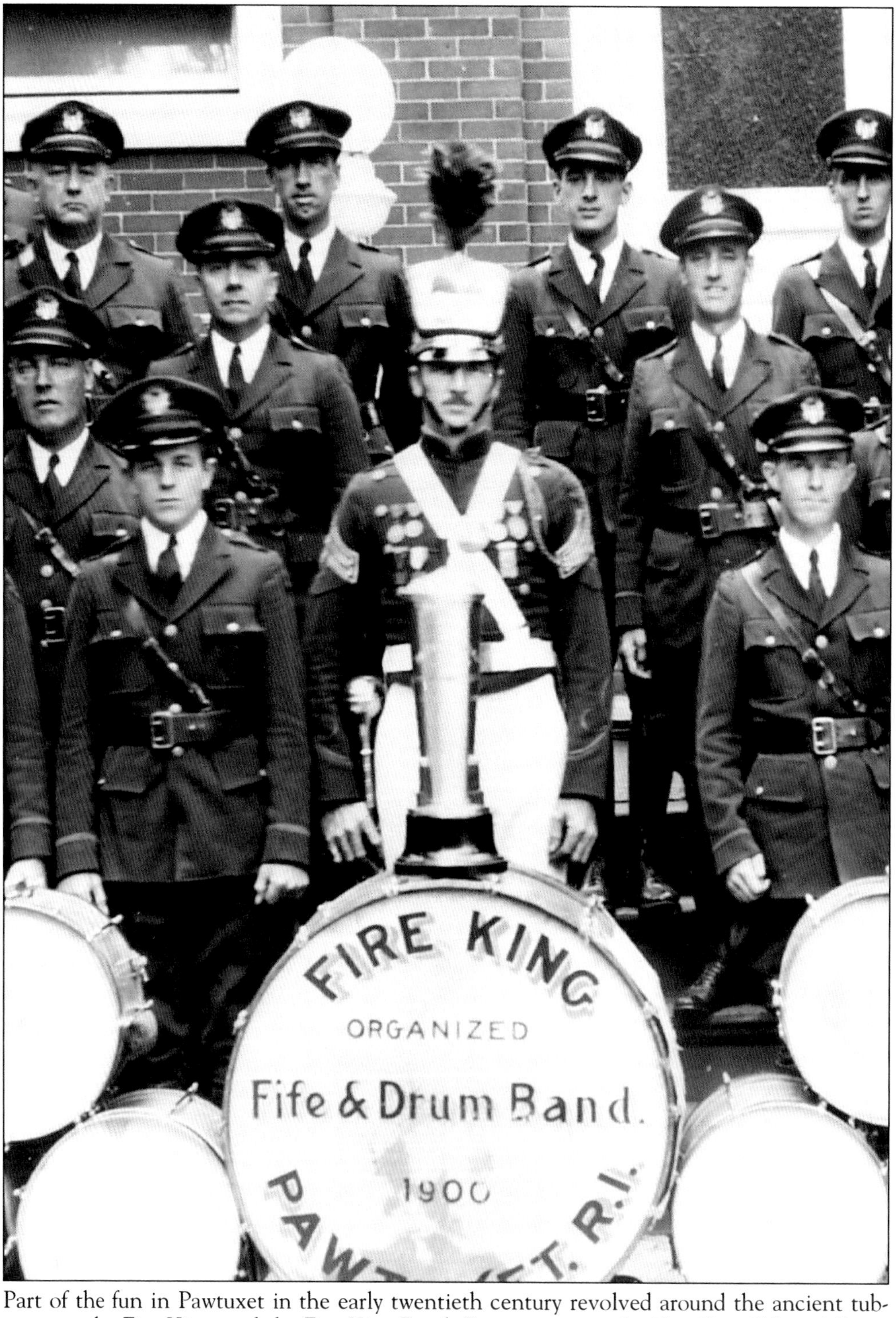

Part of the fun in Pawtuxet in the early twentieth century revolved around the ancient tub-pumper, the Fire King, and the Fire King Band. For many years the Fire King Fife and Drum Corps Band, shown here c. 1930, practiced on the second floor of the firehouse. This was the first outside band to ever play at the West Point Academy. (Henry A.L. Brown Collection.)

IMAGES
of America

PAWTUXET
RHODE ISLAND

Donald A. D'Amato and Henry A.L. Brown

ARCADIA
PUBLISHING

ISBN 978-0-7385-6409-8

Published by Arcadia Publishing
Charleston, South Carolina

Printed in the United States of America

Library of Congress Control Number: 2009920477

For all general information contact Arcadia Publishing at:
Telephone 843-853-2070
Fax 843-853-0044
E-mail sales@arcadiapublishing.com
For customer service and orders:
Toll-Free 1-888-313-2665

Visit us on the Internet at www.arcadiapublishing.com

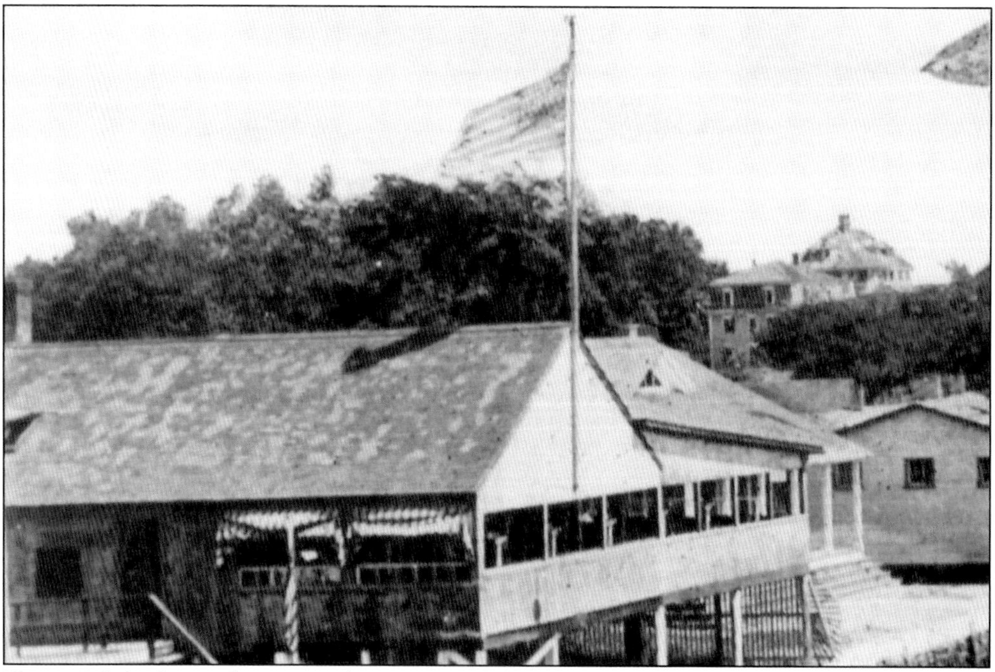

Slocum's bake house dominates this section of the landing at Pawtuxet Cove on the Cranston side *c.* 1904. At the turn of the century, a visit to Pawtuxet's famous bake house was a summer must. (Henry A.L. Brown Collection.)

Contents

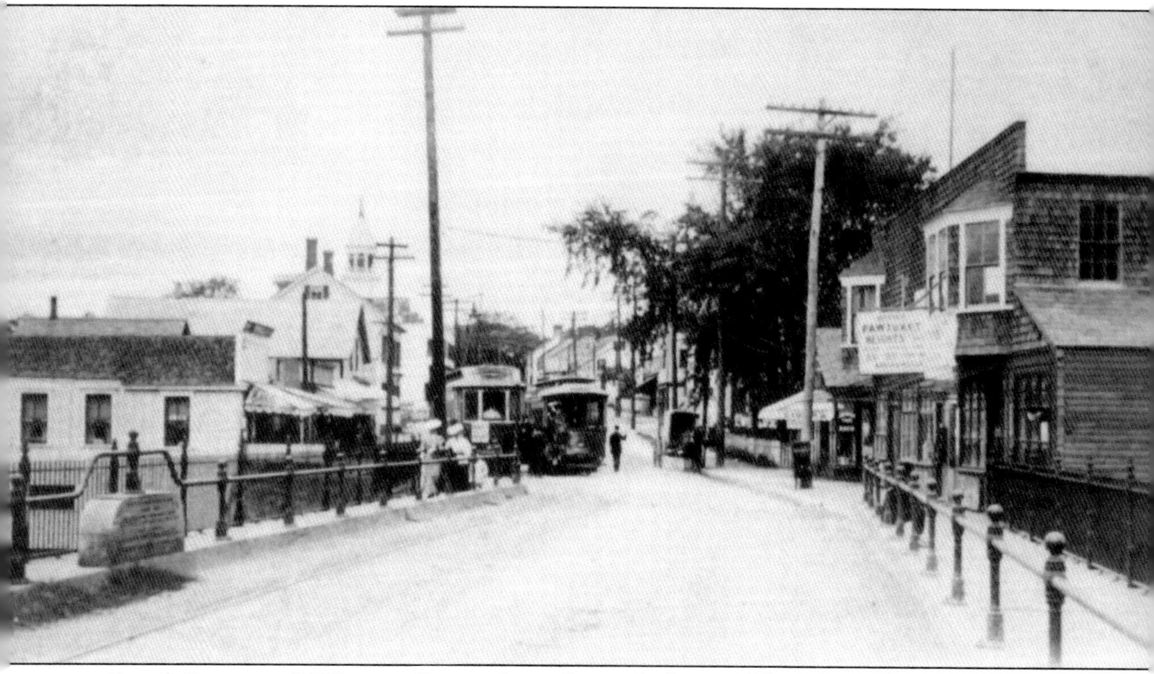

Broad Street c. 1908 was alive with traffic and places of business. The main means of transportation at the time was the trolley and it was here, at the Cranston side of Broad Street, that the lines were exchanged. The building on the right has an advertisement for a new plat in Lakewood on the Warwick side. The area was then called New Pawtuxet Heights. Note the plaque on the bridge and the iron posts and walkways. All are gone from the street today. (Henry A.L. Brown Collection.)

Introduction

Founded in 1638 by William Arnold, William Harris, William Carpenter, and Zachariah Rhodes, Pawtuxet is one of Rhode Island's oldest and most historic villages. It is unique, as the village is divided by the Pawtuxet River so that the northern section is in the City of Cranston, while the southern is in the City of Warwick. The village is an entity in itself, however, and villagers have a close bond and share a common heritage.

Today's Pawtuxet is quiet and serene, just far enough from the hustle and bustle of the major highways to retain much of its early-twentieth-century charm. It wasn't always thus, however, as the early years of the village were marked by growth, chaos, discontent, and bitter quarrels. The "Pawtuxet Men" placed the village under the jurisdiction of the Massachusetts Bay Colony because of greed and disagreements with Roger Williams and Samuel Gorton. They were involved in a "forged deed" controversy that nearly destroyed the colony. Then they weathered the horrors of King Philip's War.

By the early years of the eighteenth century, Pawtuxet emerged as a prominent Rhode Island seaport. The Sugar and Molasses Act of 1732 saw protests against Great Britain develop into smuggling, and the village gained a reputation as a haven for illegal imports. On June 9, 1772, Pawtuxet was the scene of the first act of violence in the Revolution when the British revenue schooner *Gaspee* was burned close by and the captain and crew were taken to the village.

By 1776, when the Revolution became official, Pawtuxet was well established as a leading Rhode Island seaport. After a brief setback due to the rigors of the Revolution, Pawtuxet's prosperity continued into the Federal period. Fortunately, many of the homes and buildings from that era have survived and have been beautifully restored. As a result, the village has a special charm not found in many other areas of the United States.

The early nineteenth century saw a prosperous Pawtuxet as the seaport gained a certain importance through the coastal trade. In time, trade, shipbuilding, and industry brought about the establishment of the C & W Rhodes textile company and the Pawtuxet Bank. Late in the nineteenth century, Thomas Rhodes made history by adding a casino to his bake house and the famous Rhodes-on-the-Pawtuxet was born. This famous establishment was the mecca for dancers, canoeists, and politicians for over a century.

As the village grew, problems concerning fire protection prompted the citizens to establish the Pawtuxet Volunteer Fire Company #1. Their tub, the Fire King, manned by burly quahogers and village stalwarts, gained fame for its sterling performances at musters and for the excellent Fire King band.

During the twentieth century, the village experienced steady growth as new and faster methods of transportation brought about more development. Physical changes over the years resulted in Pawtuxet's demise as a major seaport. In time, industry moved from the village, and in the late twentieth century, a major network of super highways and roads bypassed the area. As a result, Pawtuxet was able to escape the destruction and maintain the fabric that made it such a charming late-nineteenth- and early-twentieth-century village.

Today, Pawtuxet residents take great pride in their village, They have their own monthly newspaper, a village organization, and especially they have citizens who love the village and intend to keep it and preserve its rich heritage.

One

Pawtuxet Falls and Bridge

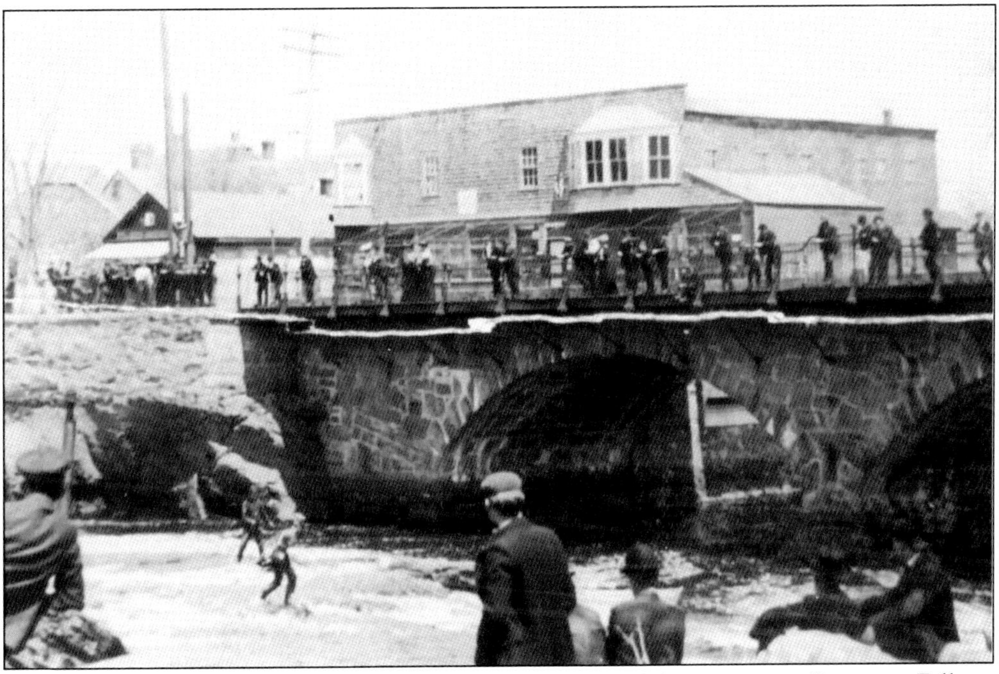

How do you spend a pleasant Sunday afternoon in 1901? Many came to Pawtuxet Falls to catch the elusive buckeyes (herring) that were spawning up river, mounting the falls. It was considered great sport. People came to Pawtuxet from Providence in streetcars to watch local boys catch the herring with nets. The water was clean then. (Henry A.L. Brown Collection.)

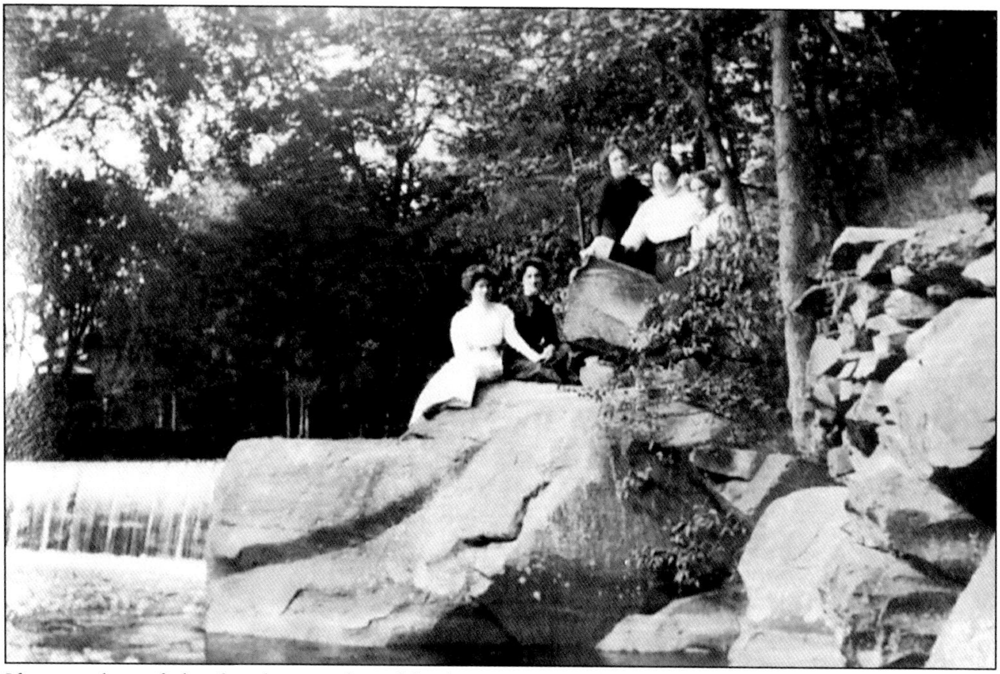

If a member of the family or a friend had a camera and you were in Pawtuxet on a Sunday afternoon around the turn of the century, chances are you would climb on this boulder on the Cranston side of the falls, just about everyone's favorite photograph location. This picture of Pawtuxet Falls was taken in 1892. (Henry A.L. Brown Collection.)

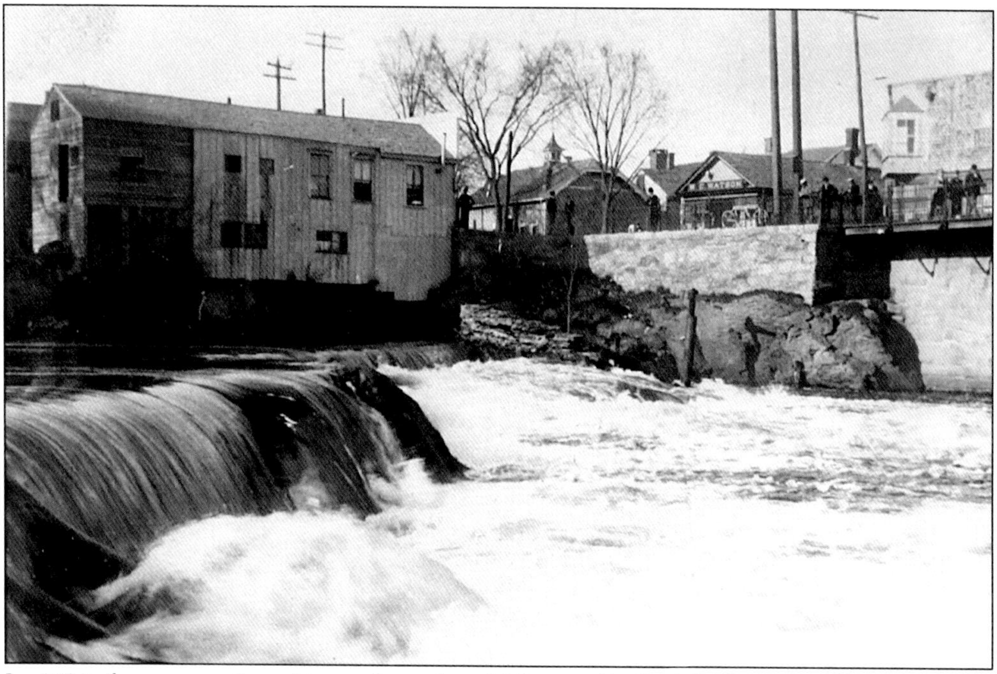

In 1904, fragments of machinery from the old Pierce Stafford Mill were still in the river. Watson's drugstore, the Pawtuxet bakery, and Haywood's carriage house (from left to right) can be seen on the Cranston side of the Pawtuxet Bridge. (William Hall Library Collection.)

This water-powered textile mill on the Cranston side of the river burned on January 15, 1875 (the sketch was made shortly before the mill's destruction). At that time, the land and mill belonged to the City of Providence. It was built in 1830 by Brown & Ives. Obviously, the mill area has changed a great deal in modern times. (Henry A.L. Brown Collection.)

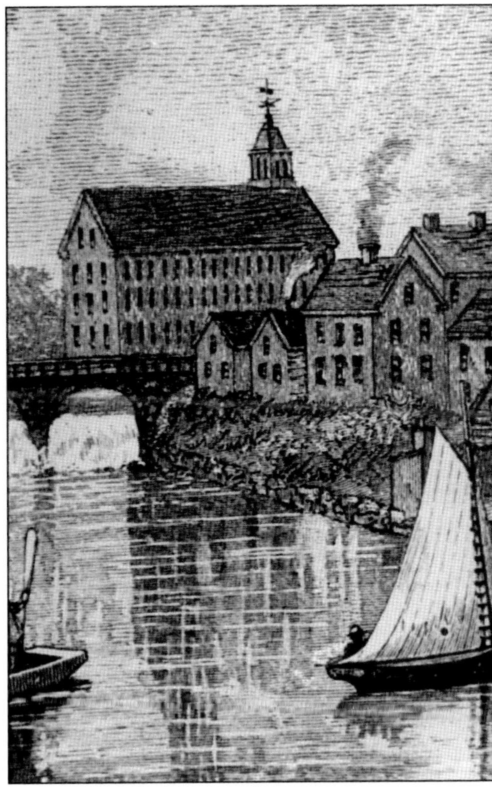

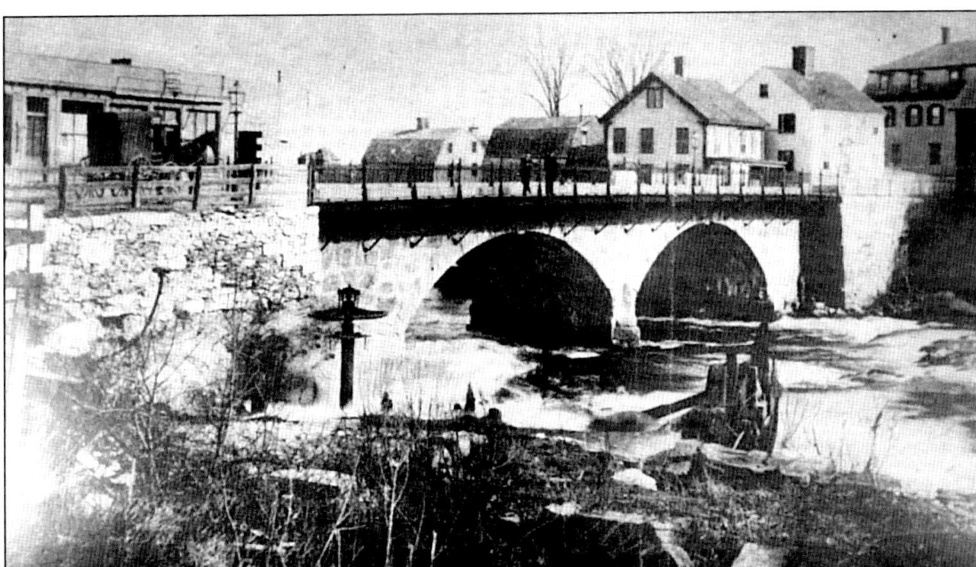

The Cranston section of Pawtuxet is to the left, and Warwick is to the right. The ruins of the Pierce Stafford Mill are in the foreground of this 1885 Pawtuxet Bridge photograph. (Cranston Historical Society Collection.)

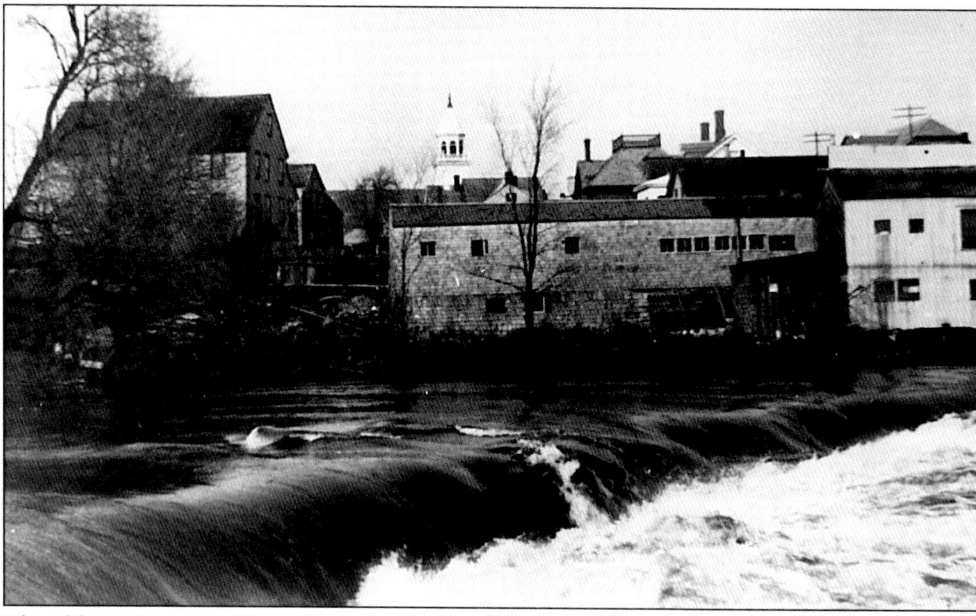

The old warehouse building (left) that survived the fire of 1875 (altered *c.* 1900), the Pawtuxet bakery building (1900), and the steeple of the Pawtuxet Baptist Church (1895) all help to date this lovely 1905 photograph of the falls. (Henry A.L. Brown Collection.)

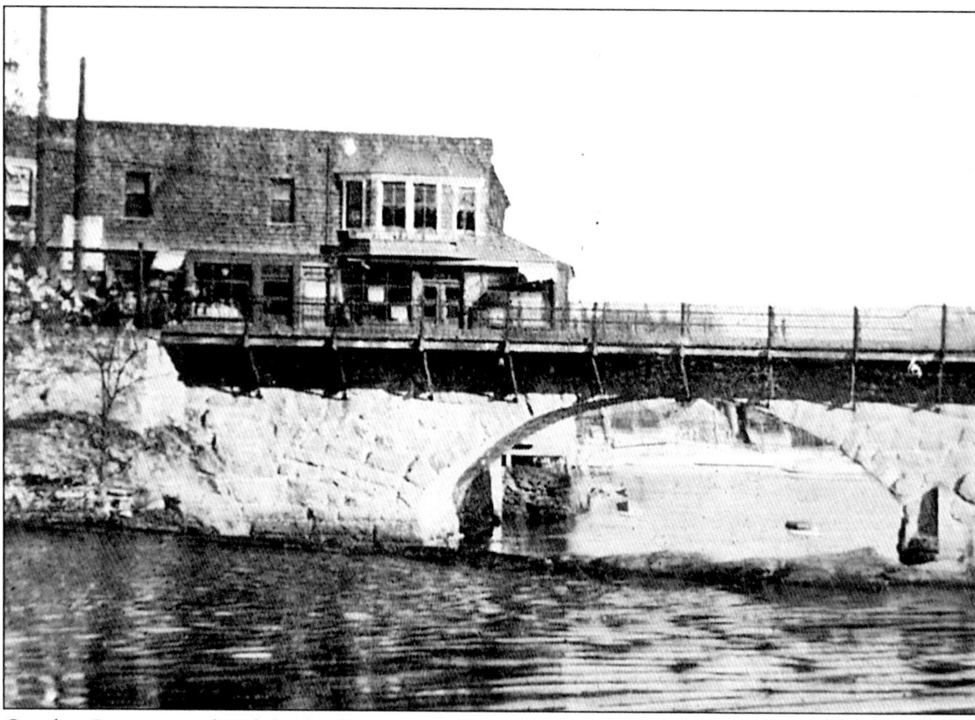

On the Cranston side of the bridge in 1910 is Wilbour's store with a barbershop upstairs. This building still stands and is owned by George and Ellen Morton. Today, Dearheart's ice-cream store is there, as well as a barbershop on the lower floor, a little restaurant, a card shop, and Twice Told Tales. (William Hall Library Collection.)

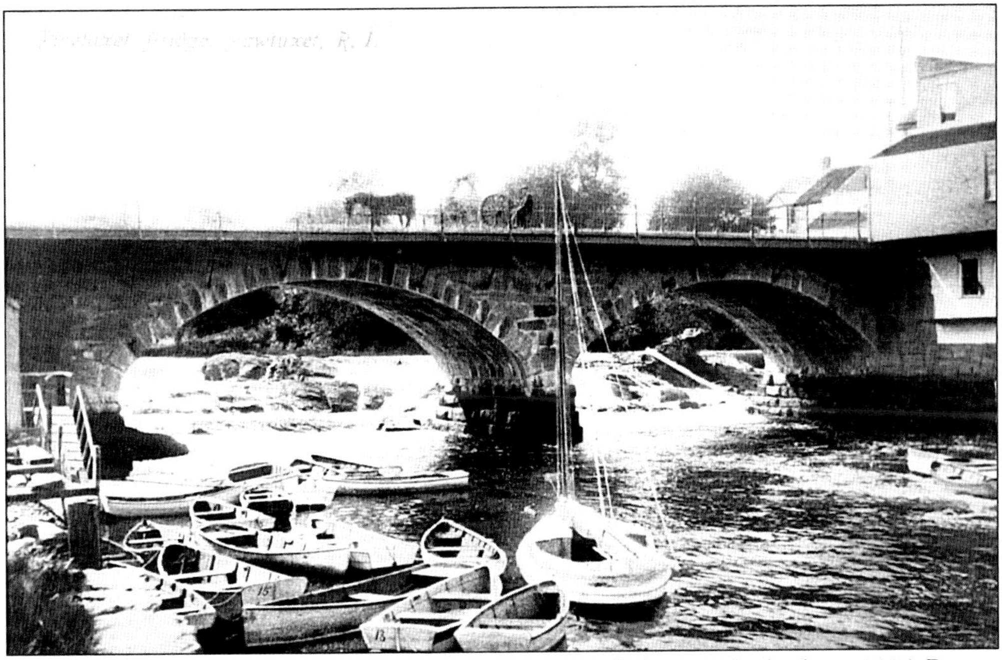

The photographer captured this old farmer's cart being pulled across the bridge c. 1906. During the late nineteenth and early twentieth centuries, this was a common sight, as this type of cart was used for hauling seaweed and fertilizer, valuable products in old Pawtuxet and the vicinity. (Henry A.L. Brown Collection.)

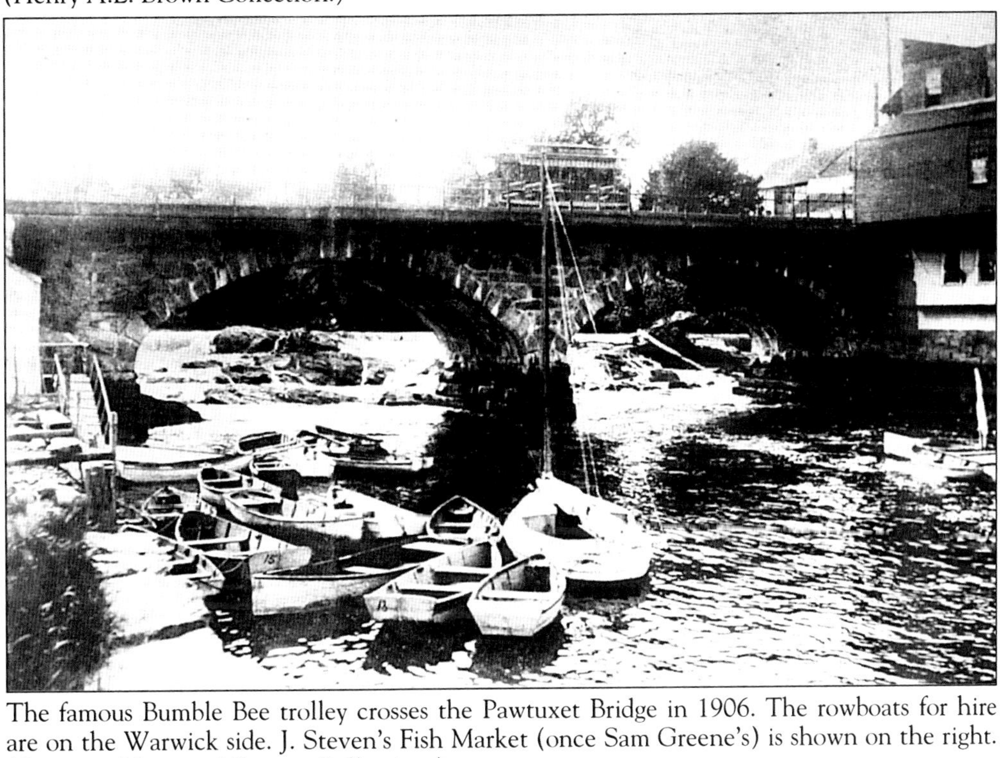

The famous Bumble Bee trolley crosses the Pawtuxet Bridge in 1906. The rowboats for hire are on the Warwick side. J. Steven's Fish Market (once Sam Greene's) is shown on the right. (Cranston Historical Society Collection.)

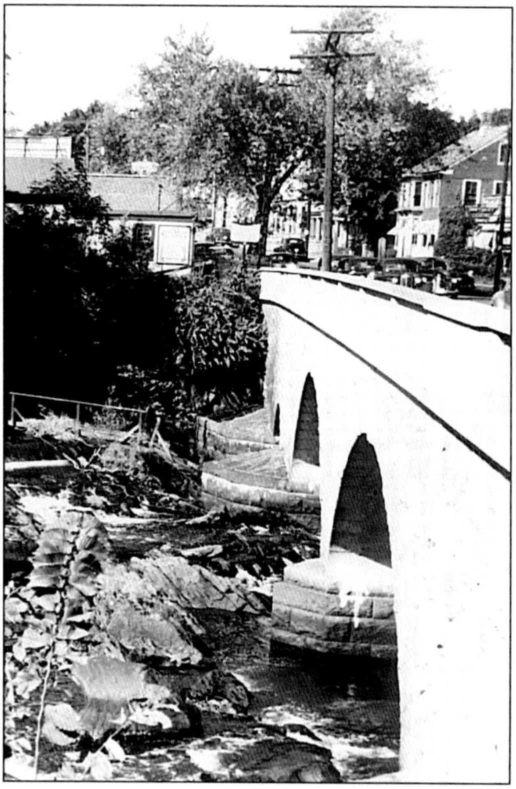

Taken before the Hurricane of 1938, this picture of the bridge captures the "catwalk" (or walkway) in the center of the river. This device enabled canoeists to take their craft from salt to fresh water or vice versa. (William Hall Library Collection.)

The village of Pawtuxet, with its bridge, falls, and charm, has always attracted artists. In 1939, these artists tried to capture the scene from the lower level of the bridge adjacent to Bishop's Garage, which is now Hunter's Garage. (William Hall Library Collection.)

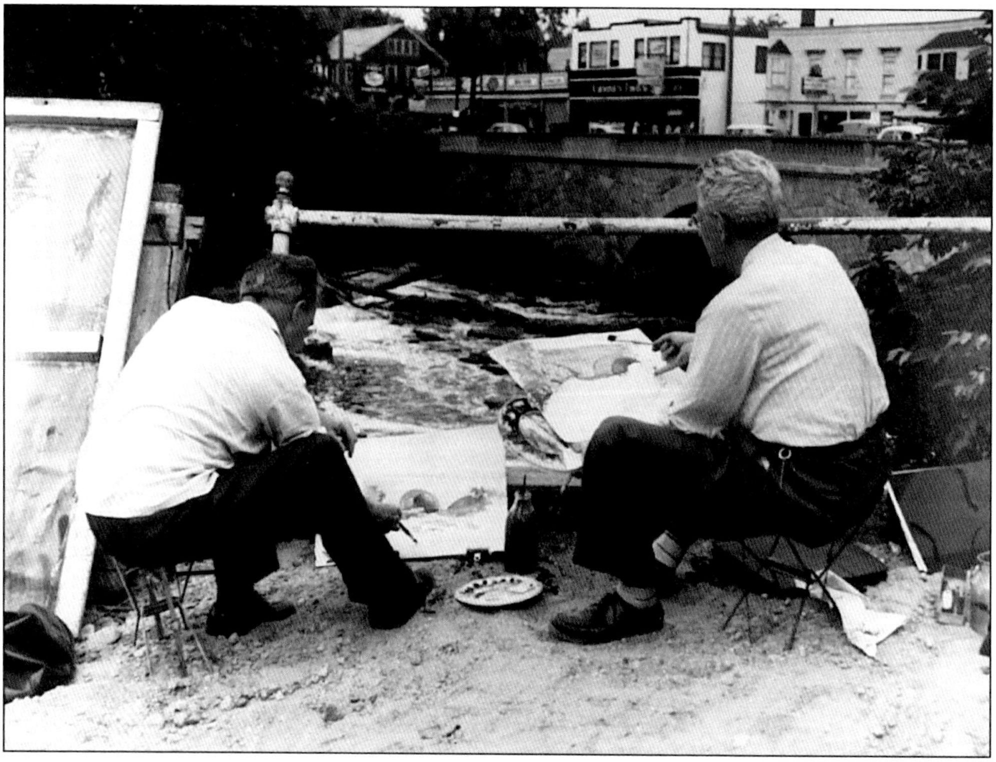

These boats were for hire in the early twentieth century. For a couple of dollars you could rent a rowboat and fish all day. Many rowed down to Greene's Island to go clamming, or to Warwick Downs for a picnic. The more ambitious could go out to the channel for several good fish, including tautog in the spring and flat fish, scup, and squeteague in the summer. (Henry A.L. Brown Collection.)

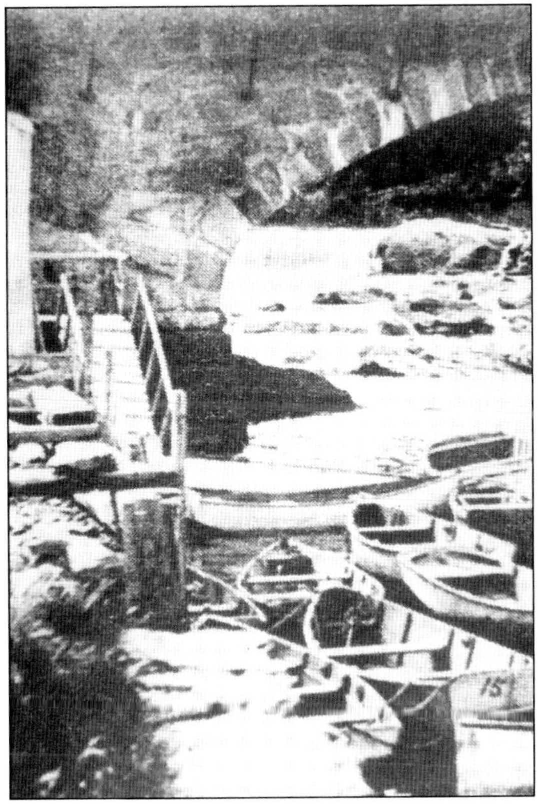

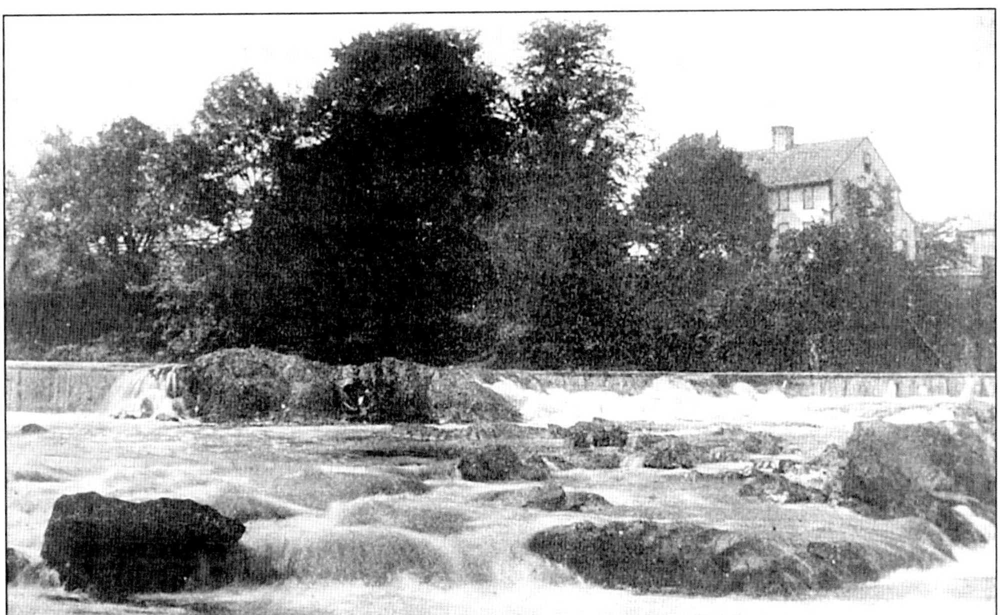

This old farmhouse dominates the Pawtuxet Falls in 1898. At that time, there was a wooden dam, which was replaced in the late 1920s by a cement spillway. (William Hall Library Collection.)

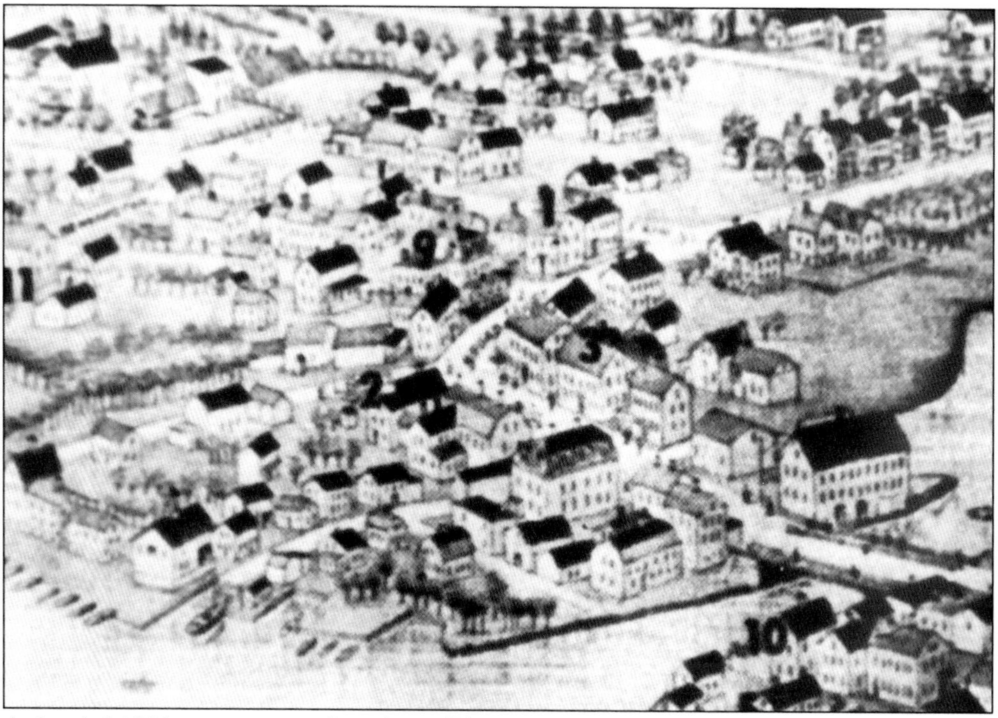

A detailed 1891 map attempted to place all houses and buildings in the village in their proper places. This section gives us a view of the houses surrounding the bridge as they were before the turn of the century. (Thomas E. Greene Collection.)

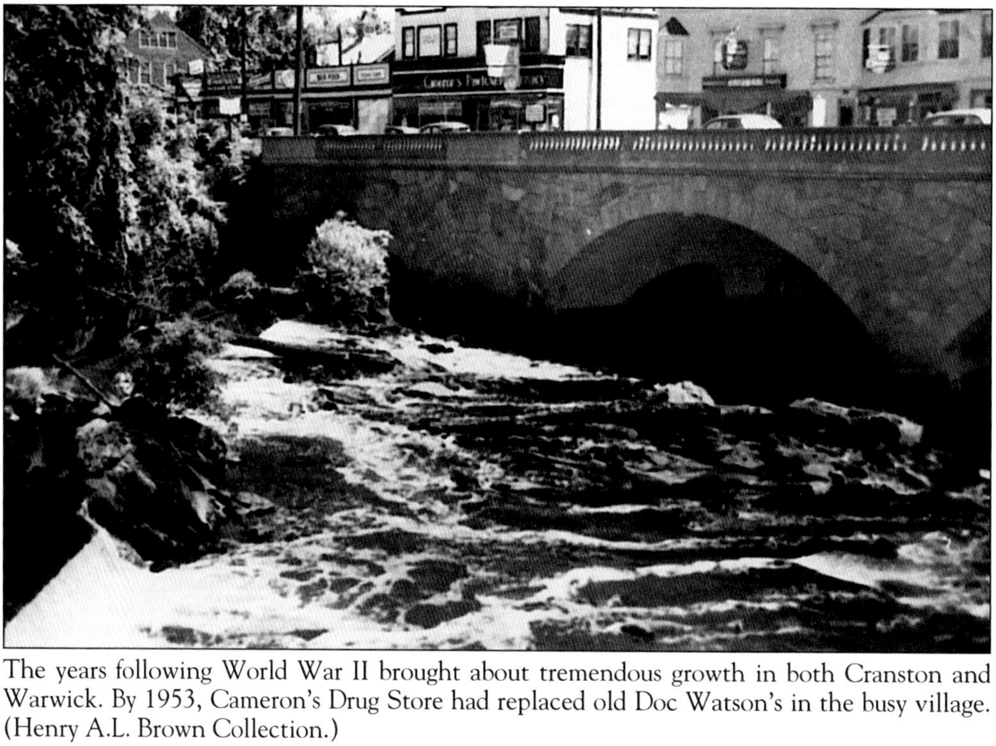

The years following World War II brought about tremendous growth in both Cranston and Warwick. By 1953, Cameron's Drug Store had replaced old Doc Watson's in the busy village. (Henry A.L. Brown Collection.)

Two

Cranston at the Bridge

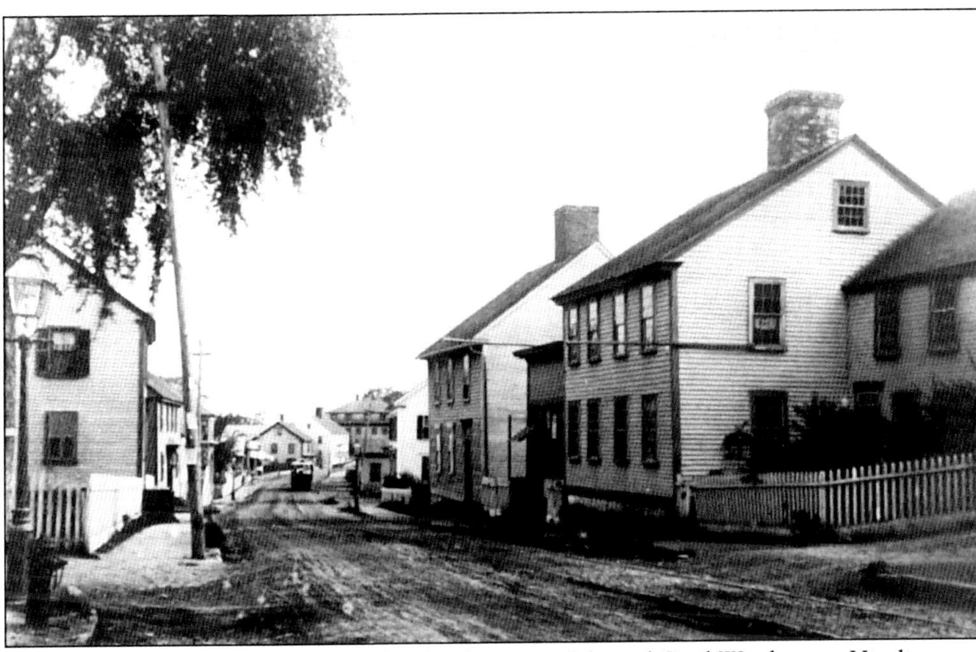

Elisha Hunt Rhodes was one of Rhode Island's most celebrated Civil War heroes. His diary was used extensively in Ken Burns's highly acclaimed television presentation on the Civil War. Rhodes took the original picture of this scene from the Pawtuxet Baptist Church looking across the bridge to Warwick in 1885. Rhodes's house is the large one on the right with the fence. (Robert Hunt Rhodes Collection.)

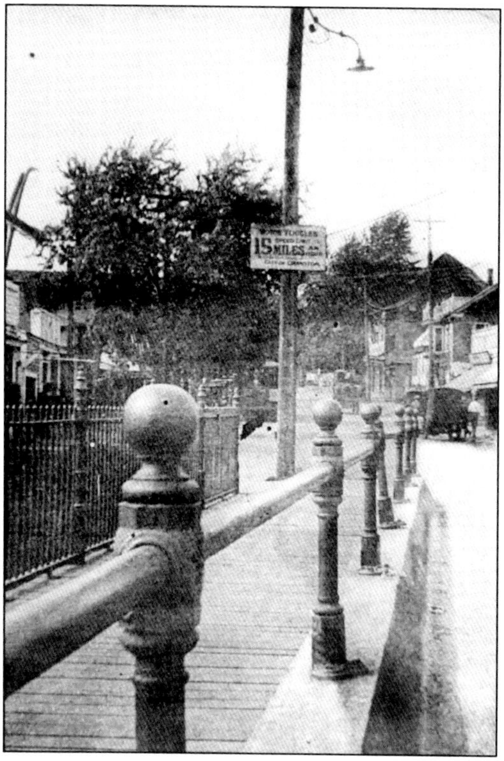

Automobiles were beginning to become more common in the old village in 1916, which prompted the posting of a "Speed Limit 15 miles per hour" sign on Broad Street. Note the lovely bridge walkway and the wrought-iron fence. (Henry A.L. Brown Collection.)

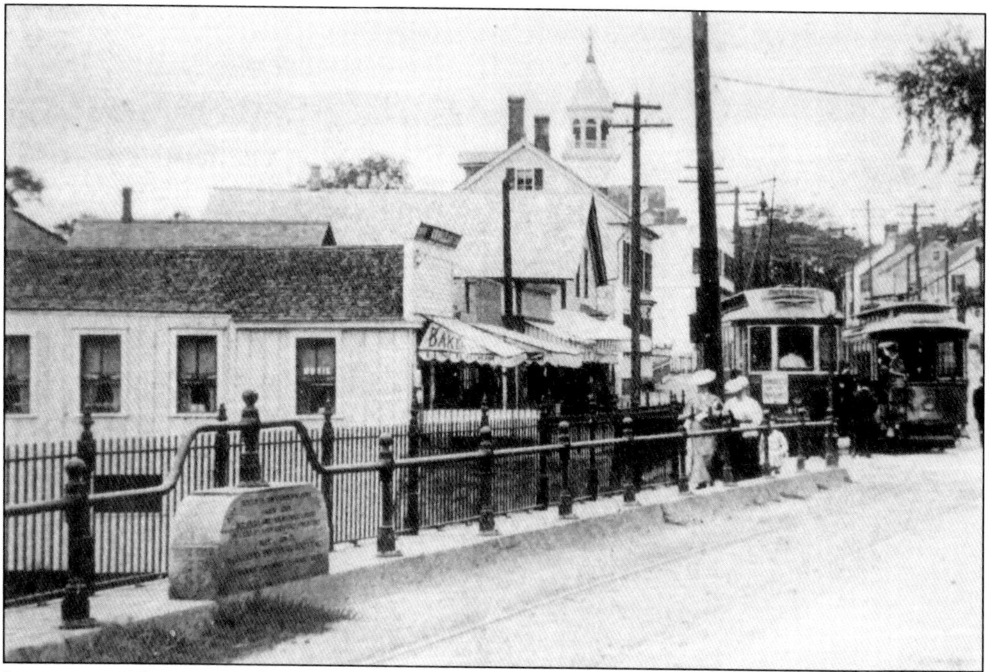

It is impossible not to acknowledge the importance of the trolley to Pawtuxet. Two streetcars, the Bumble Bee heading for Lakewood and the Broad Street car—with its familiar Rhodes-on-the-Pawtuxet sign—are side by side on Broad Street in 1908. (Henry A.L. Brown Collection.)

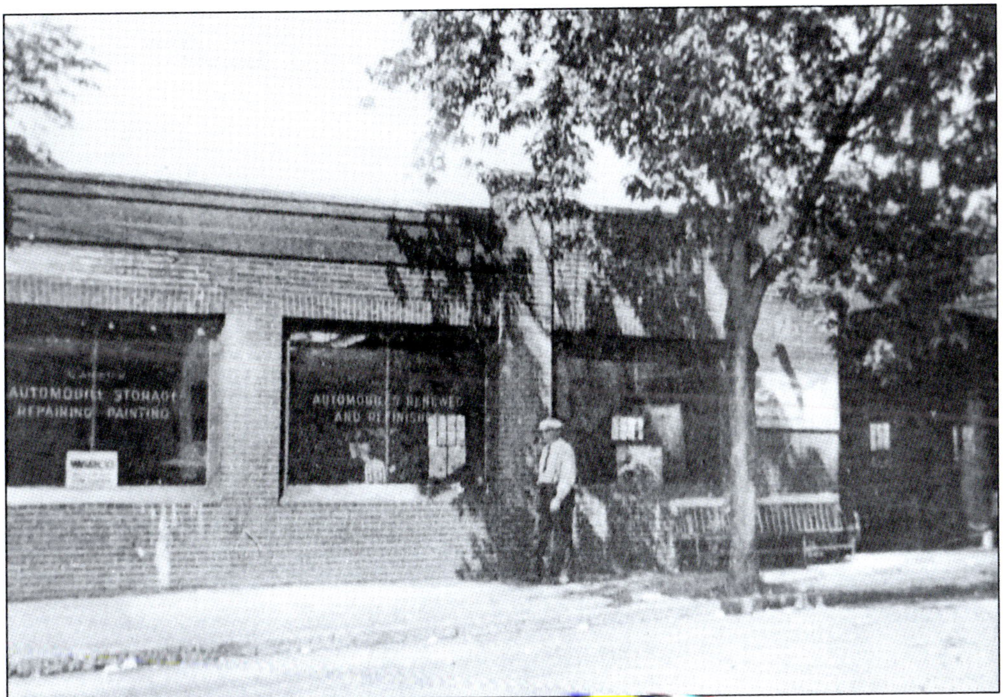

The Pawtuxet Garage and Post Office were on the site now occupied by Citizens Bank and the Basta Italian Restaurant. This block was developed by Joseph B. Hayward, a realtor who owned considerable property in Pawtuxet. (Henry A.L. Brown Collection.)

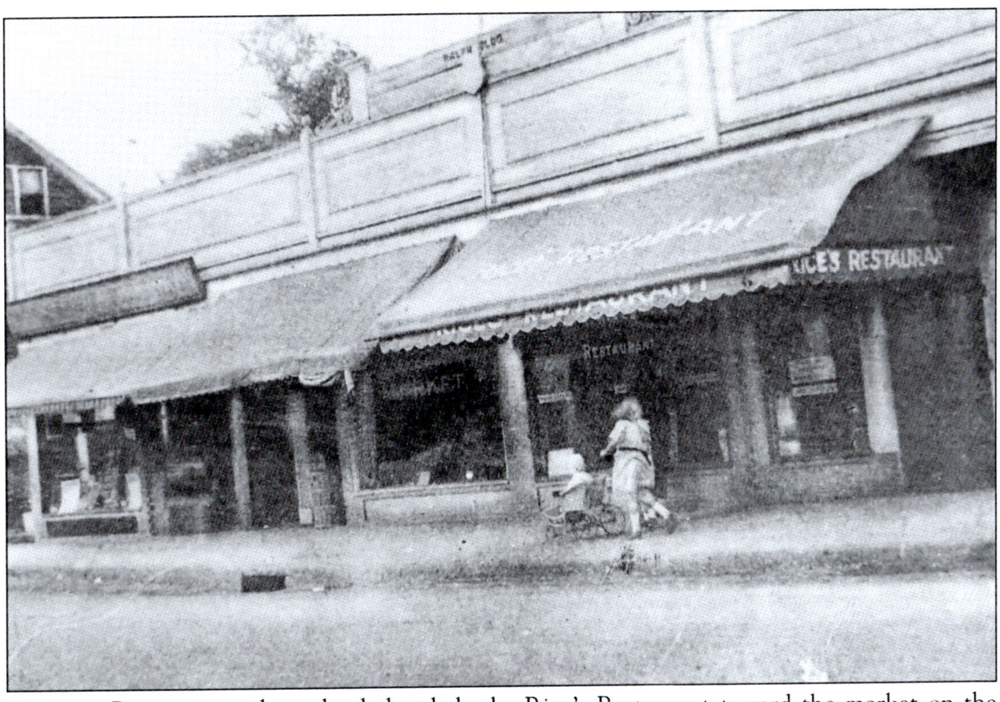

A young Pawtuxet mother wheels her baby by Rice's Restaurant toward the market on the corner of Aborn Street in 1916. (Henry A.L. Brown Collection.)

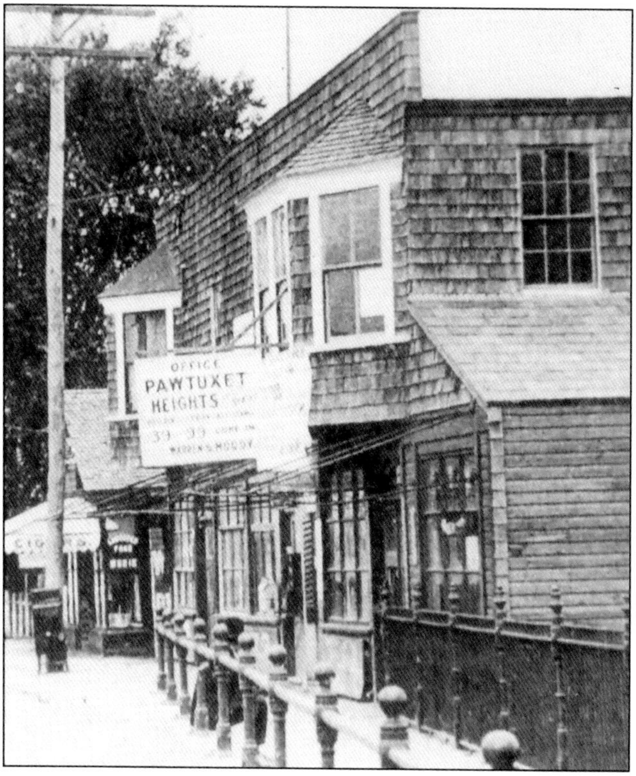

On the east side of Broad Street, just across the bridge in Cranston, the building that now houses Dearheart's ice cream was home to a fish market in 1908. On the second story was the Pawtuxet Heights Realty Office, owned by Warren Moody. There was also a barbershop on the second floor. (Henry A.L. Brown Collection.)

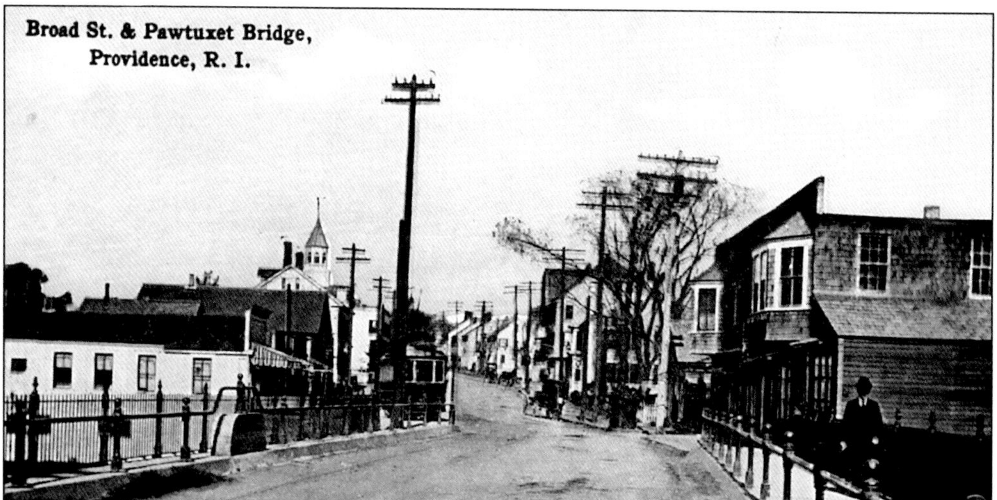

During the late nineteenth and early twentieth centuries, photographers favored the view of Broad Street across the Pawtuxet Bridge. One of the much-sought-after postcard views for visitors was this scene of Pawtuxet looking north. (Henry A.L. Brown Collection.)

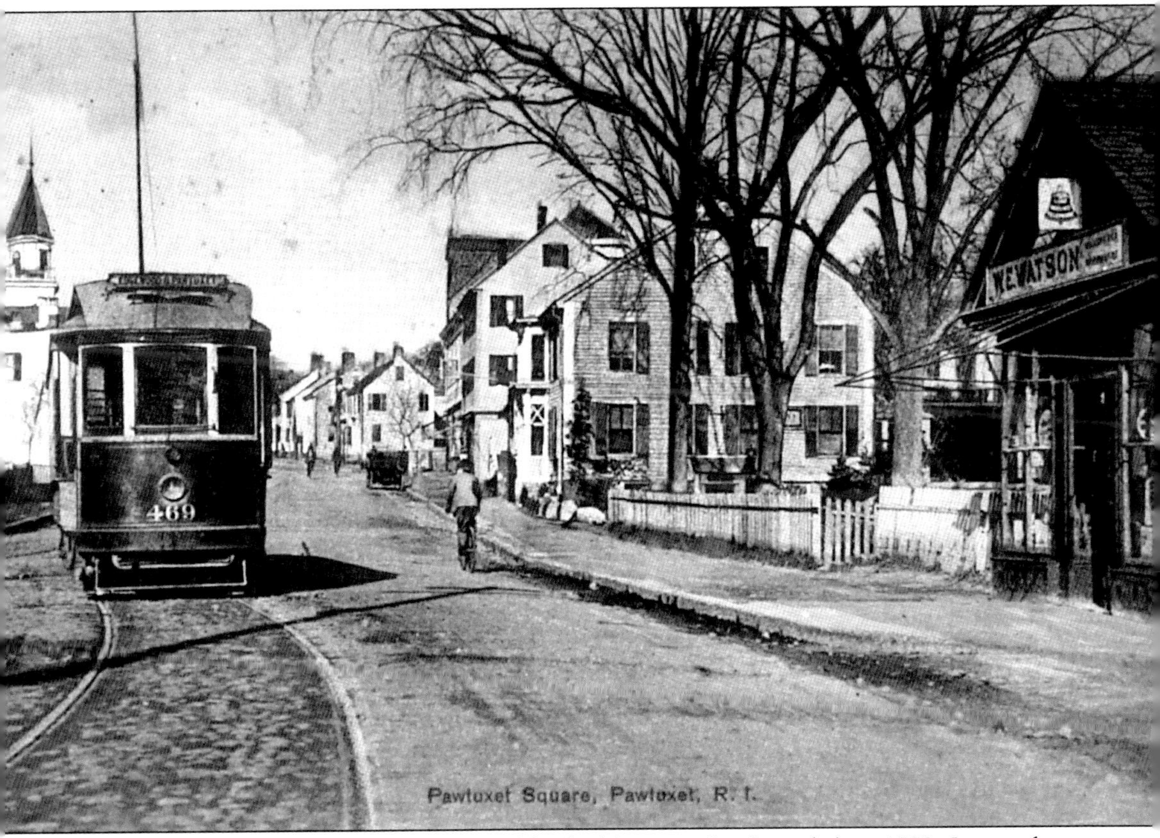

Walter E. Watson opened his pharmacy (the building on the far right) *c.* 1890. It was the only pharmacy between Thurbers Avenue and the Pawtuxet Bridge for many years. By the twentieth century, the gable-roofed structure was rebuilt with a flat roof and was known as the Pawtuxet Pharmacy and then Cameron's. Watson's was one of the few places in Pawtuxet with a phone in the early period. Unfortunately, the handsome elms are all gone, as is the Haywood home, which was demolished and replaced by Pawtuxet Paint and Hardware. (Henry A.L. Brown Collection.)

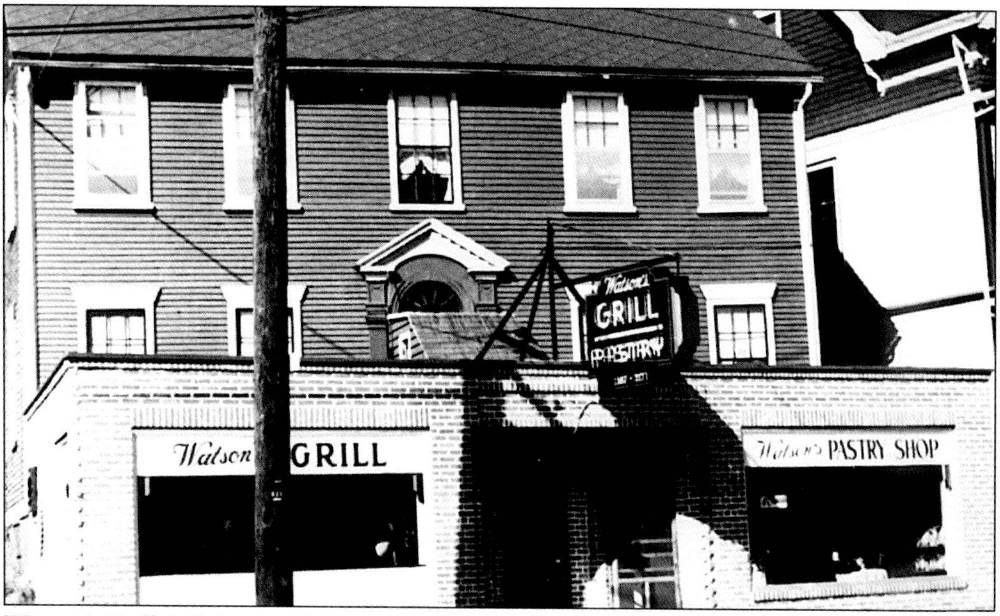

Watson's Grill & Bakery is shown here *c.* 1950. The old Sheldon house on Broad Street next to Lindsay's Market was raised and a store was built under it. Note the old doorway on the second story. The building was demolished to make room for an Esso Gas Station. Later, Mr. Lindsay bought the station, demolished it, and put in a parking lot. (Cranston Historical Society Collection.)

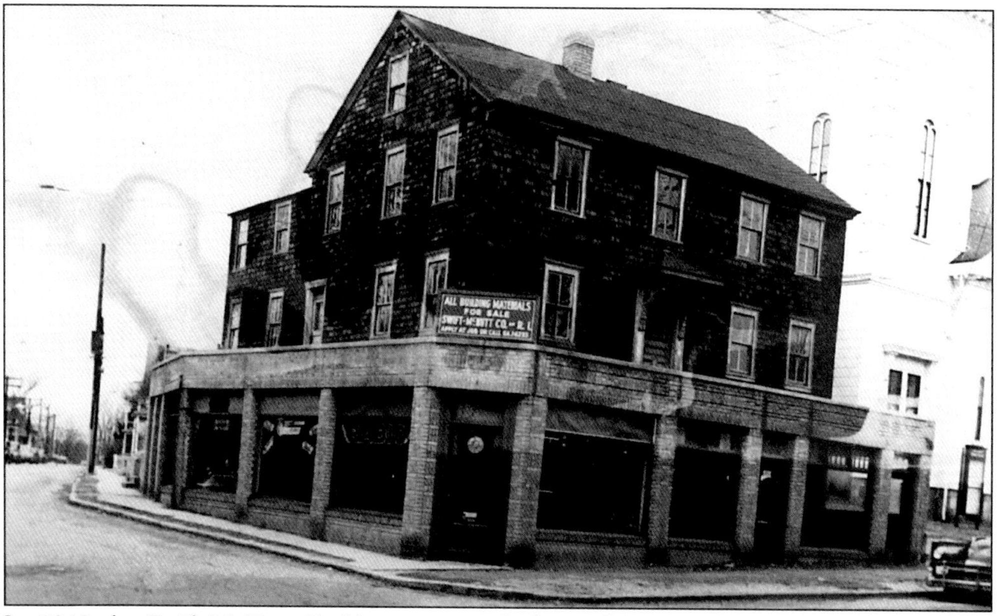

In 1948 the Swift-McNutt Building, previously located on Broad Street at the corner of Tucker Avenue, was next to the Pawtuxet Baptist Church. At its former location, the structure (previously a house) was jacked up, and Mrs. Eliza Rhodes's lunch counter restaurant was located underneath. Garry Slocum's radio and television repair shop was in the building's most recent location before the structure was purchased by the church and demolished. (Cranston Historical Society Collection.)

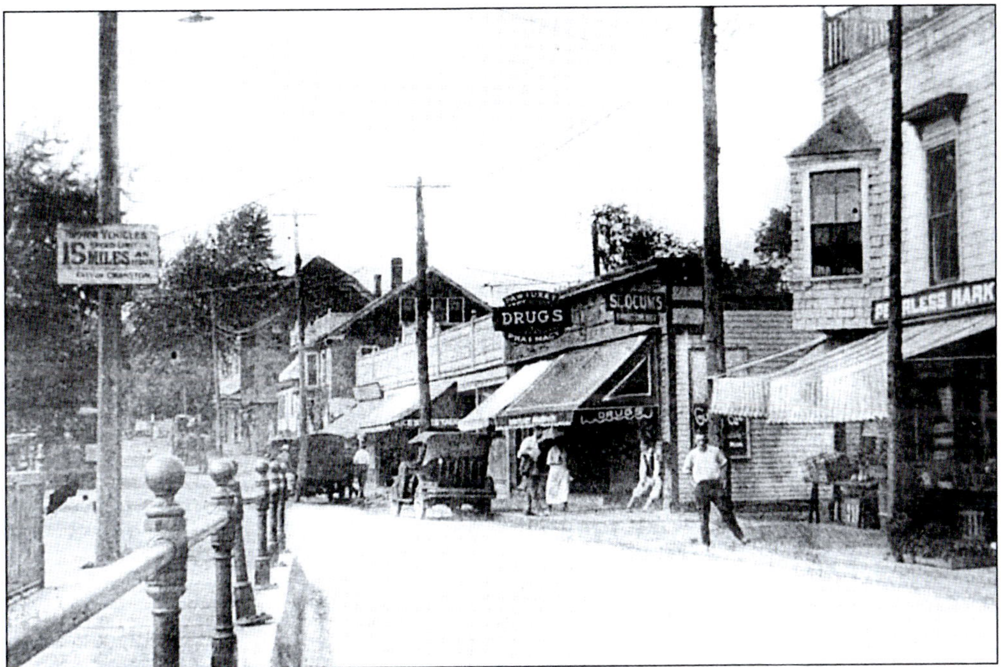

In 1908, several early motor vehicles line Broad Street in front of the Pawtuxet Pharmacy while a man waits, probably for a trolley, at the Peerless Market. The sign for Slocum's bake house is on Bridge Street. (Henry A.L. Brown Collection.)

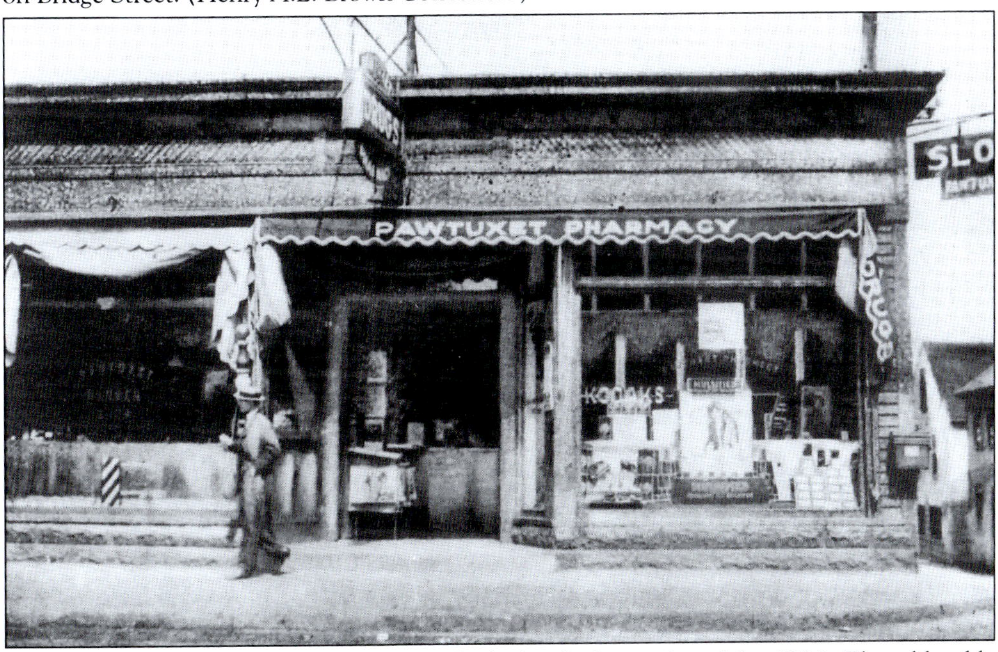

Walter E. Watson's Pawtuxet Pharmacy had already been altered by 1916. The old gable roof had been replaced by a flat one to conform to the style of the new block a little to the north. The pharmacy remained in the Watson family until 1972. It was remodeled then and expanded, overtaking the adjacent barbershop. It is now part of Cameron's Pharmacy. (Henry A.L. Brown Collection.)

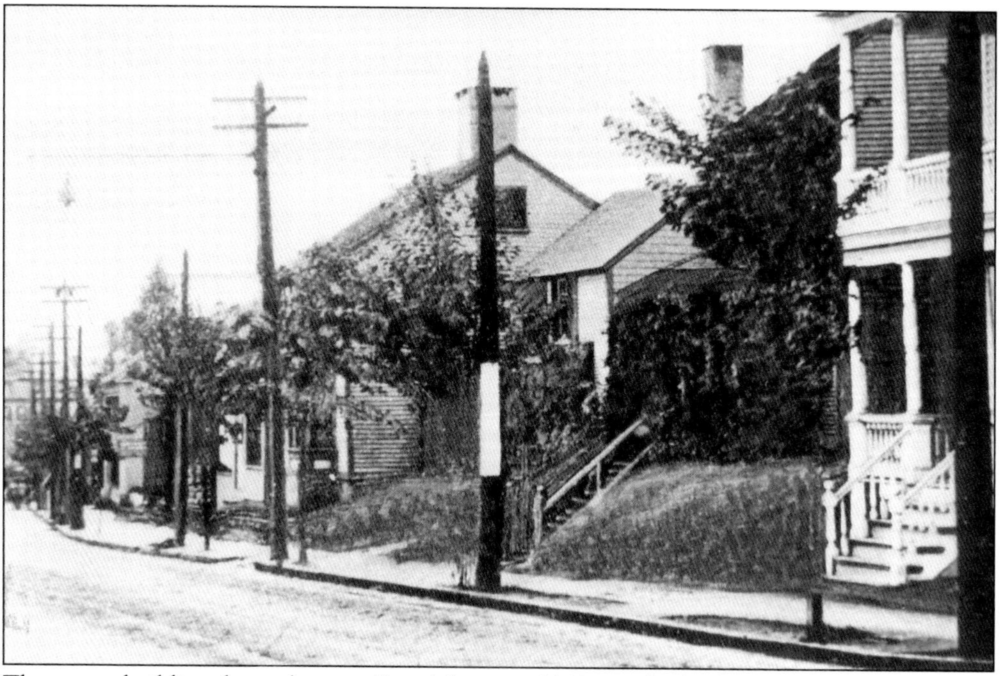

The center building shown here on Broad Street *c.* 1910 was the boyhood home of Elisha Hunt Rhodes, a celebrated Civil War hero. Rhodes maintained his connection to military service and was elected brigadier general in the Brigade of Rhode Island Militia (1878–1893). These homes were eventually demolished, and now a bank and gas station occupy the site. (Robert H. Rhodes Collection.)

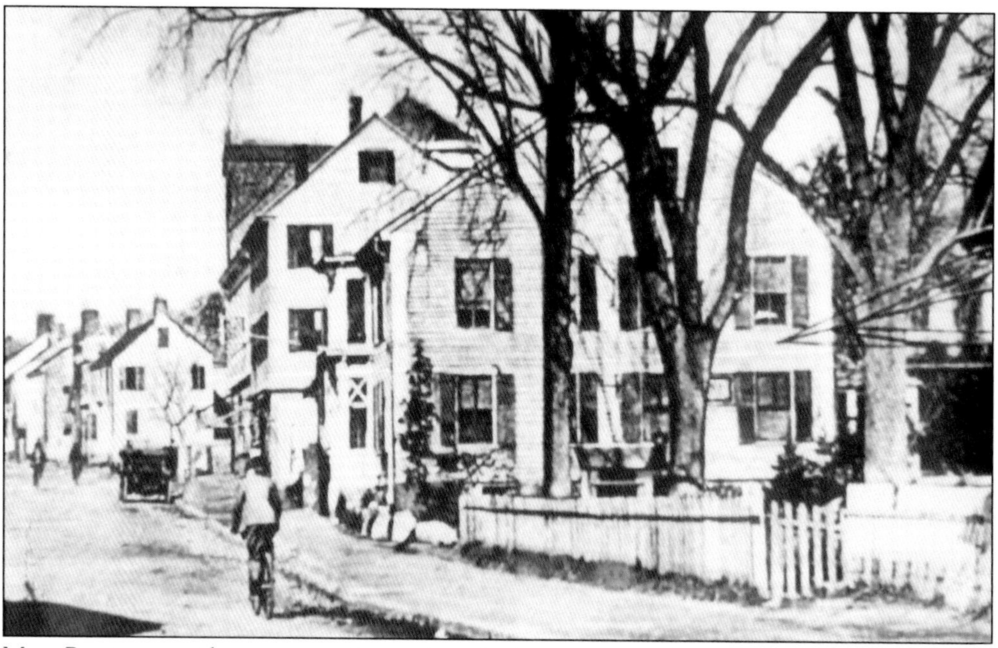

More Pawtuxet residents were on foot or bicycle than in automobiles at the turn of the century. Travel to Providence was infrequent until the electric trolley made the trip fast and inexpensive. (Henry A.L. Brown Collection.)

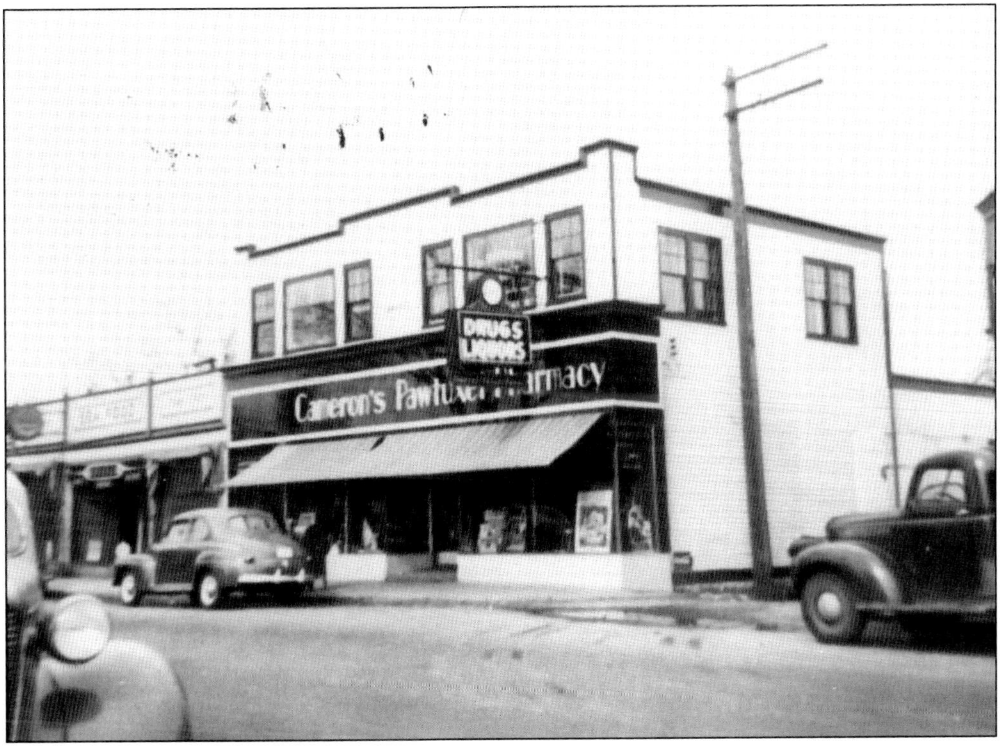

To those veterans returning from World War II, Cameron's Pawtuxet Pharmacy was a welcome sight. It emphasized the stability of the village, as a drugstore had been on that site since Walter E. Watson first opened his store in 1889. The store was remodeled in 1974. (Don Cameron Collection.)

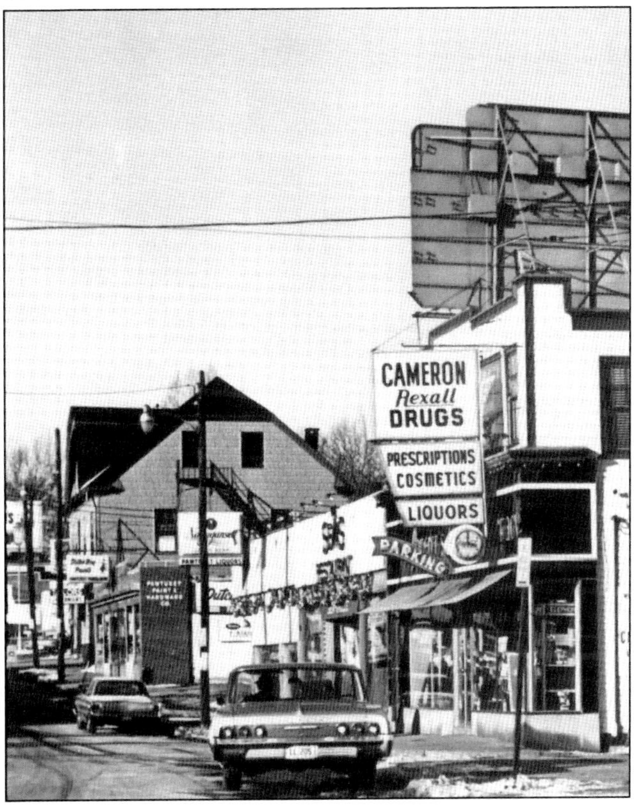

Moving well into the second half of the twentieth century, one sees that this street scene is dominated by Cameron's Drugs, the Seven Seas Restaurant, and Pawtuxet Liquors on the corner of Aborn Street. Lindsay's Market, on the opposite corner, was built in 1892 and is one of the few nineteenth-century buildings to survive in that section. (Henry A.L. Brown Collection.)

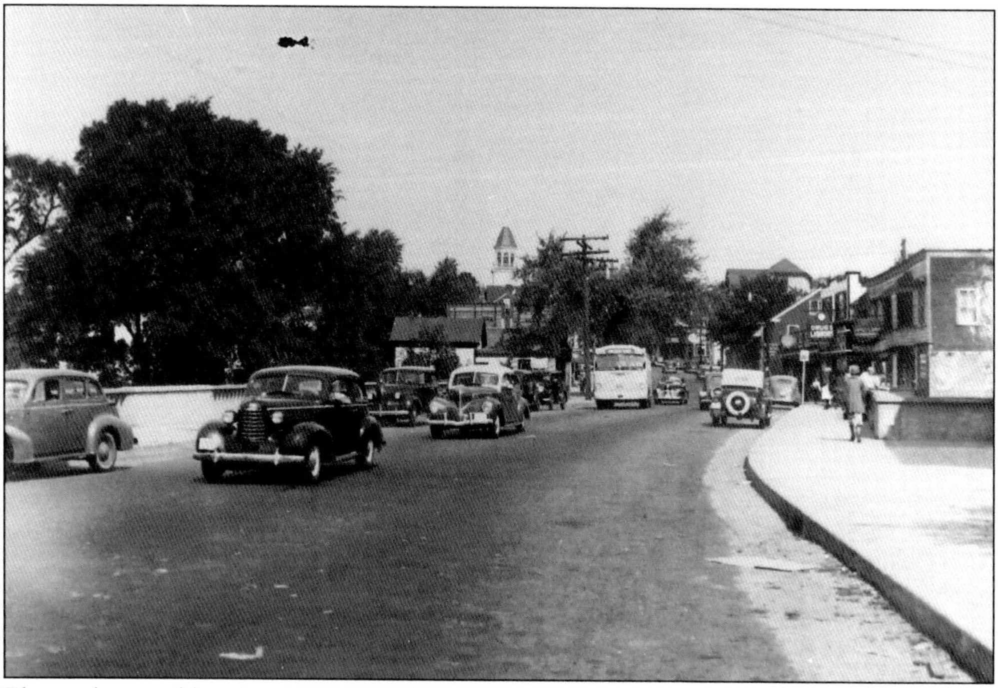

The modern world made an impact on historic Pawtuxet after World War II. The trolley tracks were removed, and bus and automobile traffic greatly increased in volume. (William Hall Library Collection.)

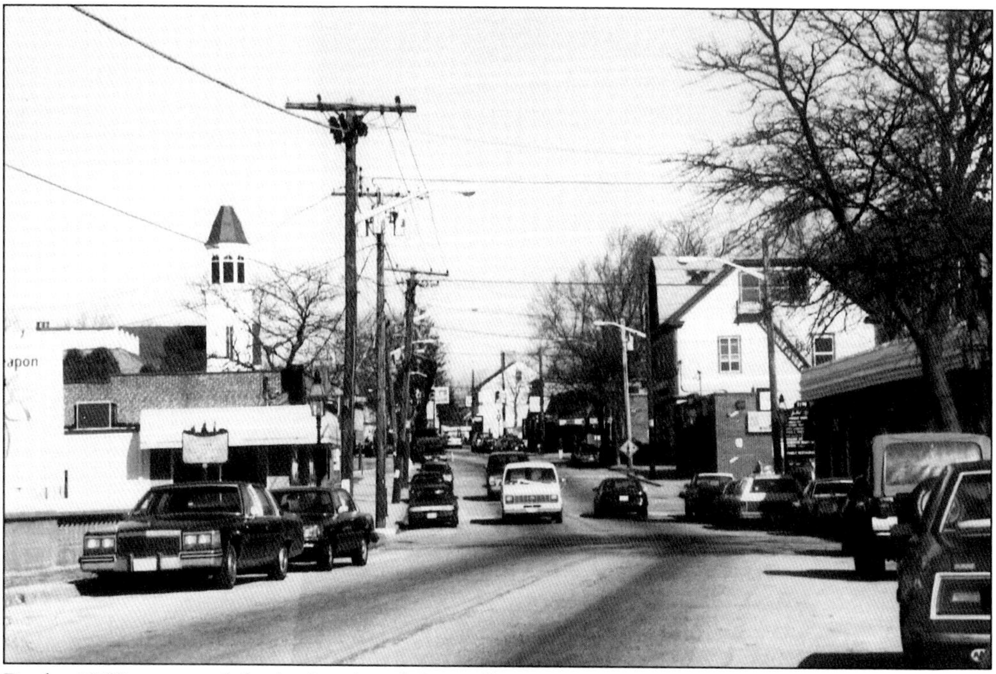

By the 1950s, automobiles had replaced the trolley in Pawtuxet. Also, by this time, the Hayward Grain, Upham's Pawtuxet Paint and Hardware, and Watson's Pharmacy all had vanished. (Don Cameron Collection.)

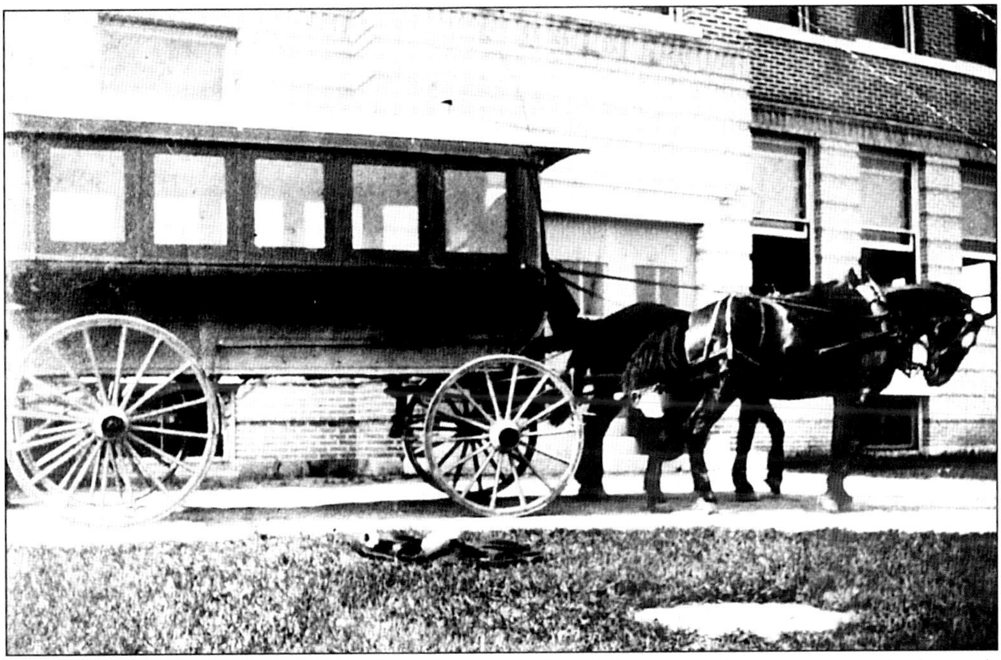

Even before the Spragues developed the Union Railroad Company, horse-drawn vehicles such as this restored wagon could be found in Pawtuxet. This public transportation service from Pawtuxet to Knightsville took pride in offering a one-hour round-trip ride. (Cranston Historical Society Collection.)

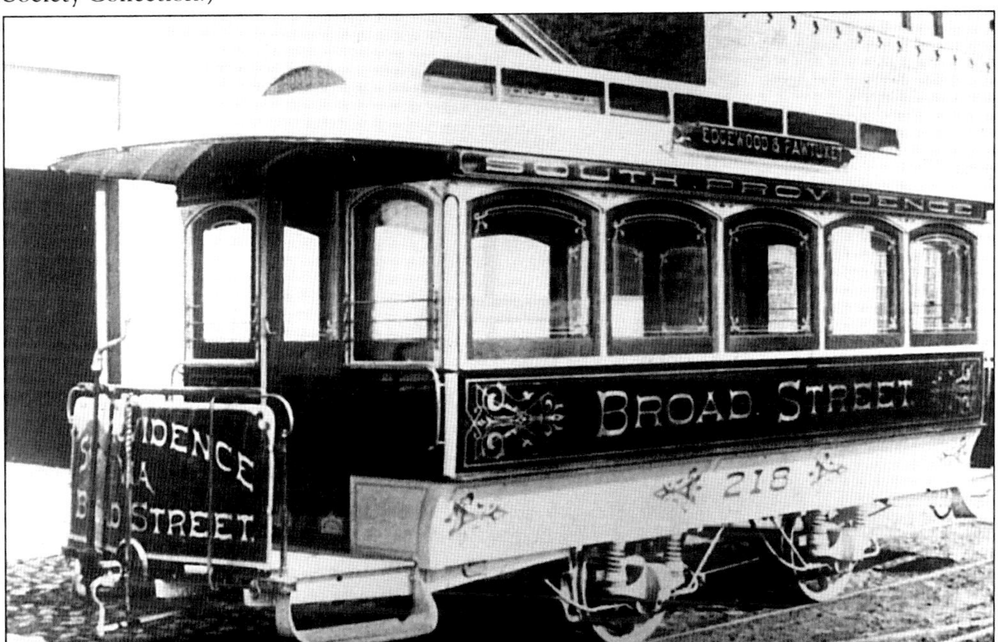

In 1870, the Sprague family extended the Union Railroad Company, which operated horsecar lines, along Broad Street to Pawtuxet. In 1892, the horsecars were replaced by the cleaner, faster, quieter electric cars. This restored horsecar helps recapture the nostalgic feel of the late nineteenth century. (William Hall Library Collection.)

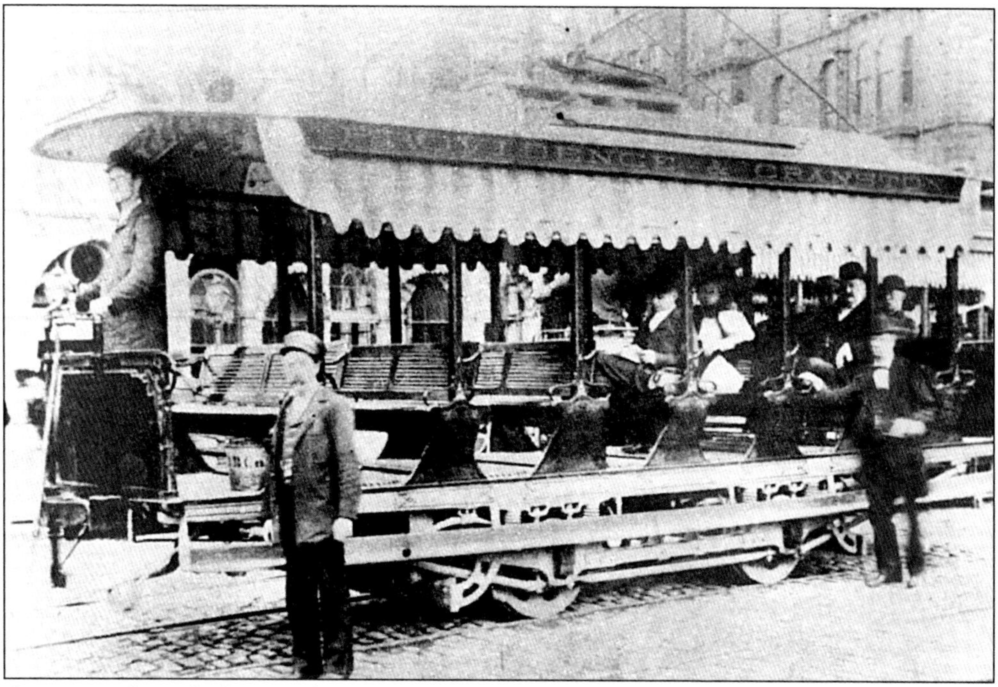

One way to beat the heat in the summertime around 1900 was to take a ride on the "bloomer" car, the open-air trolley that came from the Providence-Cranston line to the bridge in Pawtuxet. (William Hall Library Collection.)

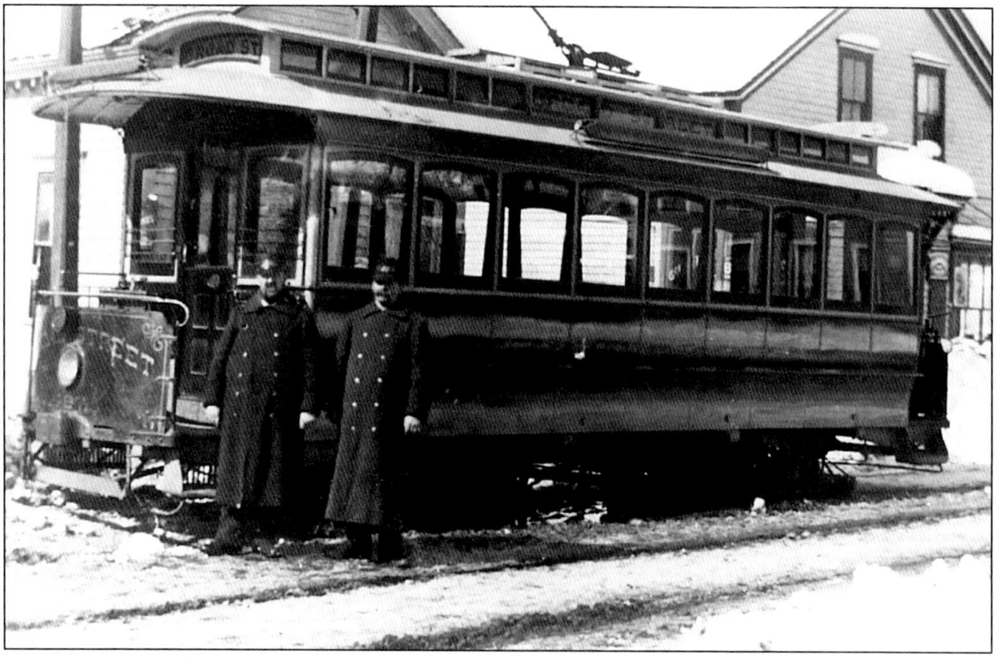

Serving as a conductor in the late nineteenth century was no job for the weak, as conductors stood at the front end of their vehicles, exposed to the weather. These conductors, dressed to face the elements, are getting ready to leave Pawtuxet in 1897/98 for Union Station. (From the Henry A.L. Brown Collection.)

The photographer has captured the motorman changing the wire on the Bumble Bee trolley in 1908. The trolley had come from Lakewood and was now going back. The horse-drawn vehicle is in front of Watson's Pharmacy. The Pawtuxet Heights sales office was located over the store that is now Dearheart's ice cream. The barber pole can be seen at the end of the picture. (Henry A.L. Brown Collection.)

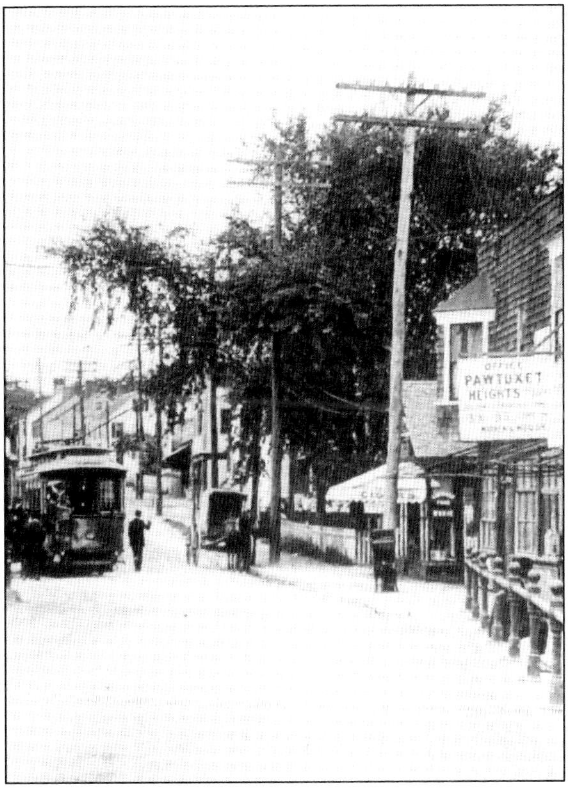

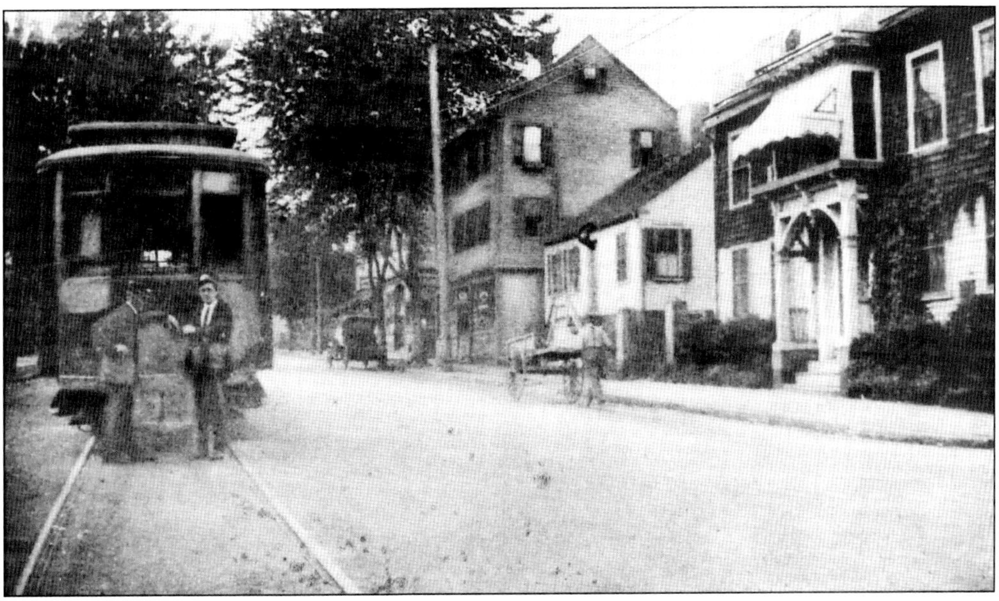

In 1916, a man with a pushcart passes in front of the Hayward house while conductors enjoy a brief chat before proceeding on their runs. The house was demolished by Murray Upham for the construction of a paint and hardware store. Today, the building houses a small mall that contains a paint store, video mailer (a mailing service), and pizza parlor. (William Hall Library Collection.)

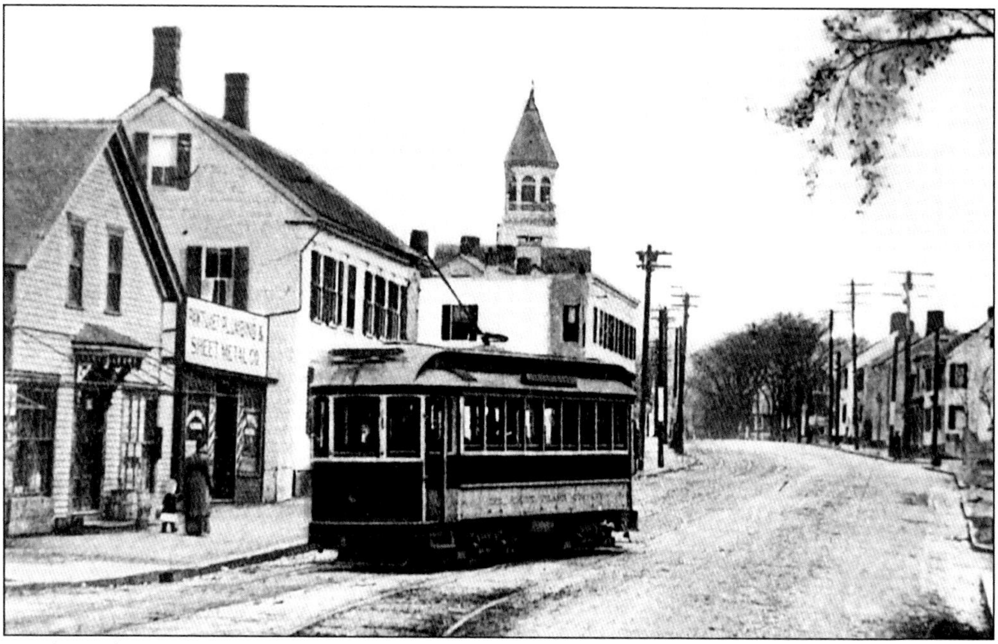

At about the time of the start of World War I in Europe (1914), almost everyone in Pawtuxet that owned a home had paid a visit to the Paint Plumbing & Sheet Metal shop, not far from the old post office. By this time, the Broad Street trolley made it possible to gain quick access to Providence from Pawtuxet. (Henry A.L. Brown Collection.)

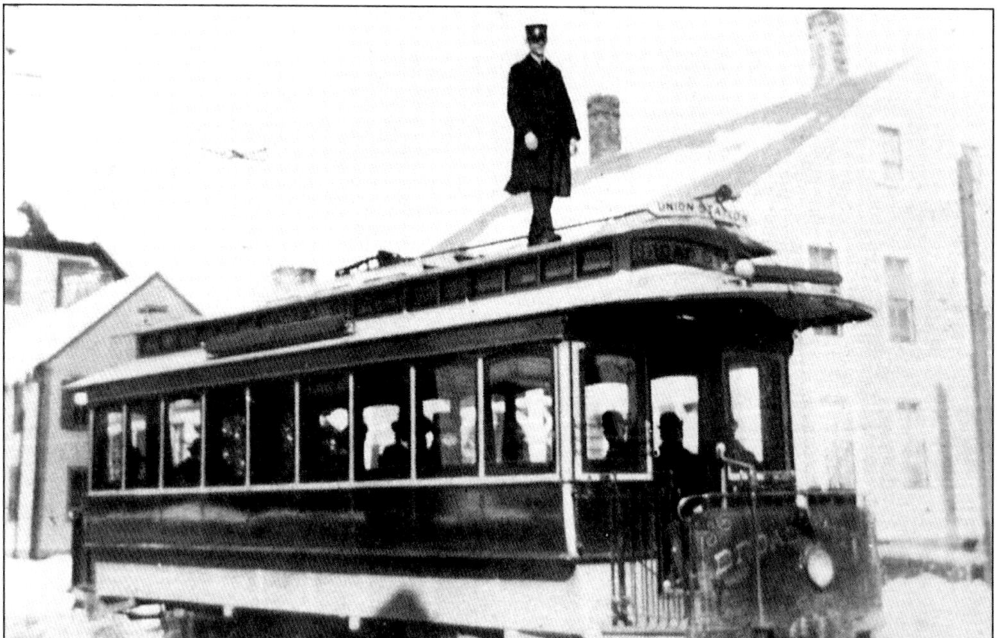

The trolley cars operated in all types of weather, sometimes causing great discomfort and danger to the conductors. This conductor had to climb on the slippery roof to reverse the car's direction by resetting the wire, which may have been frozen to the top of the car. (Henry A.L. Brown Collection.)

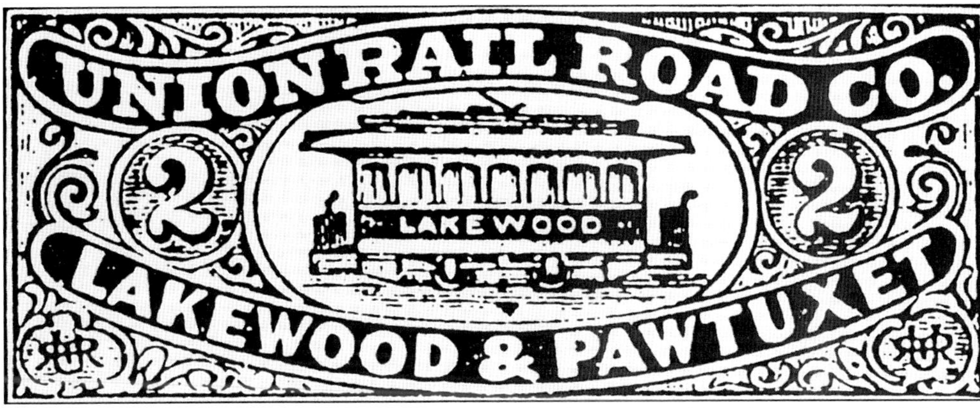

The fastest way from Pawtuxet to Lakewood, still referred to as New Pawtuxet in 1902, was via the Union Railroad's special car, the Bumble Bee. This car made so many trips that it was compared to a busy bee and the name caught on. (Henry A.L. Brown Collection.)

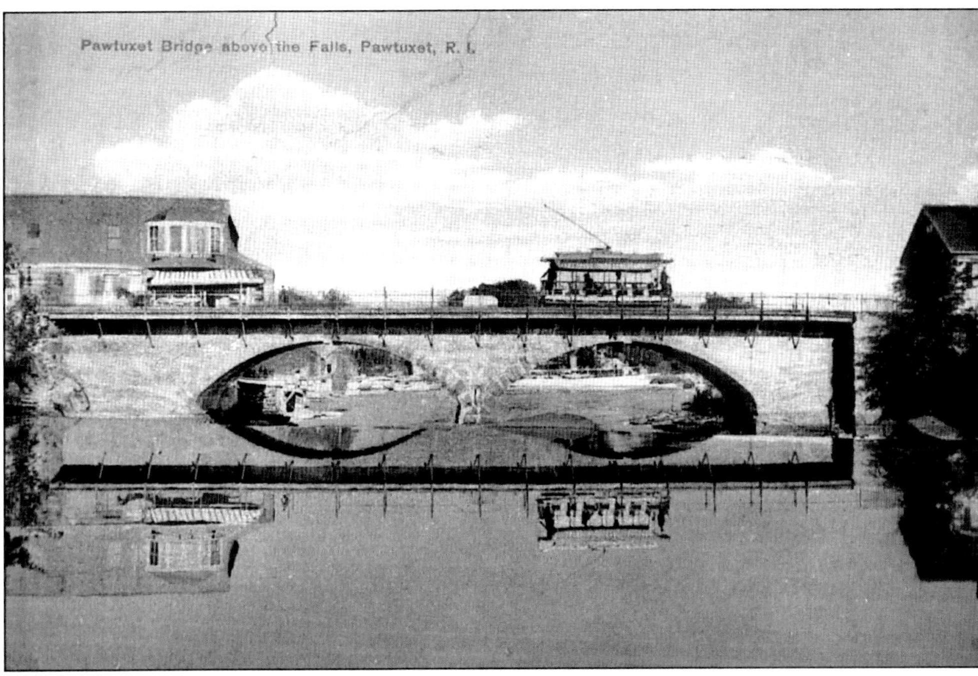

A familiar postcard captures the Bumble Bee trolley as it speeds across the bridge from Cranston on the left to Warwick on the right. It was on its way to Lakewood, taking passengers to a connection of the Warwick and Buttonwoods Railroad. The Bumble Bee started at the bridge, went up the hill, passed the bank, went on to Fair and South Fair Streets, and then to Atlantic Avenue in Lakewood. (Henry A.L. Brown Collection.)

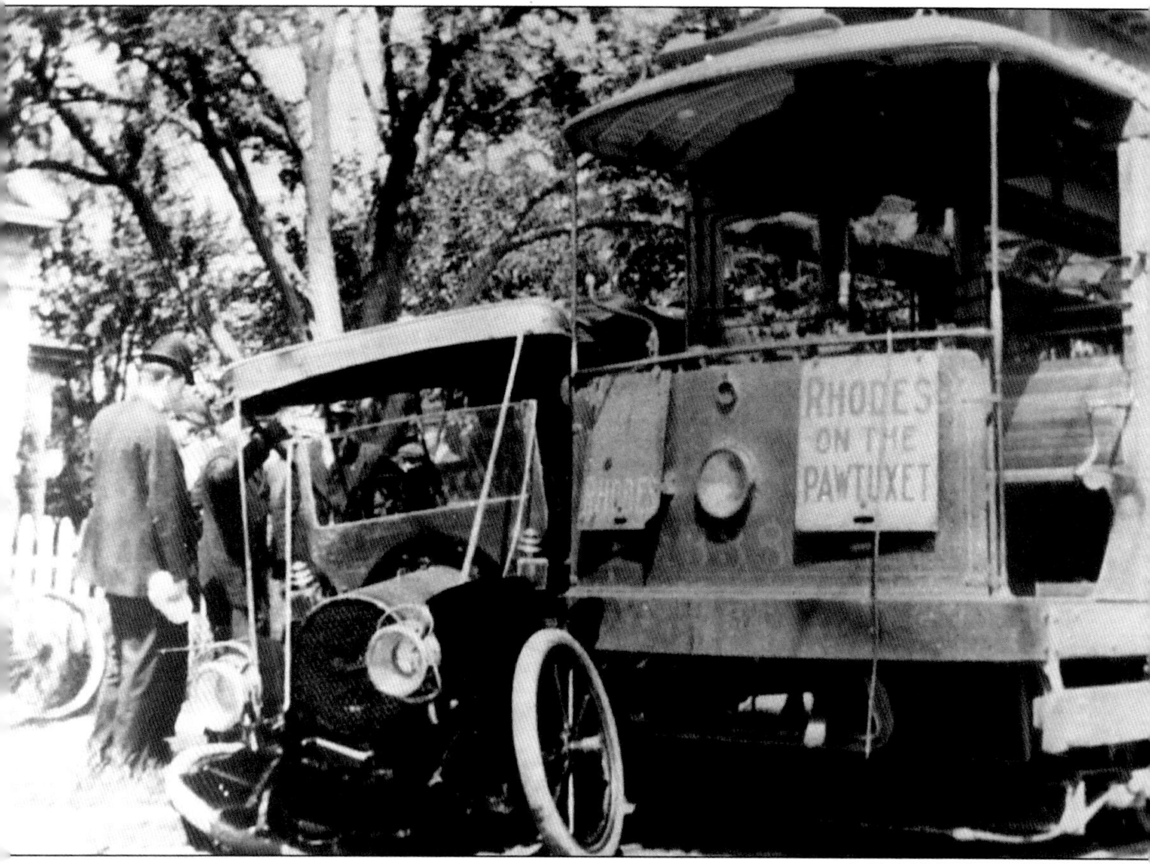

It was almost inevitable that when the automobile became more popular there would be incidents with the trolley cars that once reigned supreme. Both the trolley, an open car on its regular summertime run bound for Rhodes, and the 1912 Buick vied for the same space on Broad Street. It looks as if the trolley won. (Henry A.L. Brown Collection.)

Three

Rhodes-on-the-Pawtuxet

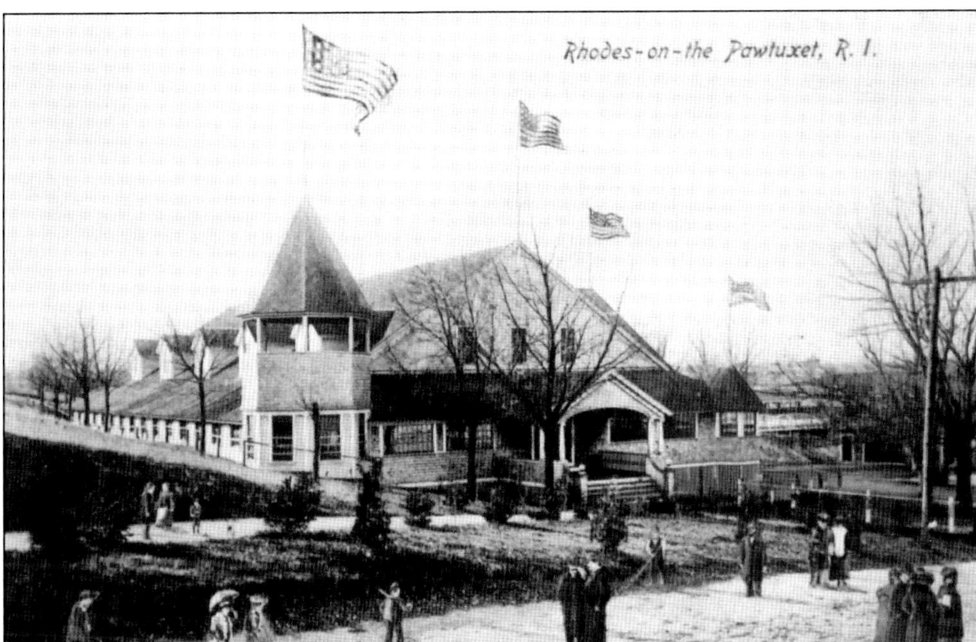

One of Rhode Island's most celebrated dance halls was the very famous Rhodes-on-the-Pawtuxet. Founded in 1872 by Thomas Rhodes, the resort went on to attract big bands and large crowds well into the twentieth century. The flag in front of the old casino at Rhodes shows only forty-five stars, as this was 1906, before Oklahoma, New Mexico, Arizona, Alaska, and Hawaii came into the Union. The lovely old building, which gave pleasure to so many, was destroyed by fire in 1915. (The Henry A.L. Brown Collection.)

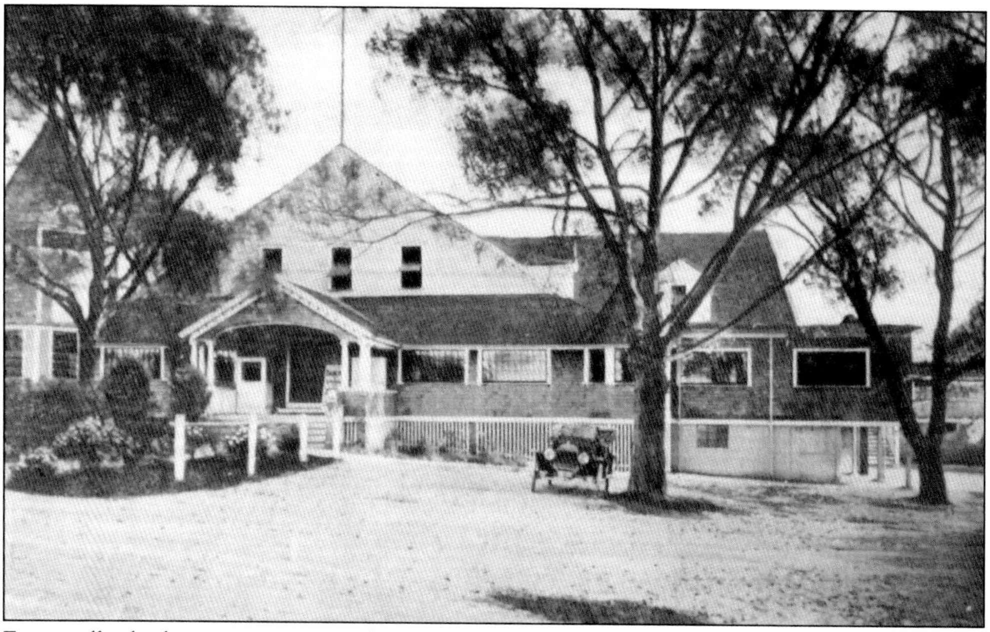

Eventually the horse gave way to the trolley and the trolley to the automobile as the mode of transportation for both young and old to the beautiful Rhodes-on-the-Pawtuxet. The Model T Ford is parked in front of the old Rhodes Casino. The casino and most of the surrounding buildings were destroyed in the devastating 1915 fire. (Henry A.L. Brown Collection.)

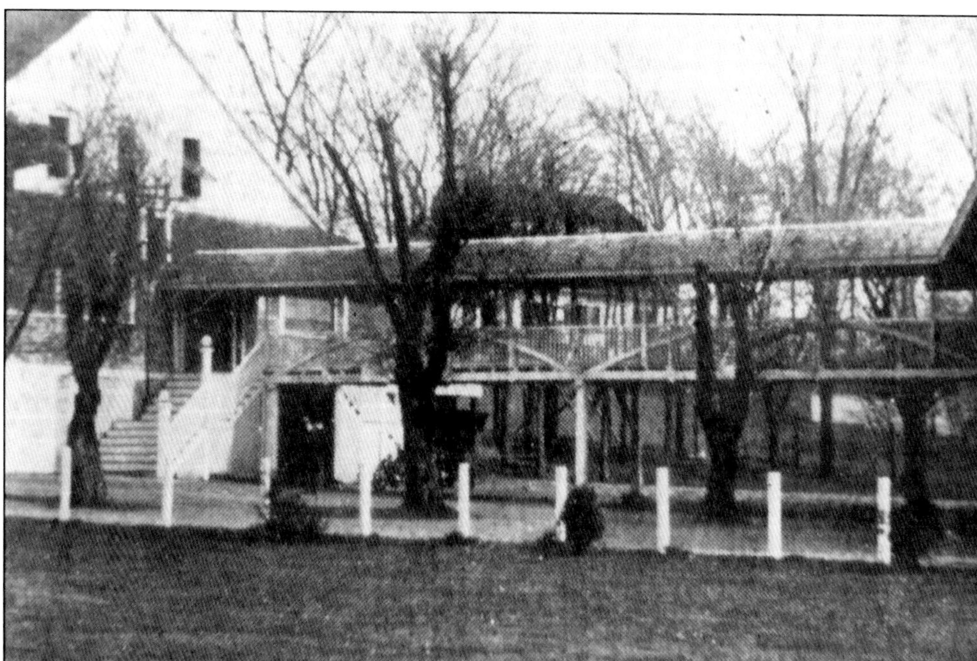

For those not interested in the canoe or the rowboat as vehicles of romance, a stroll along Lovers' Walk (shown here in 1907) was always an option at Rhodes-on-the-Pawtuxet. (Henry A.L. Brown Collection.)

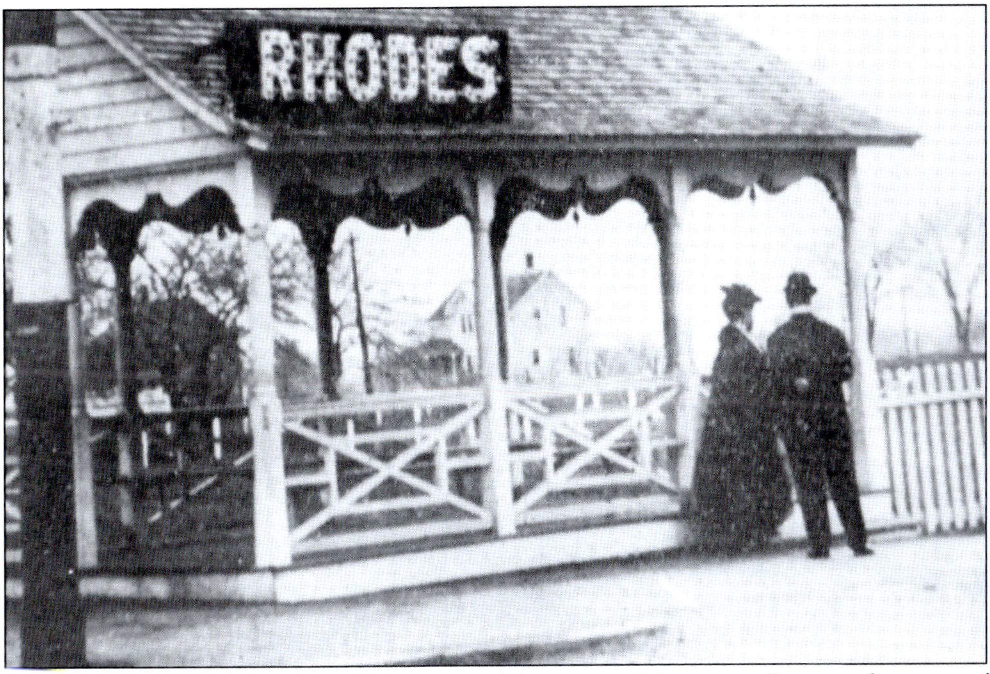

The Rhodes Waiting Station in 1904 was one of the most well-known trolley stops for scores of dance enthusiasts. This couple looks as if they were leaving Rhodes and awaiting the trolley ride home. (Henry A.L. Brown Collection.)

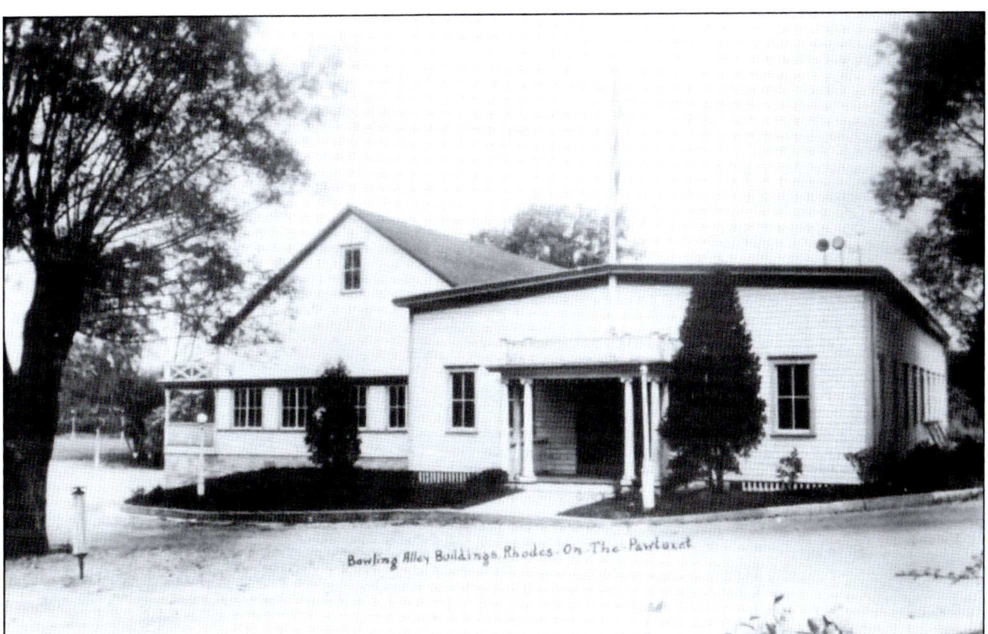

After the fire of 1915, Rhodes had a new look, which included these bowling alleys. After years of use, the alleys burned in 1965/66. (Henry A.L. Brown Collection.)

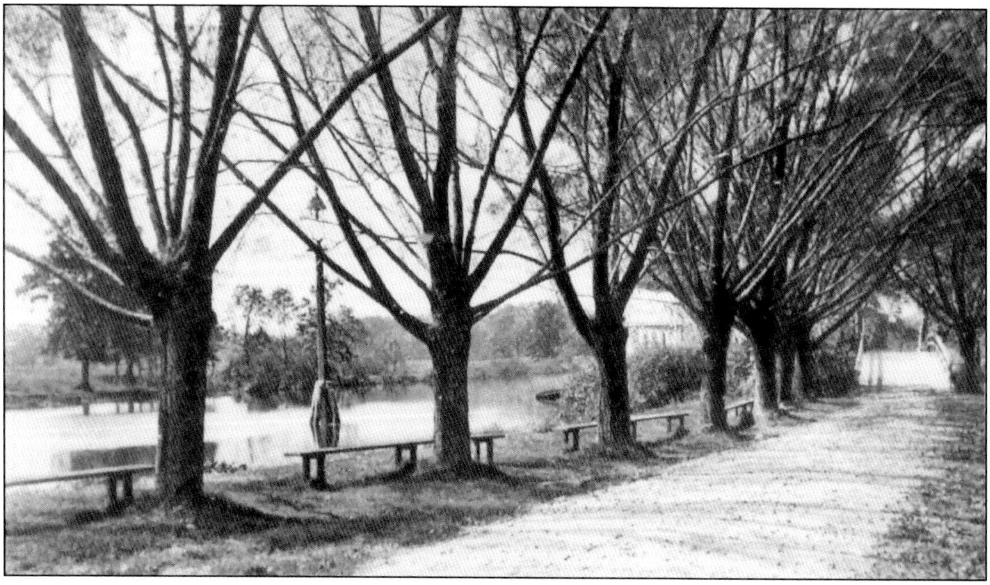

Many a marriage could trace its origins to a romantic stroll along the old Lovers' Walk at Rhodes. The lovely, tree-lined path, illuminated with flickering gaslight, caught the imagination and placed the cares of the world far away for at least a little while when the world was young in 1908. (Henry A.L. Brown Collection.)

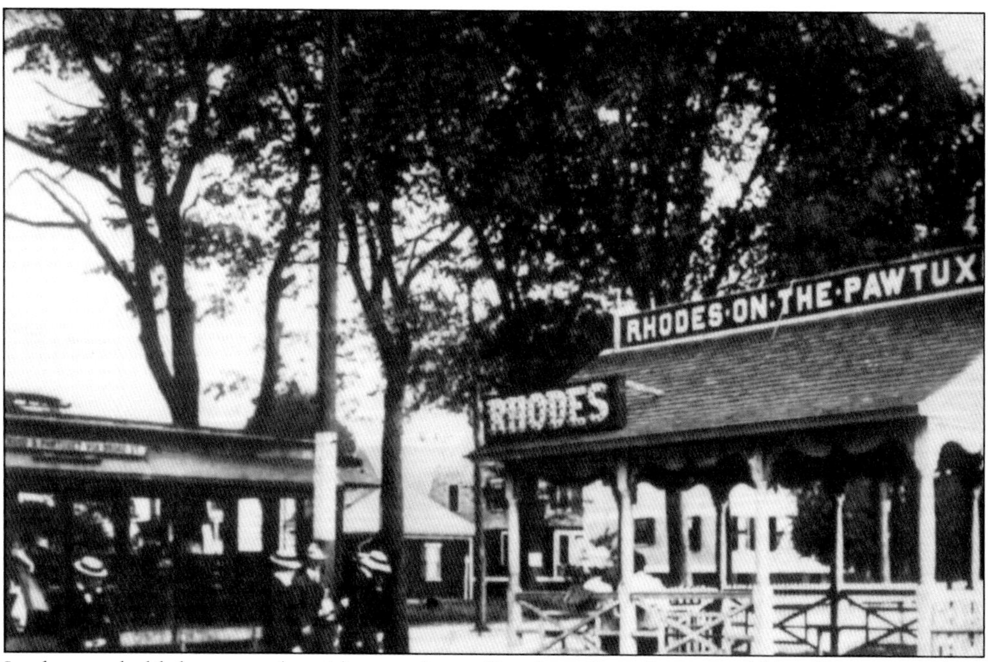

In the good old days gone by, riders on the trolley from Providence could hardly contain their excitement as the Rhodes Waiting Station (shown here in 1908) came into view. Rhodes was a place of enchantment where everyday trials and tribulations disappeared for a while. (Henry A.L. Brown Collection.)

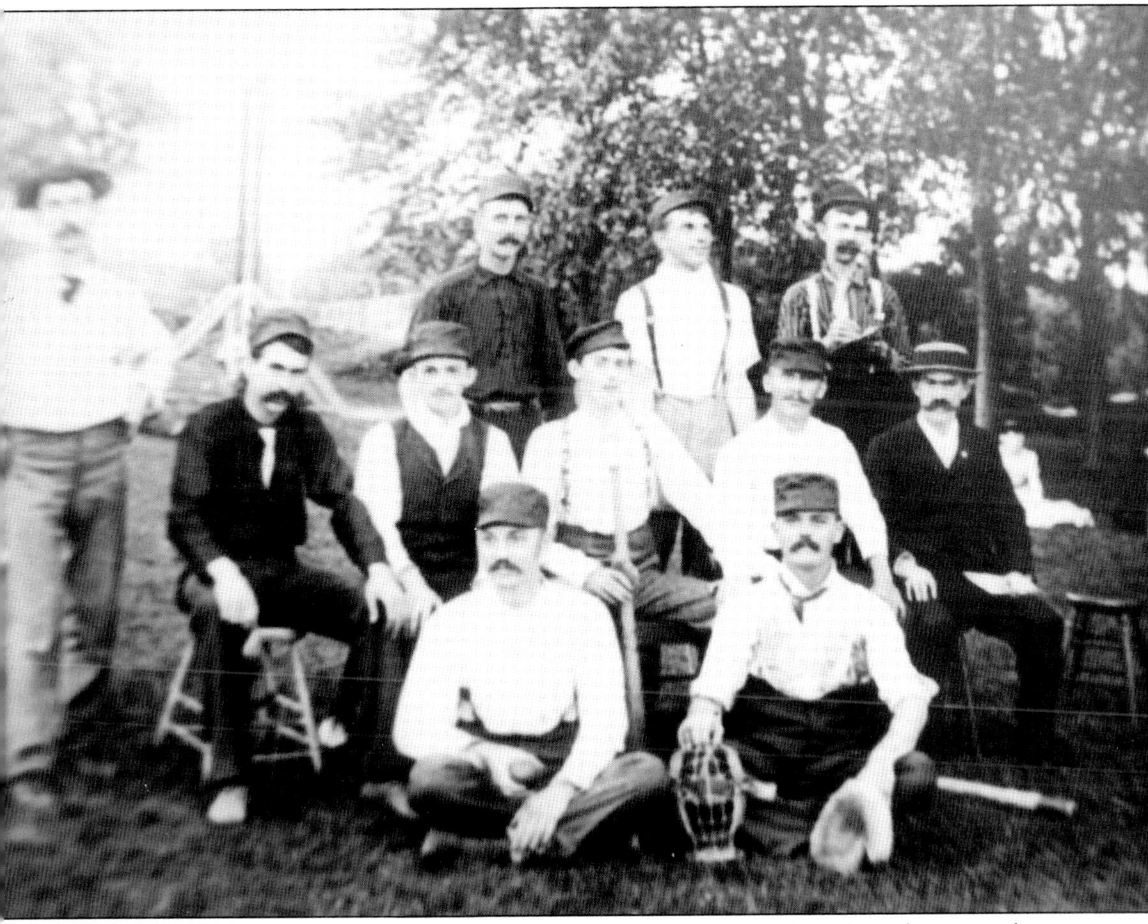

Baseball was beginning to become the great American sport by 1892, when the stalwart members of the Swat & What Cheer Baseball Club came to an outing and ballgame at Rhodes-on-the-Pawtuxet. (Henry A.L. Brown Collection.)

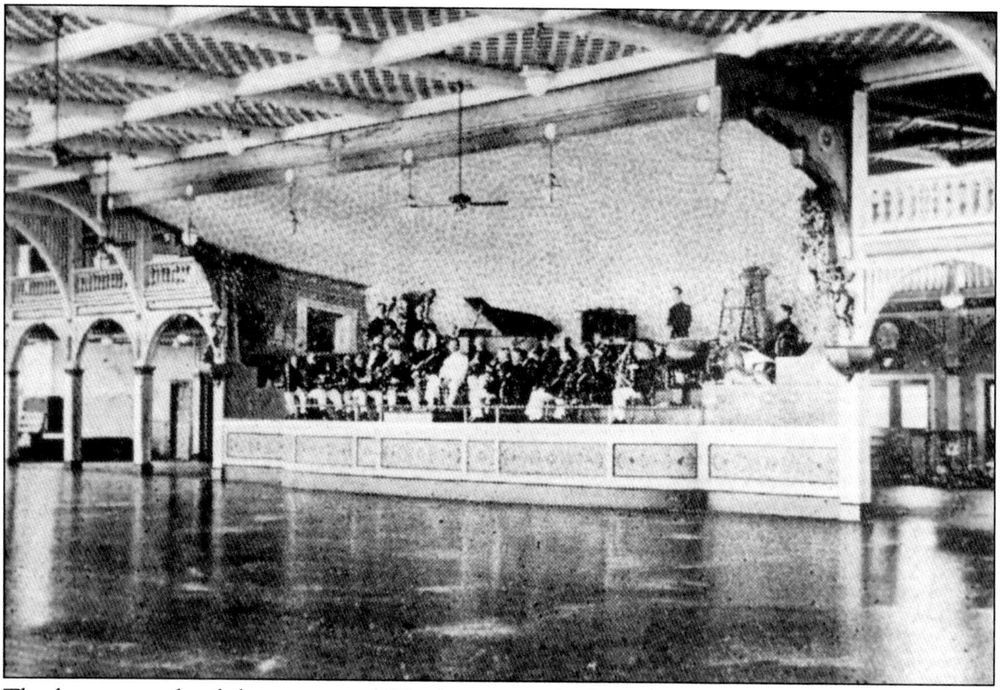

The key to much of the success of Rhodes was its high-quality entertainment. In this 1924 photograph, this orchestra was getting ready for the large crowds that were sure to come. (Henry A.L. Brown Collection.)

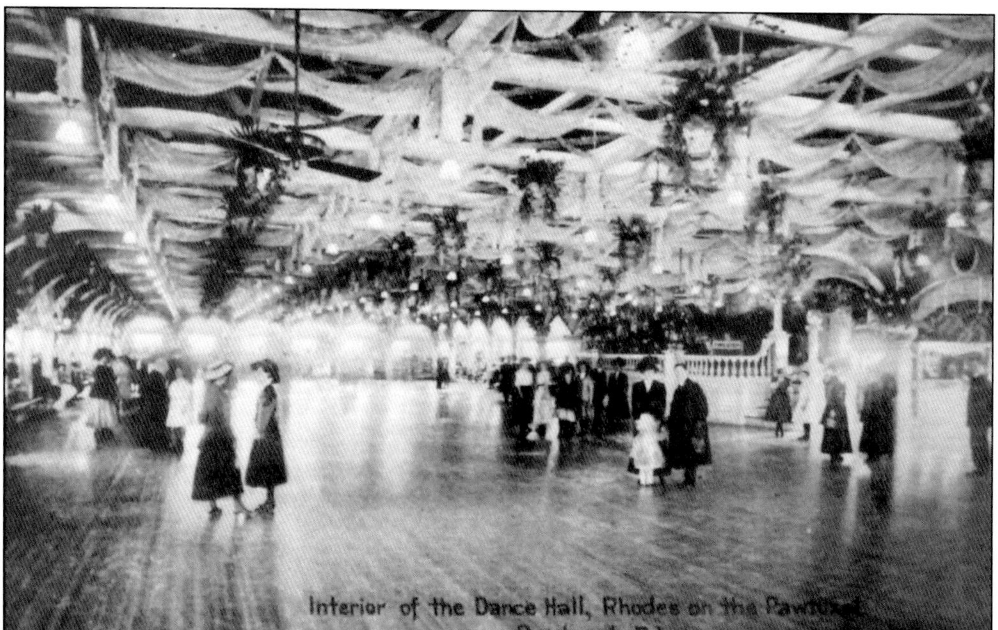

Rhodes was quickly rebuilt after the fire of 1915. This new interior ballroom drew its share of "oohs" and "ahhs" from the loyal patrons, who quickly flocked to the ballroom once the doors were opened in 1916. (Henry A.L. Brown Collection.)

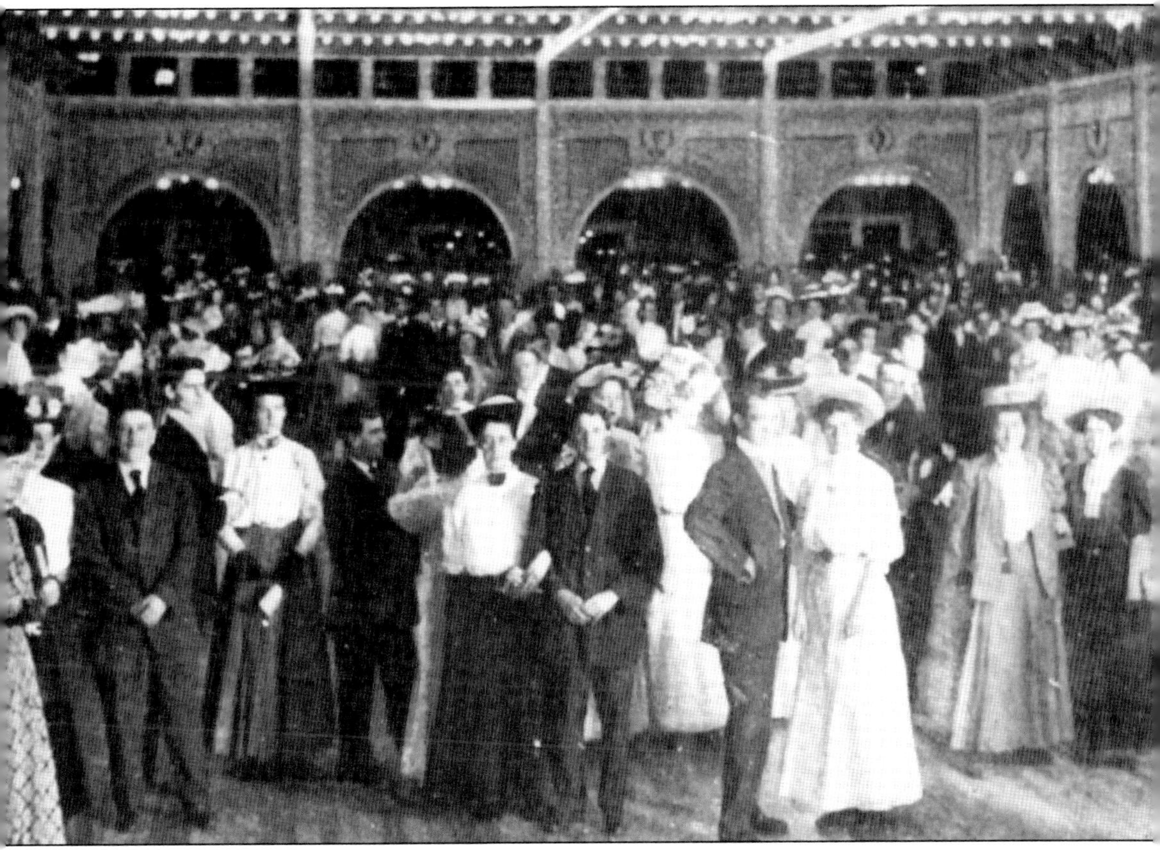

Judging by the size of the crowd gathered here in the Rhodes Casino in 1908, dancing was the main attraction of the evening at the turn of the century. What a lovely way to spend an evening! (Henry A.L. Brown Collection.)

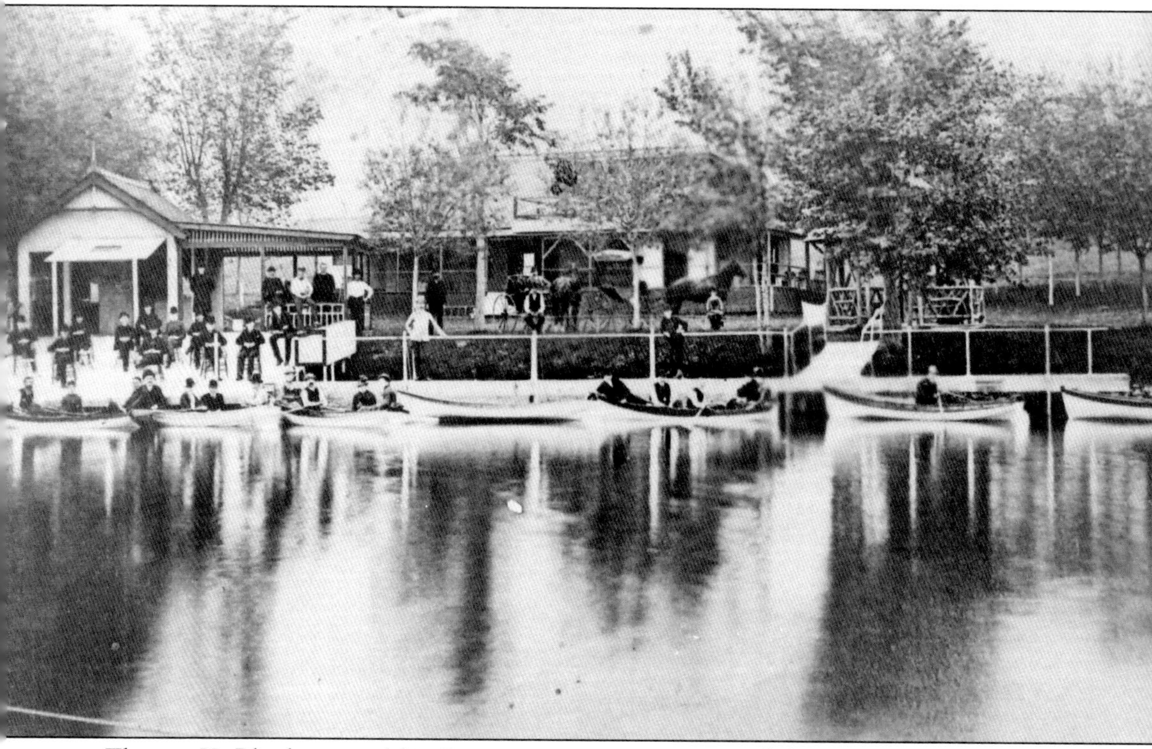

Thomas H. Rhodes turned his Pawtuxet property into one of the most fashionable summer recreational sites on the Atlantic Coast. He made provisions for bakes, dancing, and water sports. Nineteenth-century fun-seekers came here from far and wide to enjoy the facilities. Much of what is seen in this 1890 photograph was destroyed by fire in 1915. (Henry A.L. Brown Collection.)

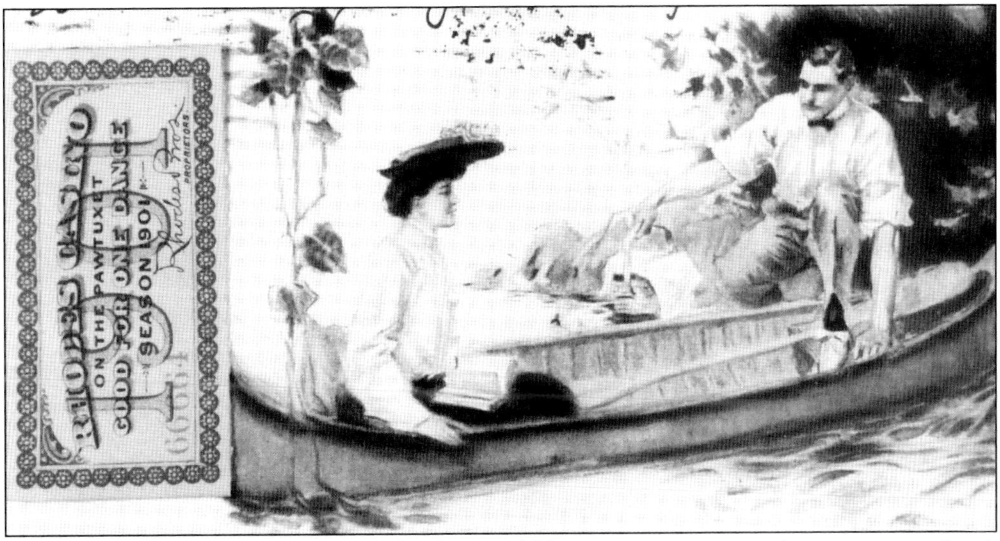

For those with romance on the mind, what could be more appropriate than a canoe ride. A rented canoe for the afternoon and a ticket for dancing at the casino at night were surefire ways to romance in the early twentieth century. (Henry A.L. Brown Collection.)

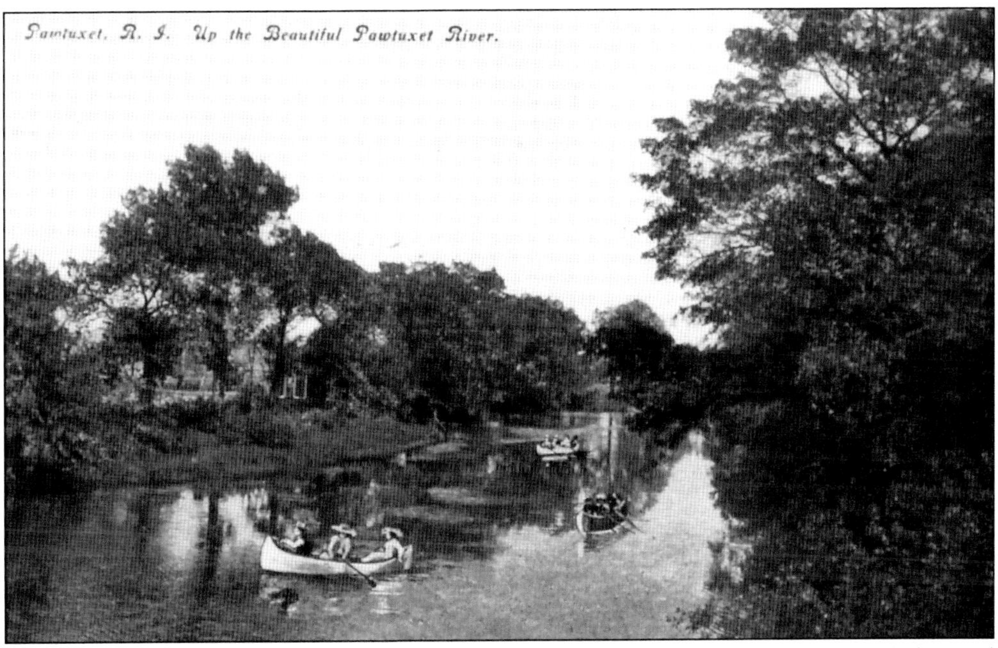

On summer Sundays, canoes and rowboats on the Pawtuxet River not only provided a cool respite after a hot work week, but they were also great for courting the lady of your choice. (Henry A.L. Brown Collection.)

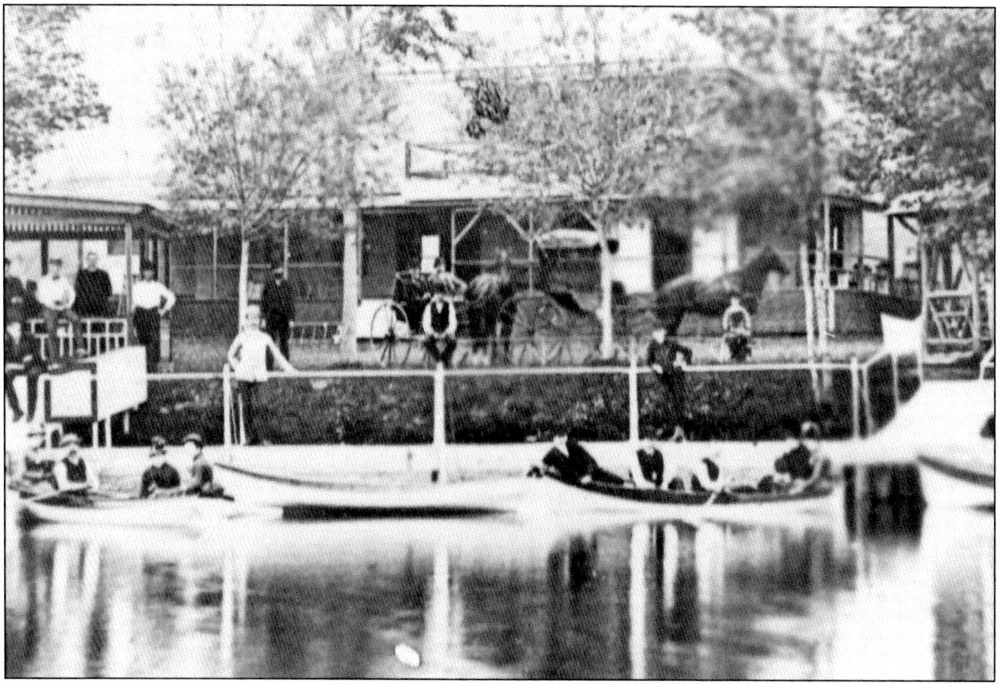

The trolley had made its appearance by the time this photograph was taken in 1890, but the horse-drawn vehicles were still the most common means of transportation. Getting to Rhodes was a bit more complicated in the nineteenth than in the twentieth century. (Henry A.L. Brown Collection.)

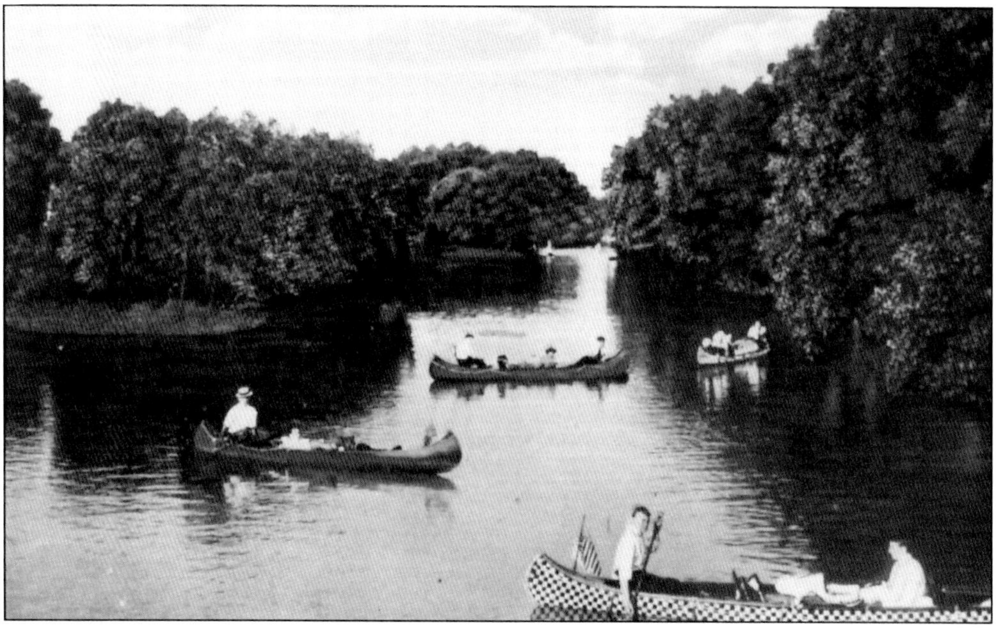

Traffic on the river increased dramatically on the weekends as canoes popped up everywhere. Canoes have come from Rhodes to the area opposite Belmont, a summer resort area with a few cottages. Belmont cottages often felt the full impact of the spring flooding along the Pawtuxet. (Henry A.L. Brown Collection.)

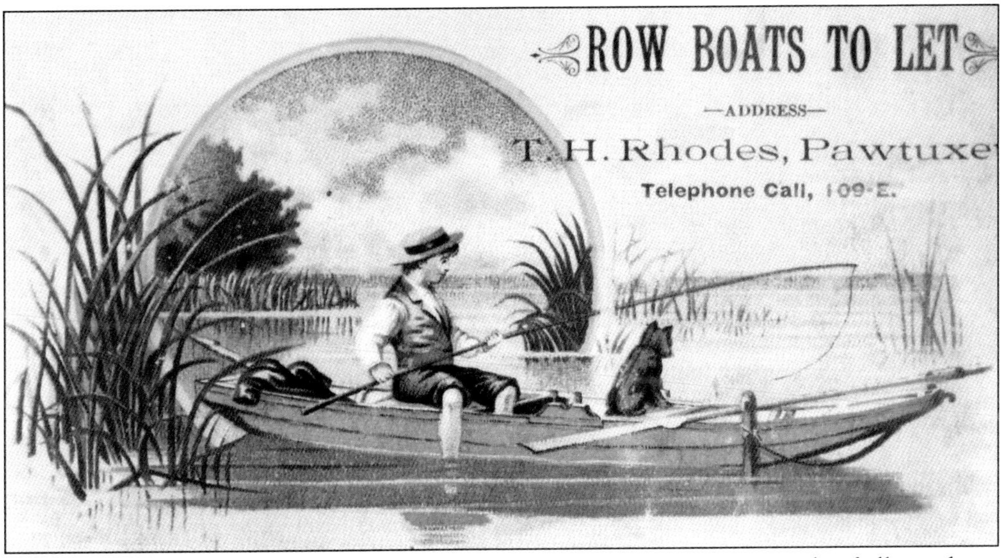

Ever since Thomas Rhodes founded Rhodes-on-the-Pawtuxet in 1872, people of all ages have been attracted to Pawtuxet for various summer activities. Postcards, such as this 1889 classic, advertised the resort. Rhodes had one of the first telephones in the state. With only three numbers and a letter, the exchange was a far call from today's area code and seven digits. (Henry A.L. Brown Collection.)

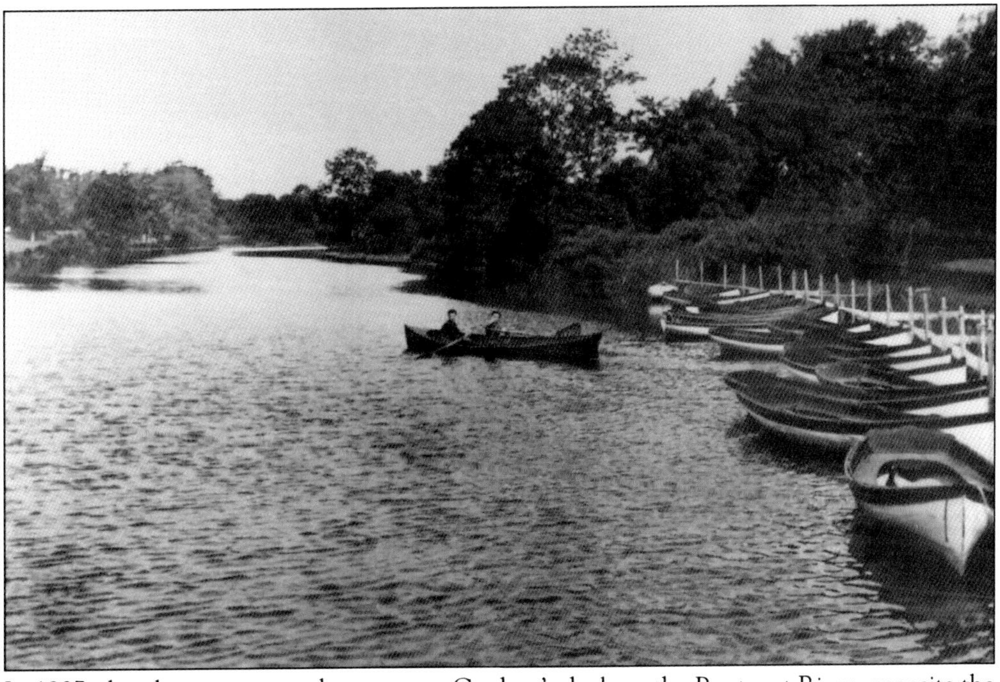

In 1907, the place to rent rowboats was at Gardner's dock on the Pawtuxet River, opposite the Rhodes Casino and Boat House. For a relatively small fee, you could rent the boat for the entire day of fishing or exploring the small islands in the vicinity. (William Hall Library Collection.)

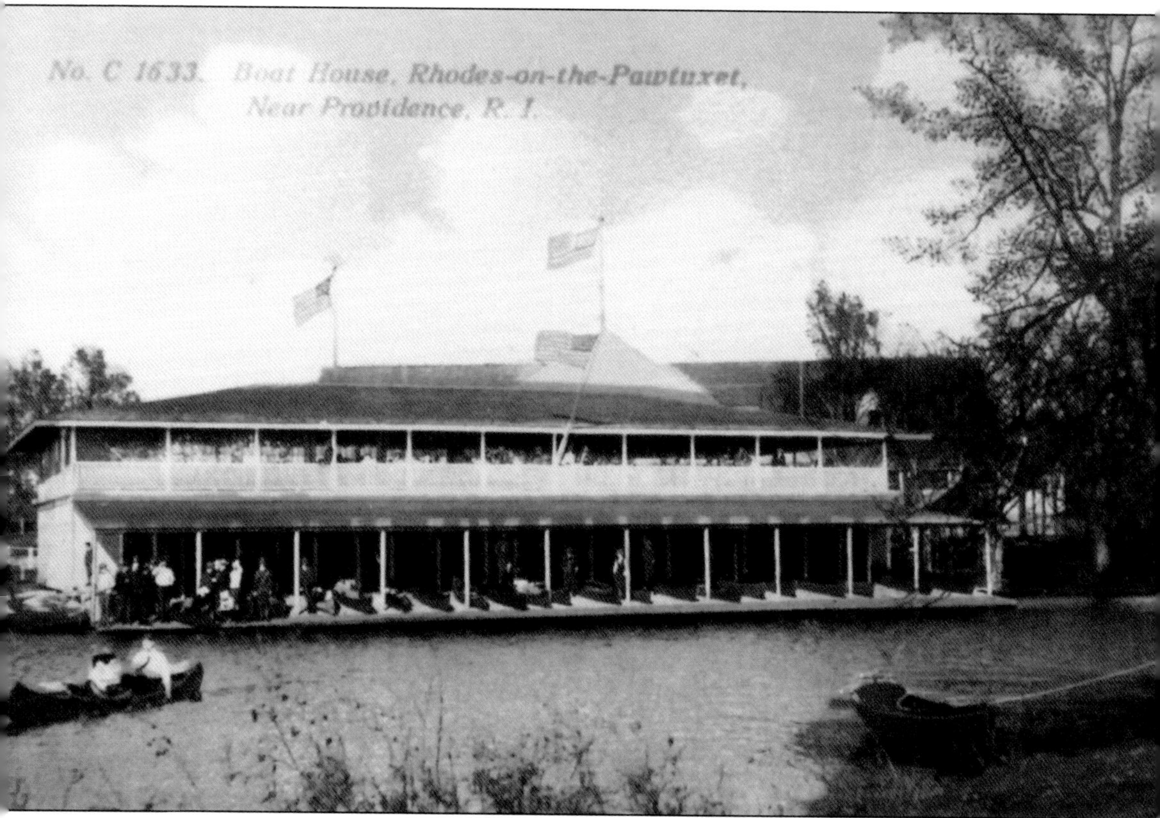

In the halcyon days before World War I, Rhode Island enjoyed the distinction of being the "Gateway to New England" and took pride in Rhodes and the Rhodes Boat House. This *c.* 1913 boathouse was destroyed by the devastating fire of 1915. (Henry A.L. Brown Collection.)

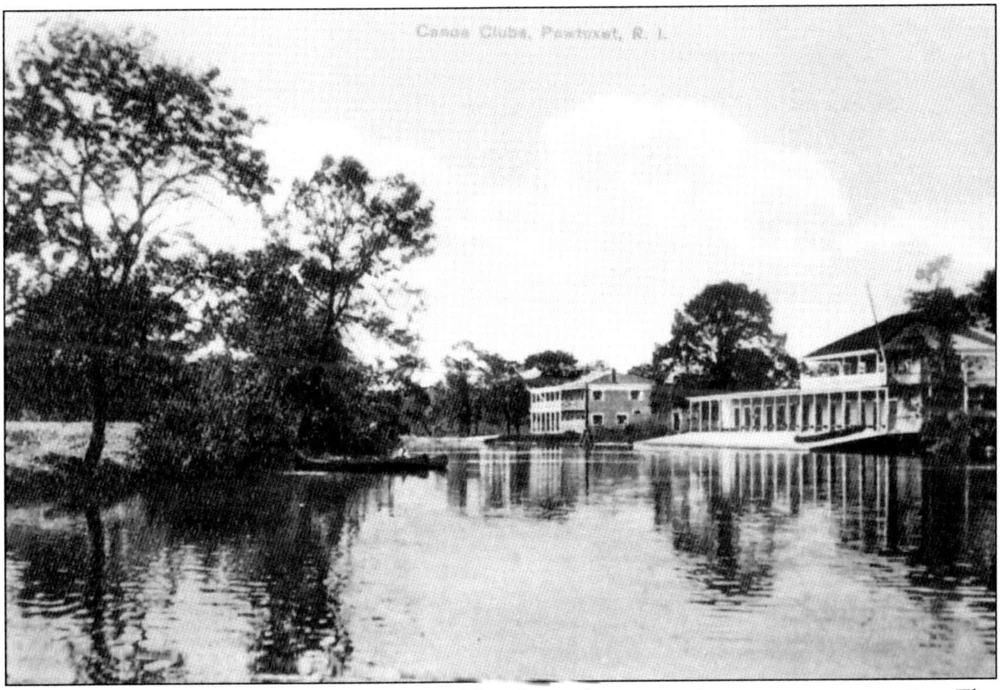

A more popular pastime than baseball or golf in the early twentieth century was canoeing. The Rhodes Canoe Clubs, adjacent to the casino and shown here in 1912, were an active social and sporting center for all ages. (Henry A.L. Brown Collection.)

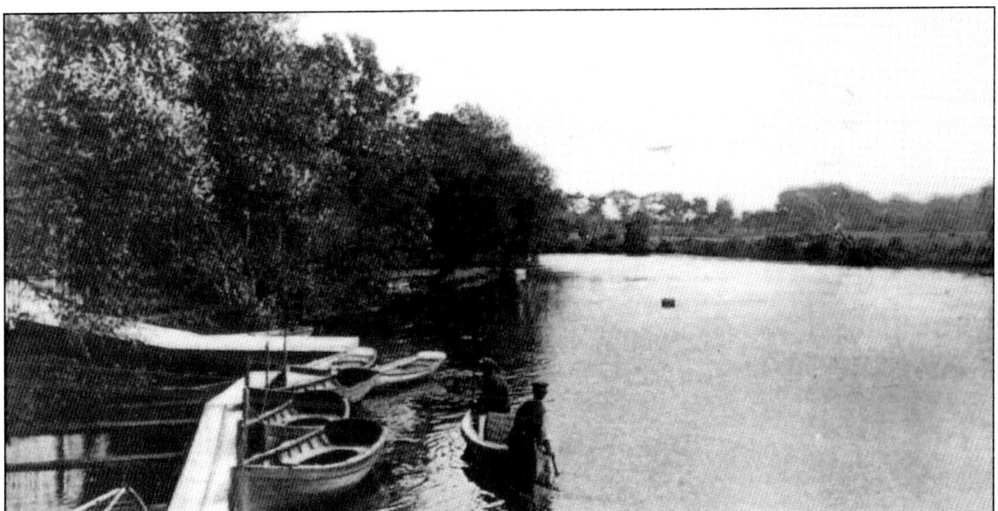

The Cole Dairy Farm, famous for its clambakes for many years, can be seen on the opposite side of the Pawtuxet River from the Rhodes Boat House in 1909. (Henry A.L. Brown Collection.)

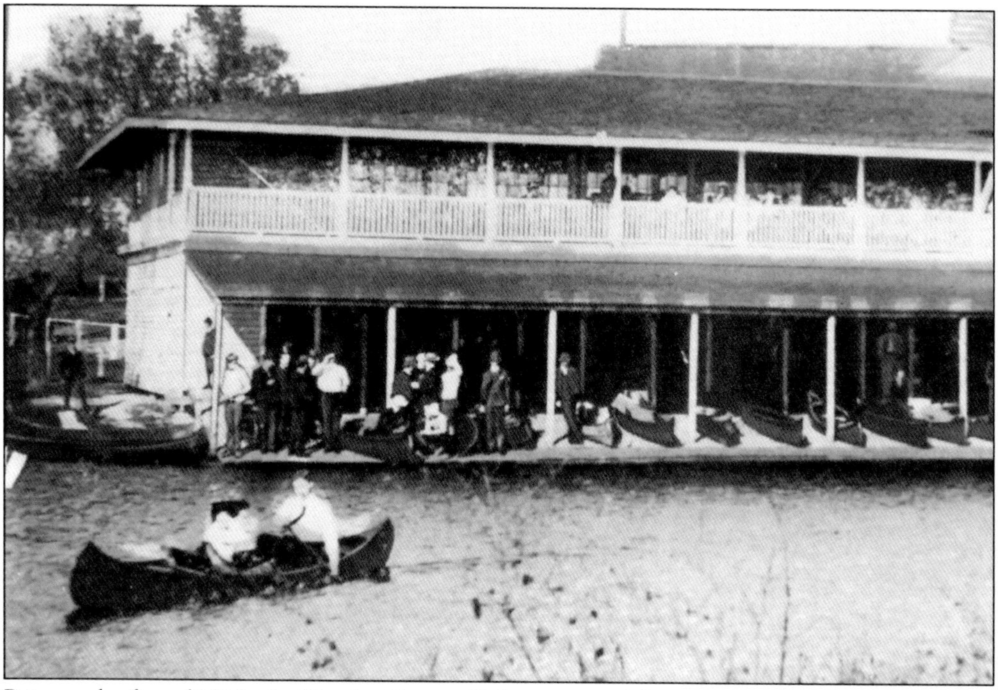

Prior to the fire of 1915, the Rhodes Canoe Club was one of the most popular in New England. The fire destroyed the club and much of the area around it. (Henry A.L. Brown Collection.)

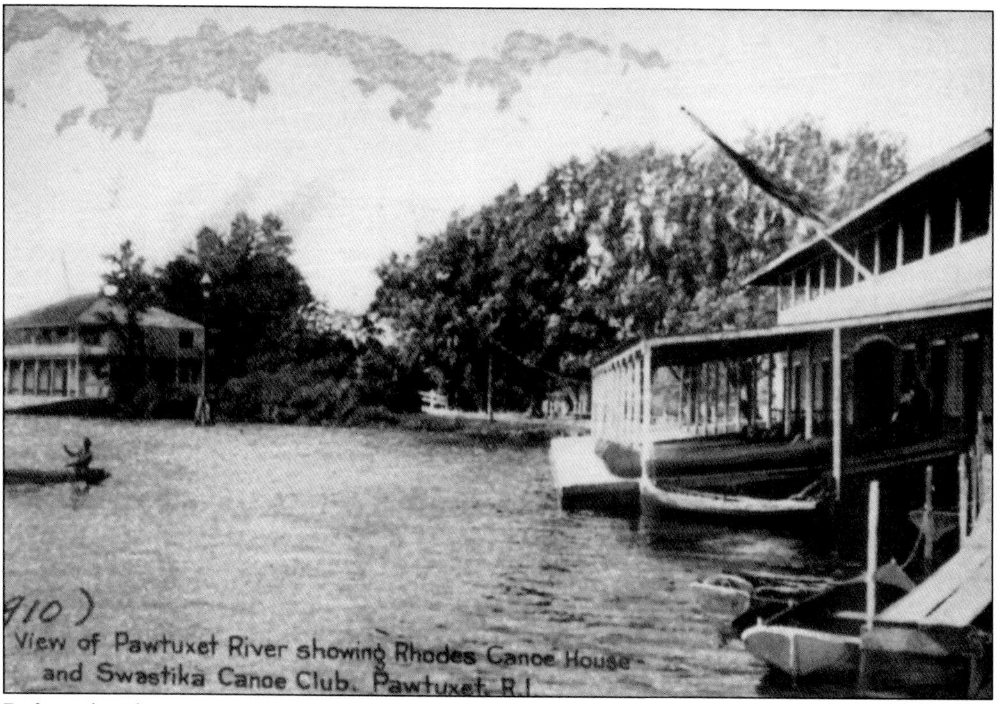

Before the devastating changes brought about by time and fire made their impressions on Pawtuxet, the Rhodes Canoe House (right) and the Swastika Club (left) were friendly rivals in 1910 for the prizes given in canoe races. (Cranston Historical Society Collection.)

Two staunch members of the Pawtuxet Canoe Club, *c.* 1926, were Madeline and William Peterson. The large white "P" on Bill's tank top was as prestigious a symbol as any high school athletic letter of later years. (Ray Peterson Collection.)

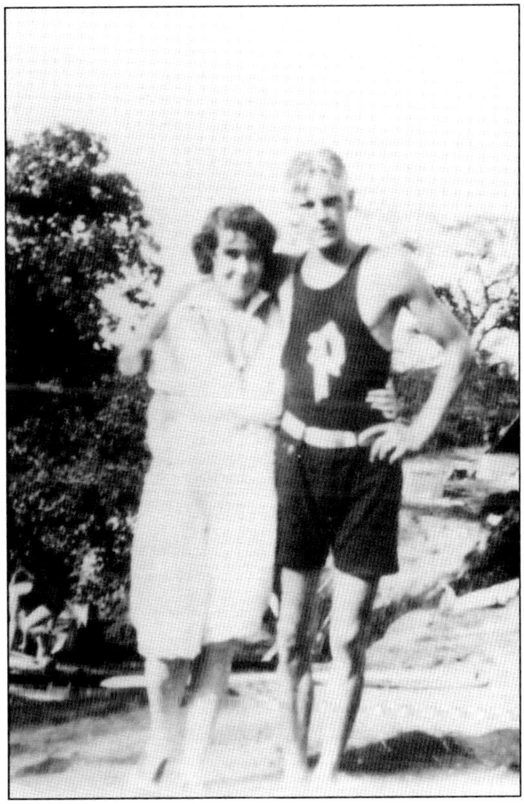

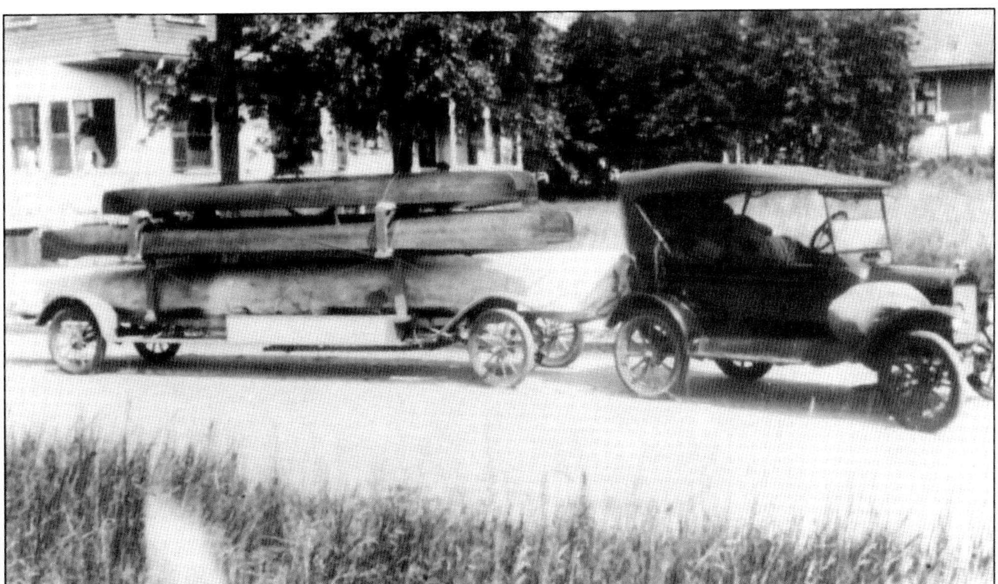

Here, members of the Pawtuxet Canoe Club get ready to compete with other clubs from Rhode Island and elsewhere in Worcester, Massachusetts, in 1926. (Ray Peterson Collection.)

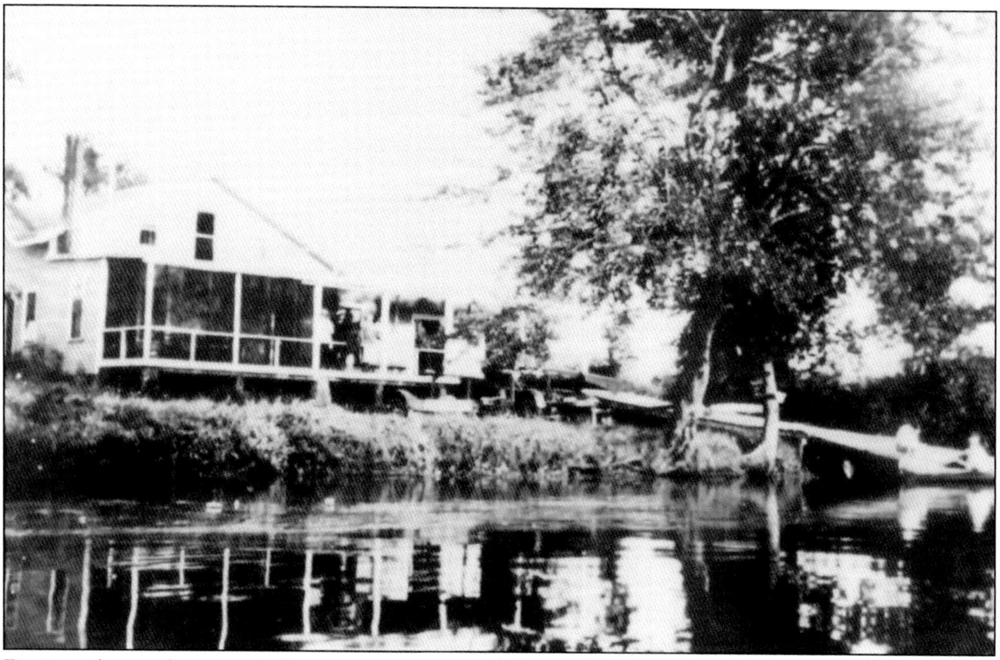

During the early twentieth century, canoe clubs such as the Pawtuxet Canoe Clubhouse conducted races and took part in the yearly canoe carnival, which was a very popular affair and drew spectators from all over New England. This photograph was taken *c.* 1926. (Henry A.L. Brown Collection.)

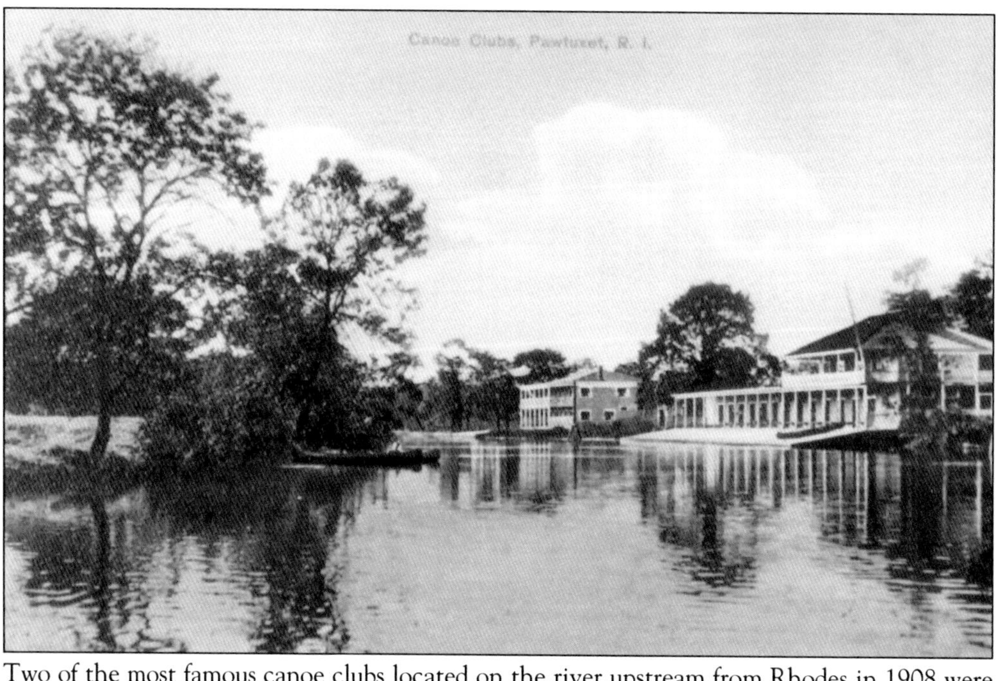

Two of the most famous canoe clubs located on the river upstream from Rhodes in 1908 were the Saskatchewam (left) and the Swastika Canoe Clubs. (Henry A.L. Brown Collection.)

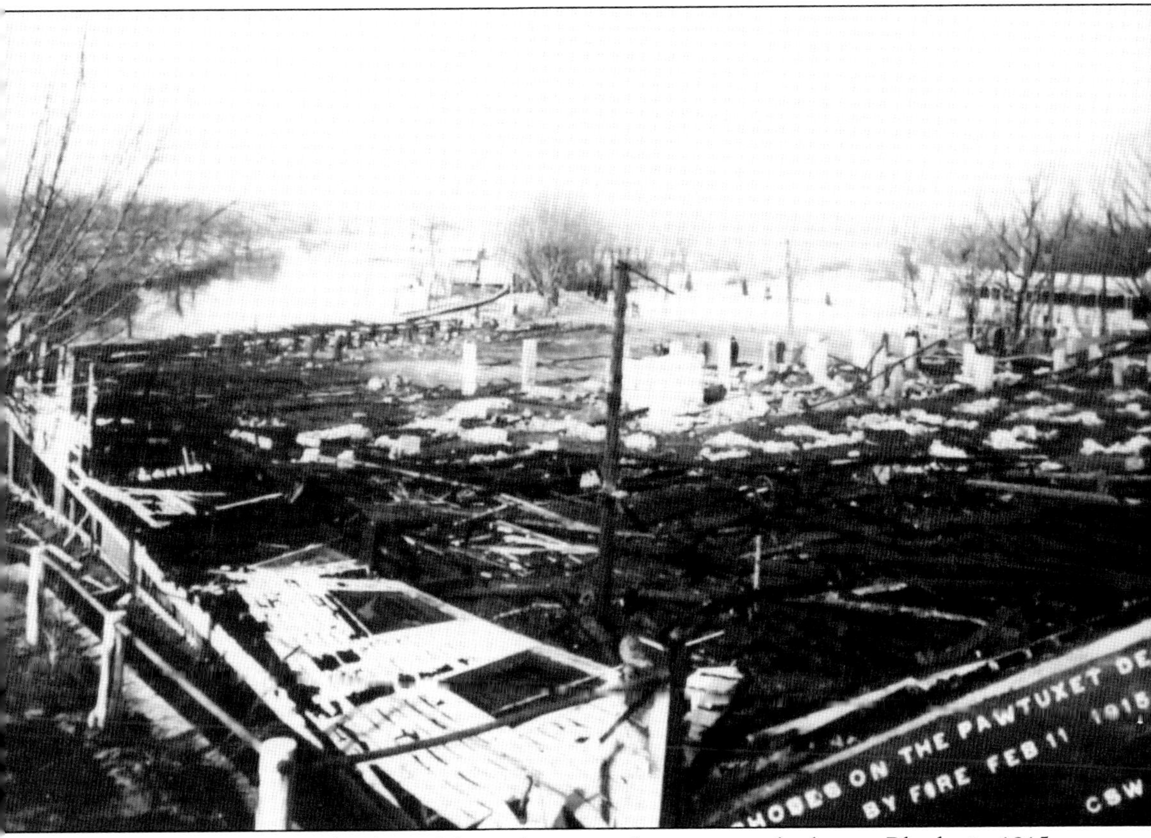

One of the most spectacular fires of the early twentieth century took place at Rhodes in 1915. The canoe club was at the center of the picture. The bake house seen on the right managed to survive the fire. (Ginnie Leslie Collection.)

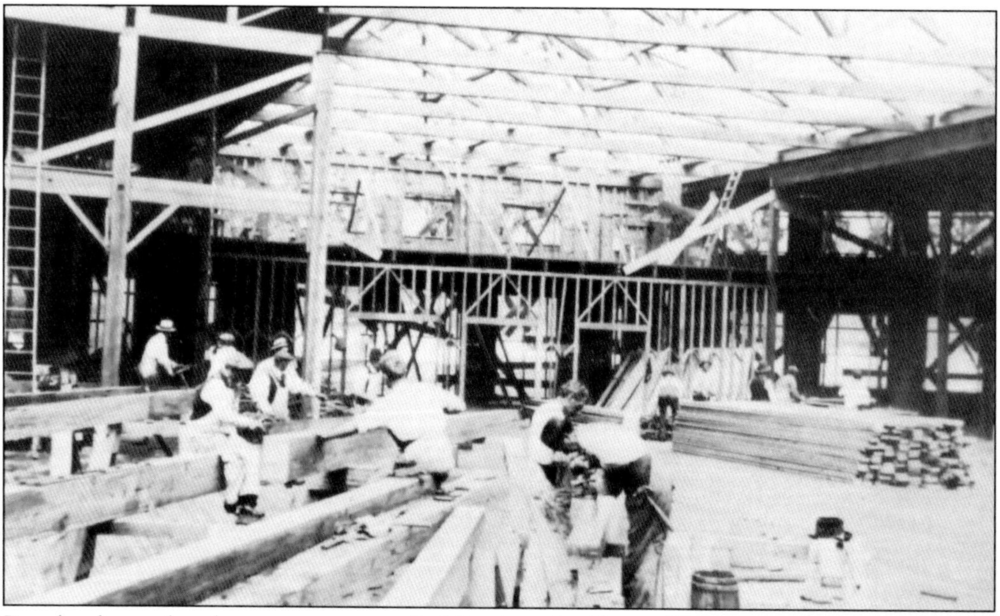

Popular demand and common sense called for the rebuilding of Rhodes-on-the-Pawtuxet after the 1915 fire. Workmen converged on the site in large numbers and quickly built a new and better casino at Rhode Island's favorite summer playground. (Henry A.L. Brown Collection.)

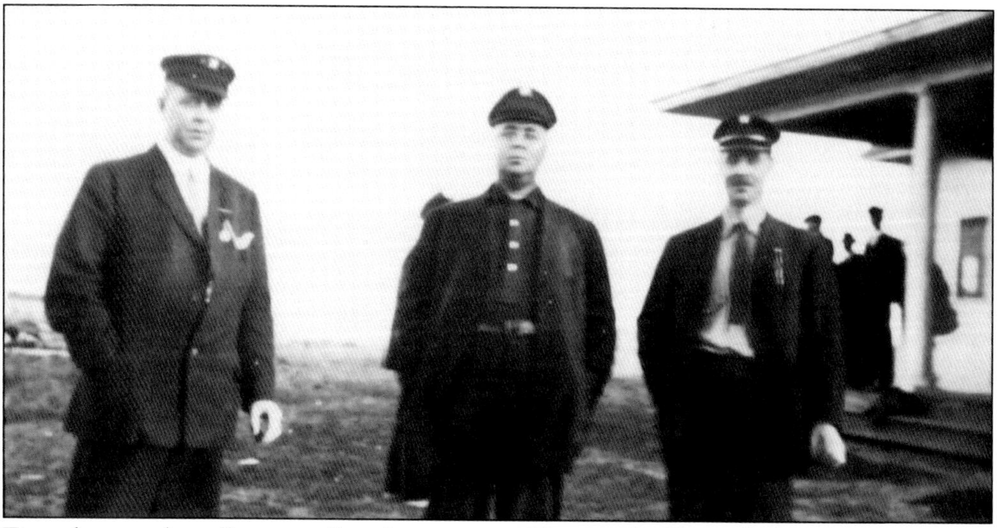

To make sure that all went well and to stop vandalism and pilferage before they could start, Rhodes hired these security guards while the enterprise was being rebuilt in 1915. (Henry A.L. Brown Collection.)

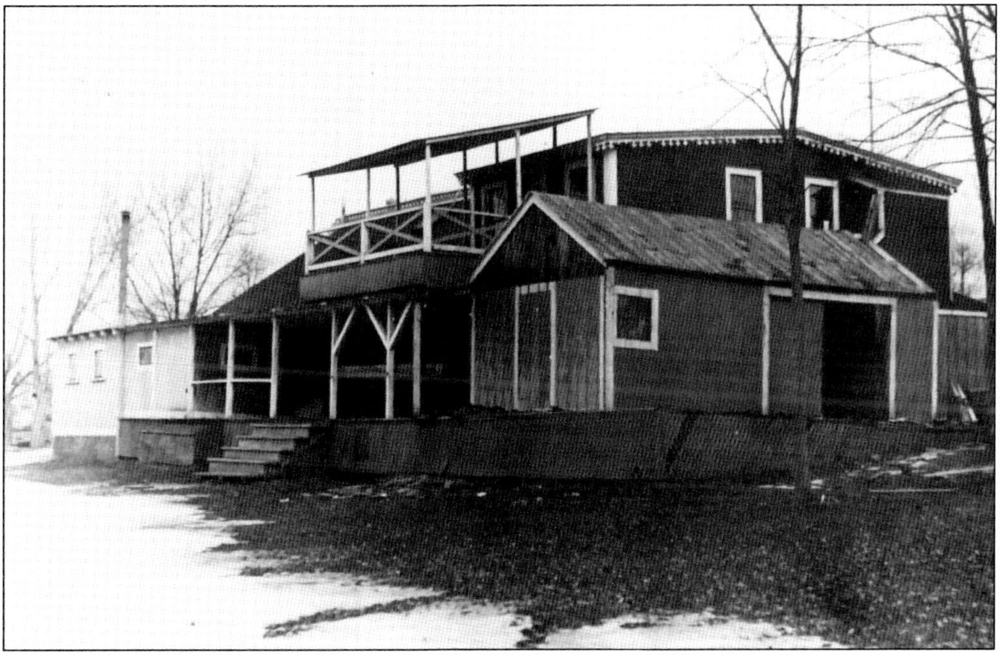

One of the few buildings that survived the fire of 1915 was the Rhodes Bake House. In 1930, it was still serving large numbers of summer visitors. (Henry A.L. Brown Collection.)

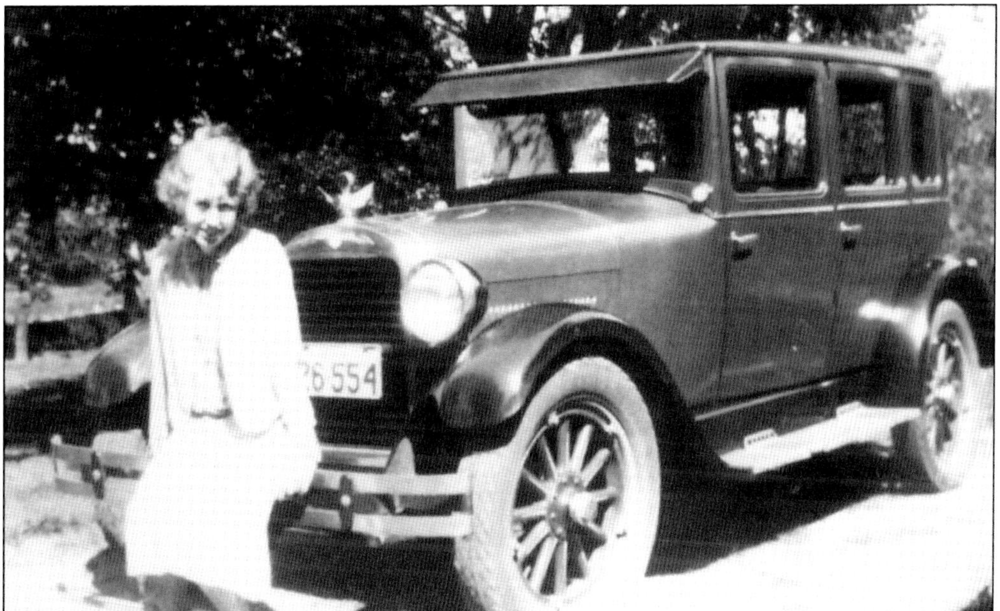

Bessie Nye seems to be enjoying her outing at Rhodes-on-the-Pawtuxet in 1928. She is perched on the bumper of a seven-passenger classic Packard. It had mohair upholstery and jump seats. (Henry A.L. Brown Collection.)

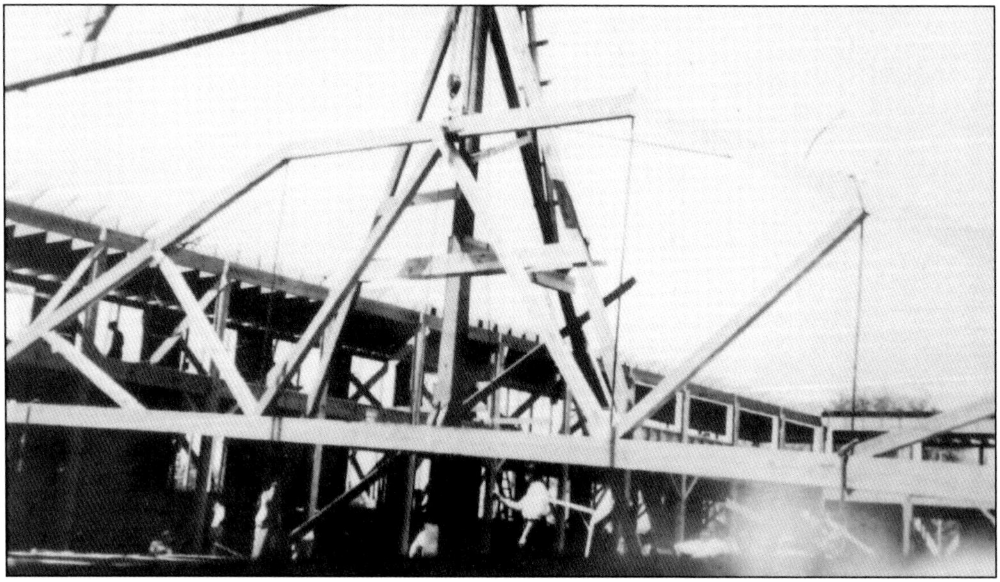

Thomas Rhodes, who founded the historic resort, would have been amazed to see how quickly the complex was rebuilt after the devastating fire of 1915. (Henry A.L. Brown Collection.)

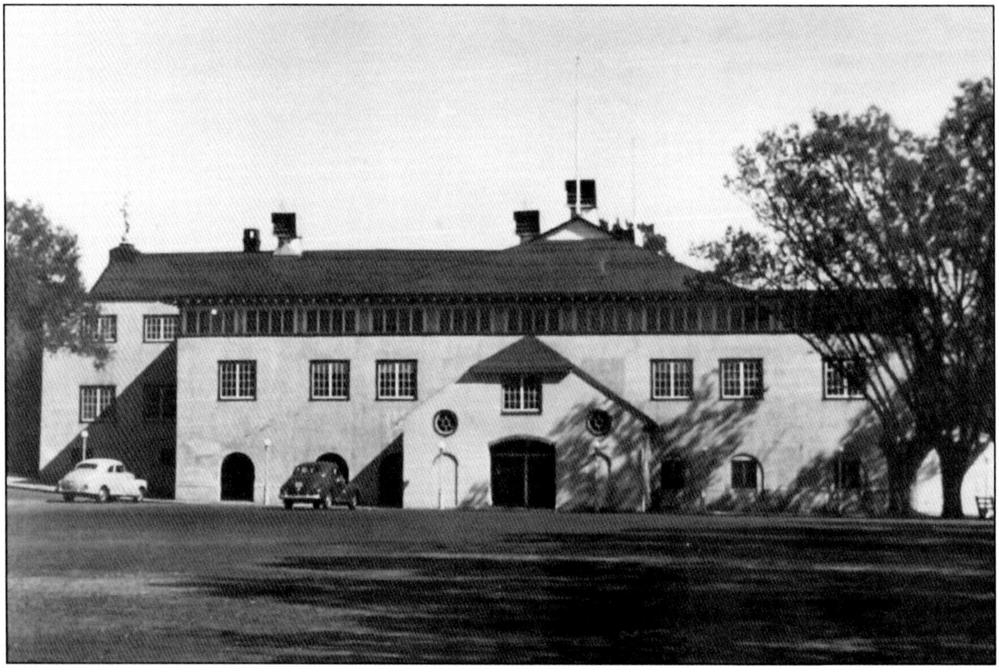

After World War II, Rhodes-on-the-Pawtuxet enjoyed another period of prosperity as returning servicemen and women tried to recapture the pre-war romance. In 1948, the casino looked like this on the side facing the parking lot. (Cranston Historical Society Collection.)

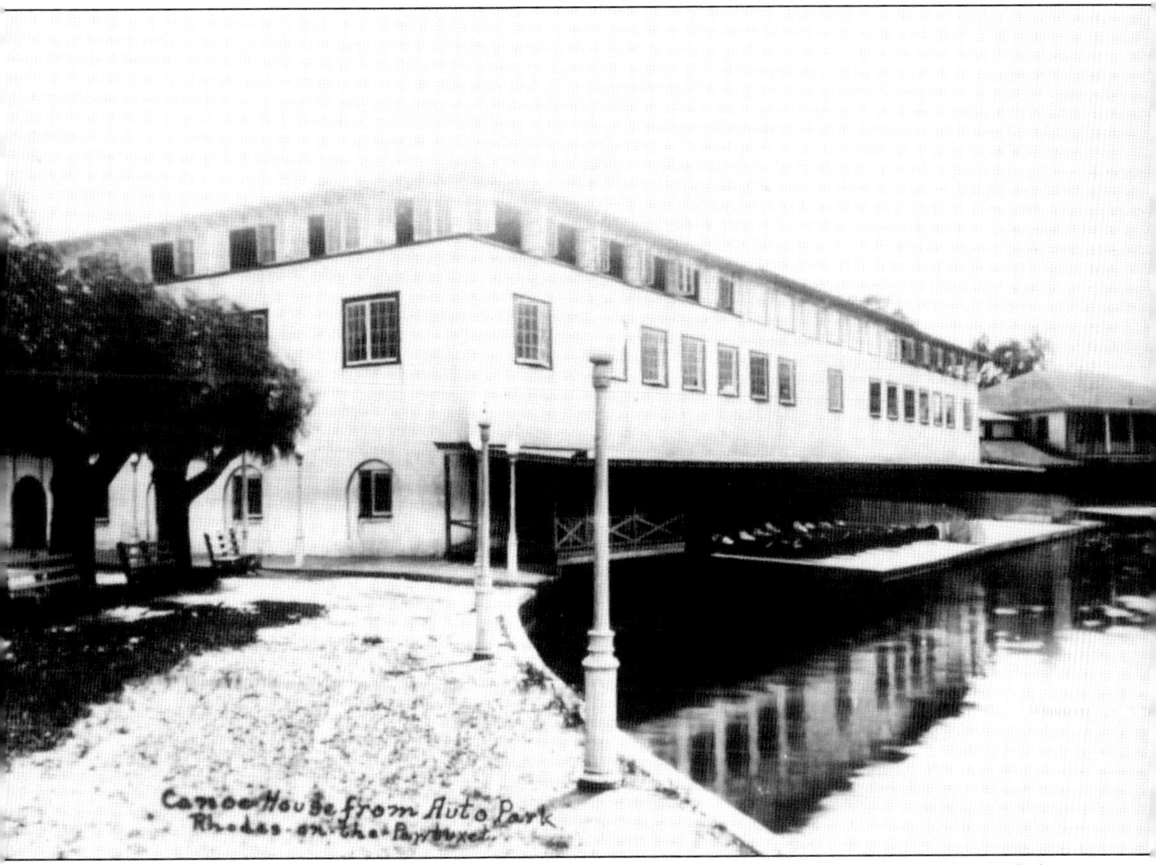

The new Rhodes Canoe House is shown here looking from the auto park in 1916. While the fire caused a serious loss, the new construction at Rhodes-on-the-Pawtuxet gave Rhodes a chance to improve and expand as the establishment ushered in a new era. (Henry A.L. Brown Collection.)

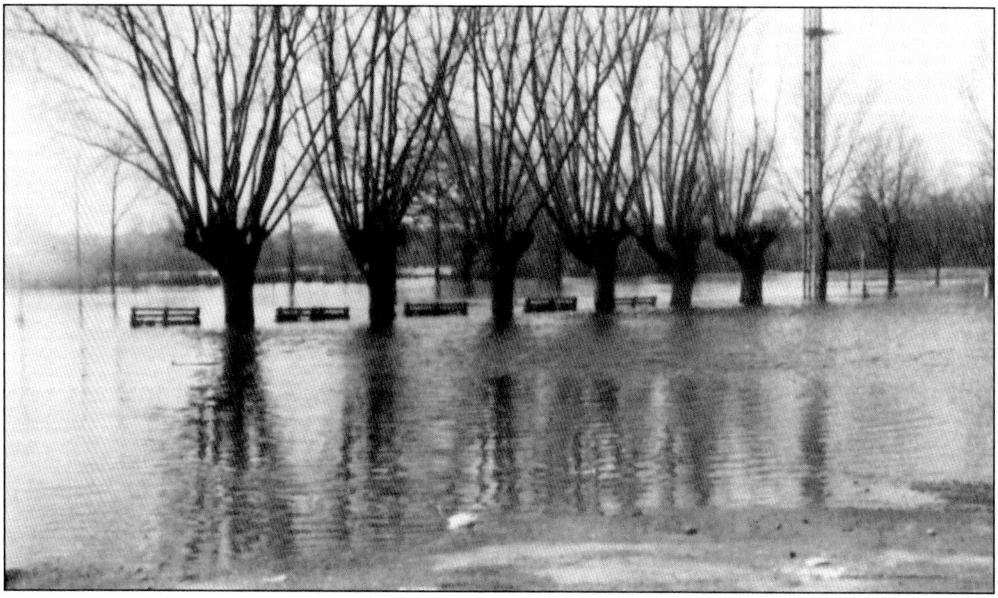

Although Mother Nature was usually Rhodes-on-the-Pawtuxet's greatest ally, she could sometimes cause distress. This freshet in March 1936 made life a little difficult for the management at the resort. (Cranston Historical Society Collection.)

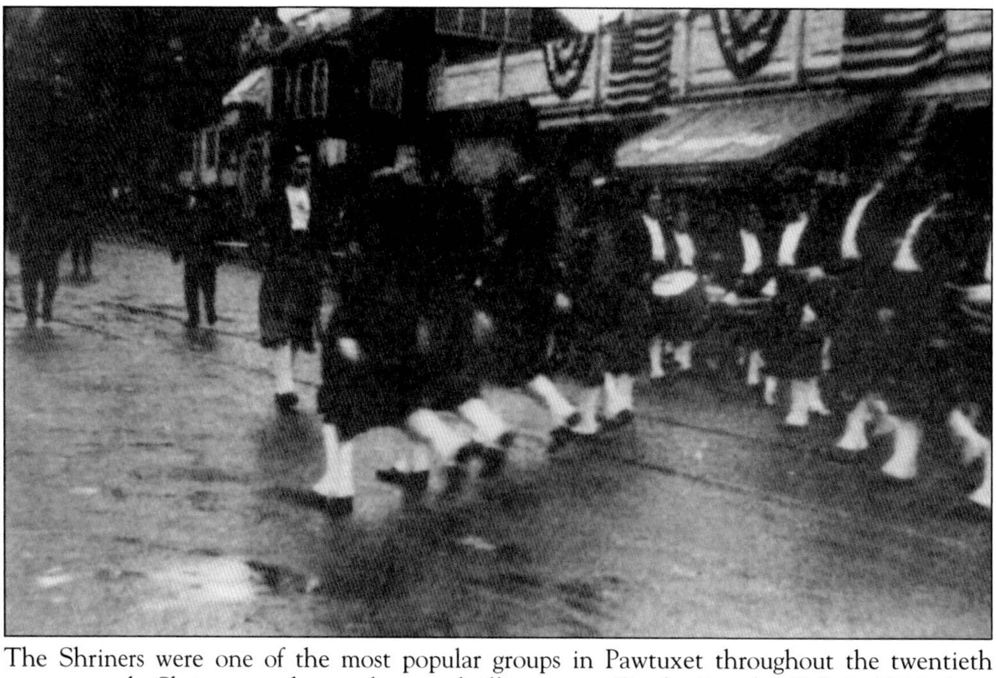

The Shriners were one of the most popular groups in Pawtuxet throughout the twentieth century, and a Shriner parade was always a thrilling event. On the Fourth of July in 1916, these Shriners turned out to parade for the spectators, who were sure to come to the village for the celebration. (Henry A.L. Brown Collection.)

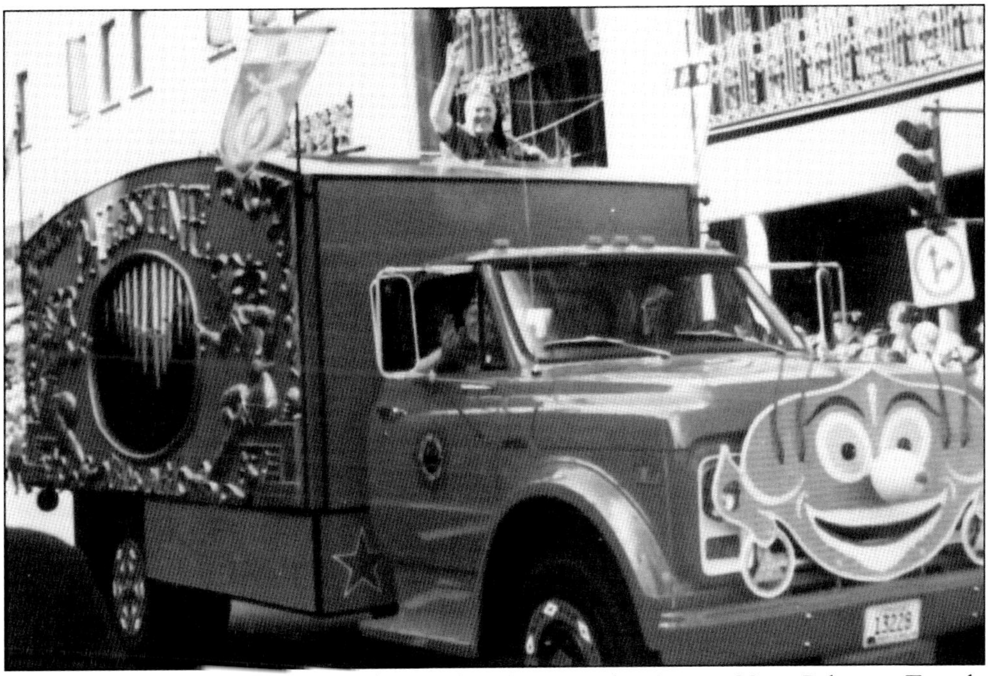

Pawtuxet has always been a special place for Shriners. The Artisan Unit, Palestine Temple Shrine Calliope, has been a consistent feature and popular attraction in all Gaspee Day Parades since 1966, when the contingent was first organized. The group is shown here in 1970. (Henry A.L. Brown Collection.)

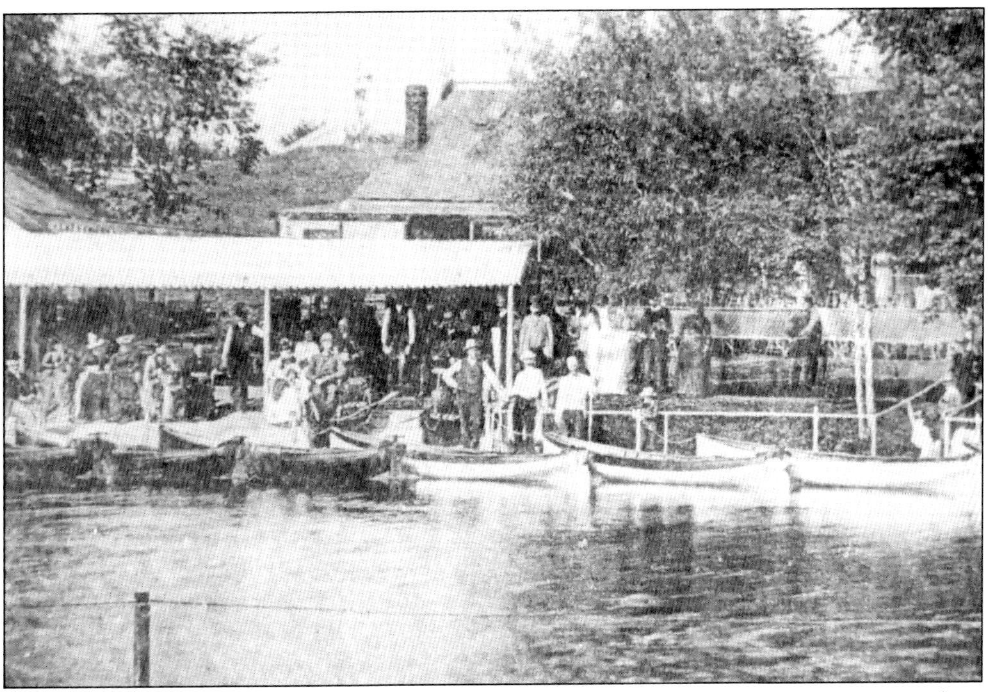

The authors wonder if the large table in the background with a net over it was set up for a catered party. Perhaps a wedding in 1890? (Henry A.L. Brown Collection.)

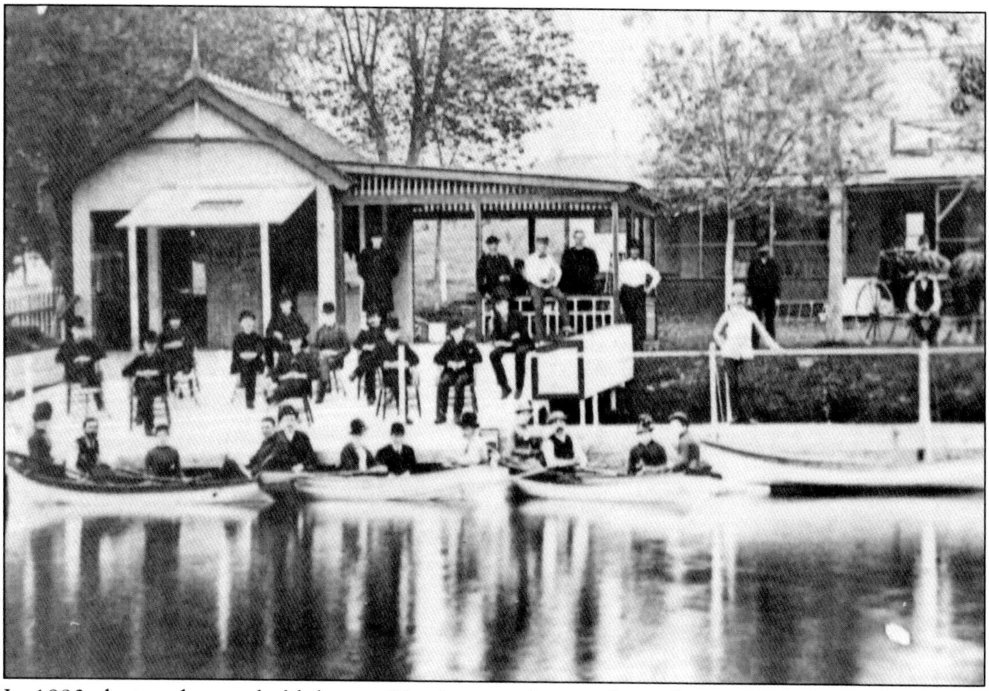

In 1890, during the good old days at Rhodes, people were formally attired despite the weather. Both men and women seemed overly dressed and wore hats even in the summer months. Of course, it was always a little cooler on the river at Rhodes. (Henry A.L. Brown Collection.)

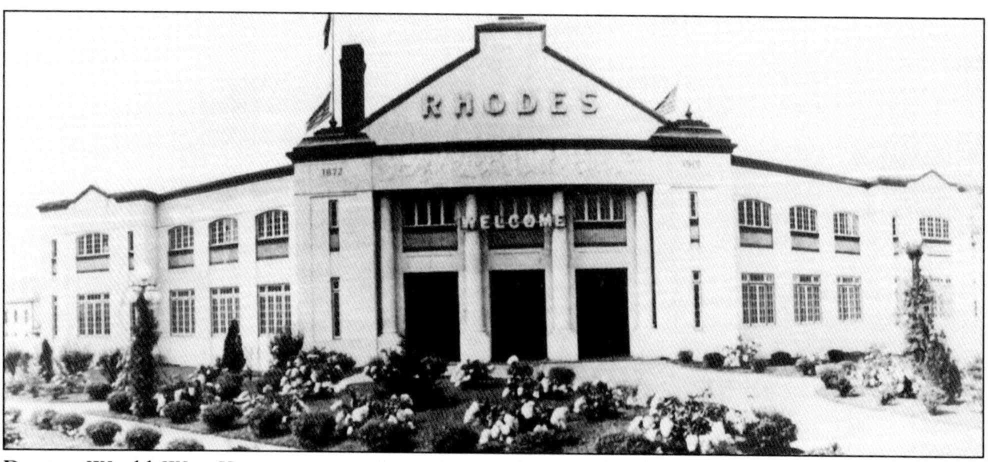

During World War II, a certain sadness lingered over Rhodes-on-the-Pawtuxet as everyone awaited the return of the men and women in the armed services and the big bands. In 1945, the flag was at half mast to mourn the death of President Franklin Delano Roosevelt. (Cranston Historical Society Collection.)

Four

Pawtuxet Cove

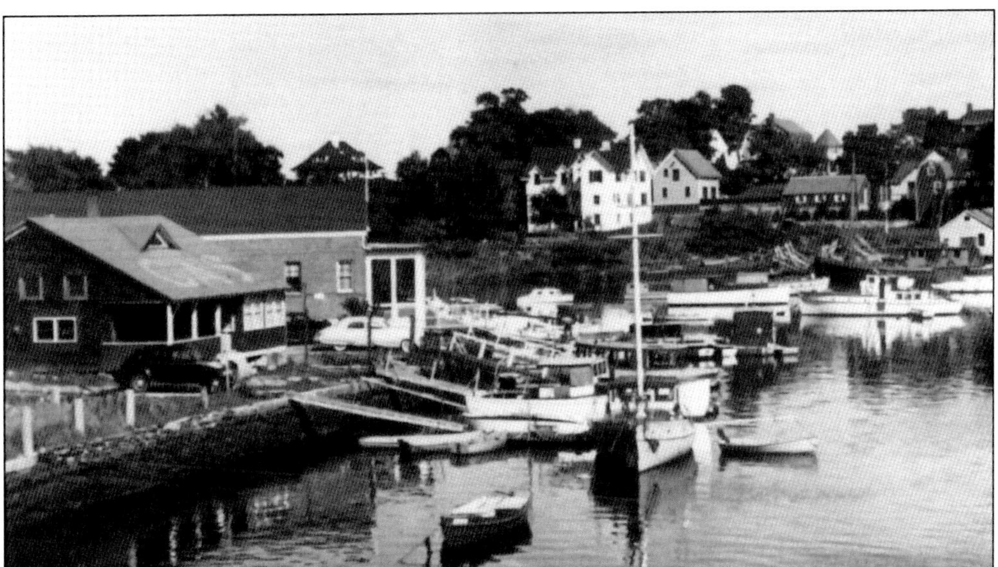

In the early 1960s Pawtuxet Cove presented a different vista. The building that says "gas" is now a house that belongs to Ray McGarrity. The brick Pawtuxet Athletic Club can be seen at the end of Bridge Street on the right. (William Hall Library Collection.)

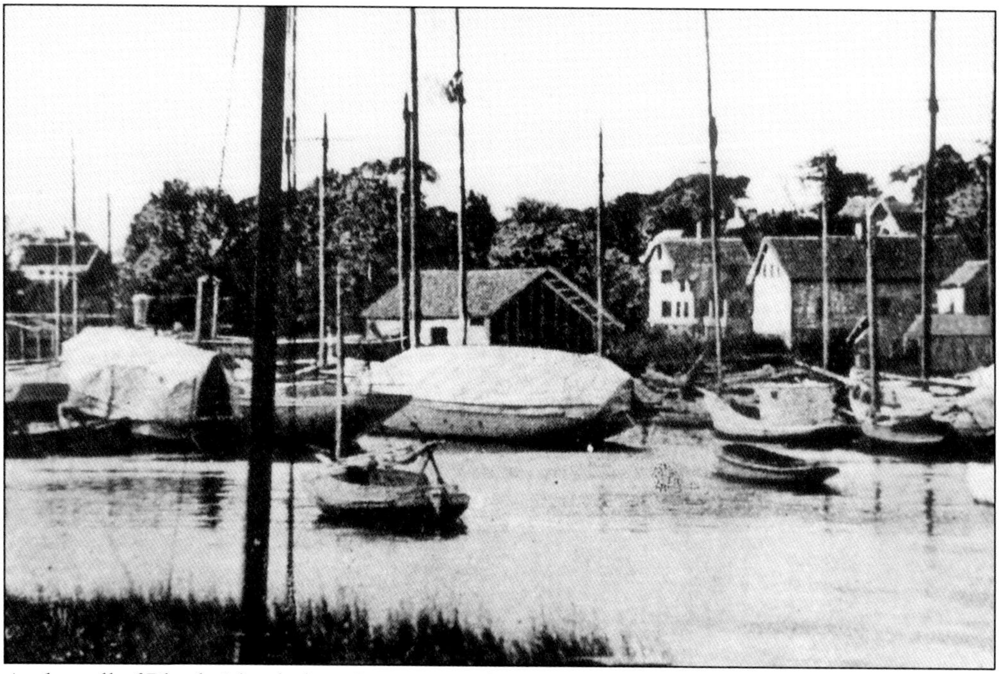

As does all of Rhode Island, these boats await the coming of summer. They still have the canvas on them, so the photograph was most likely taken before Memorial Day in 1907. (Henry A.L. Brown Collection.)

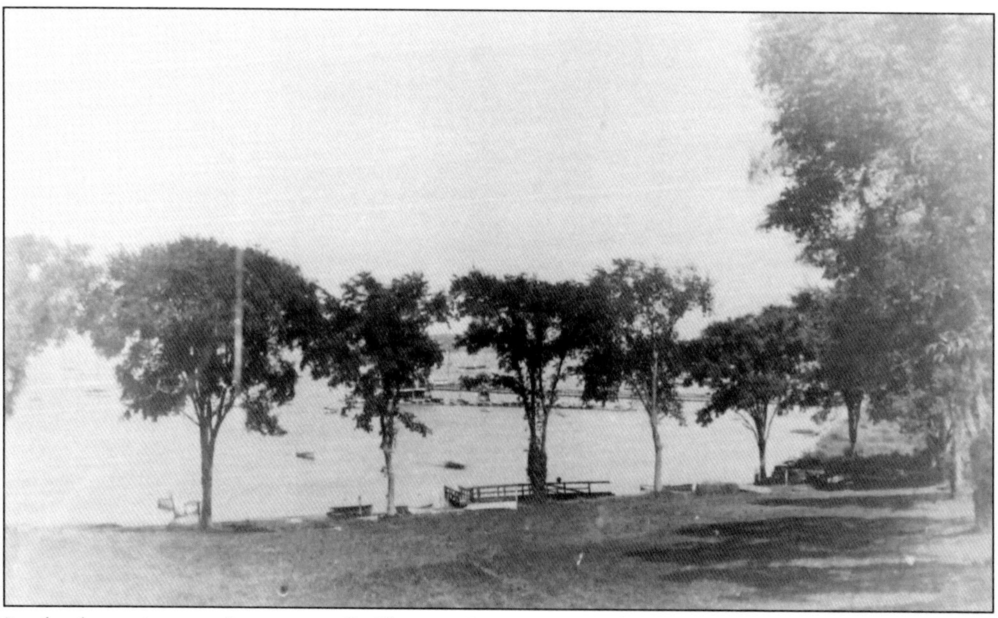

In the late nineteenth century, Stillhouse Cove presented one of the nicest vistas in Rhode Island. The photographer captured this scene in 1891, before the state acquired the land. The photograph was taken from the Edward Taft estate looking down Stillhouse Cove toward the Rhode Island Yacht Club. (Mirian Snapp Collection.)

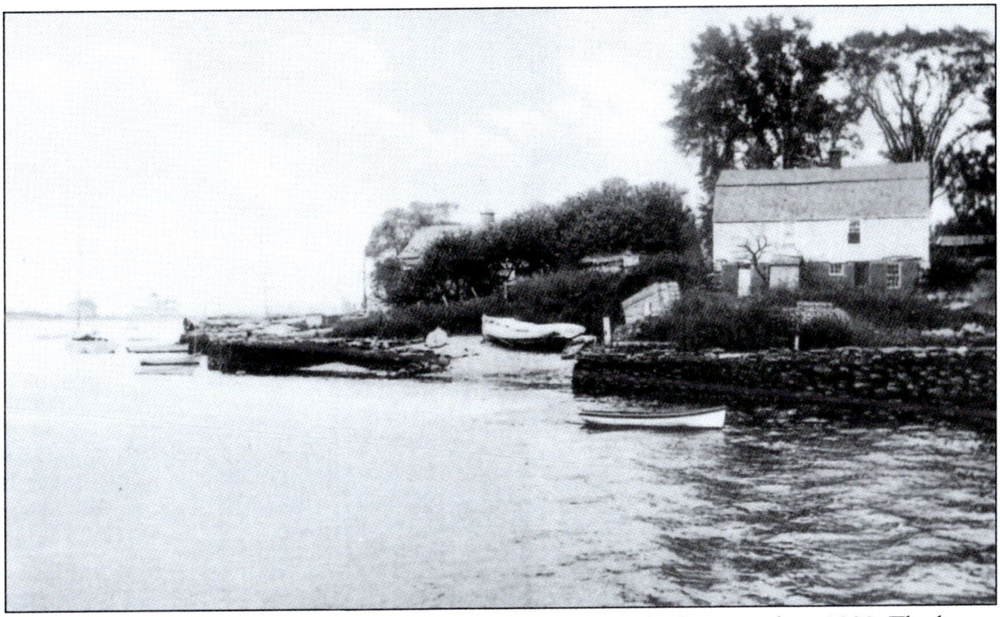

The Peter Rhodes house can be seen here at Pawtuxet Cove, looking south in 1908. The house belonged to a descendent of Zachariah Rhodes, one of the founders of Pawtuxet. (Henry A.L. Brown Collection.)

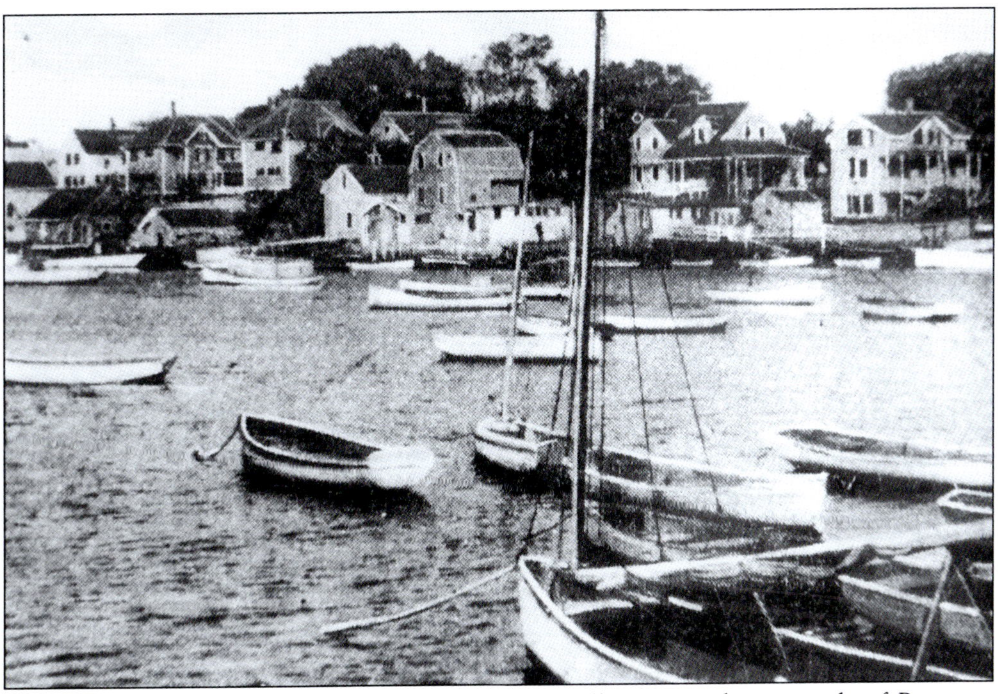

A number of the buildings depicted here in 1908 still exist on the west side of Pawtuxet Neck. The house with the gambrel roof, once a boathouse, has been renovated. (Henry A.L. Brown Collection.)

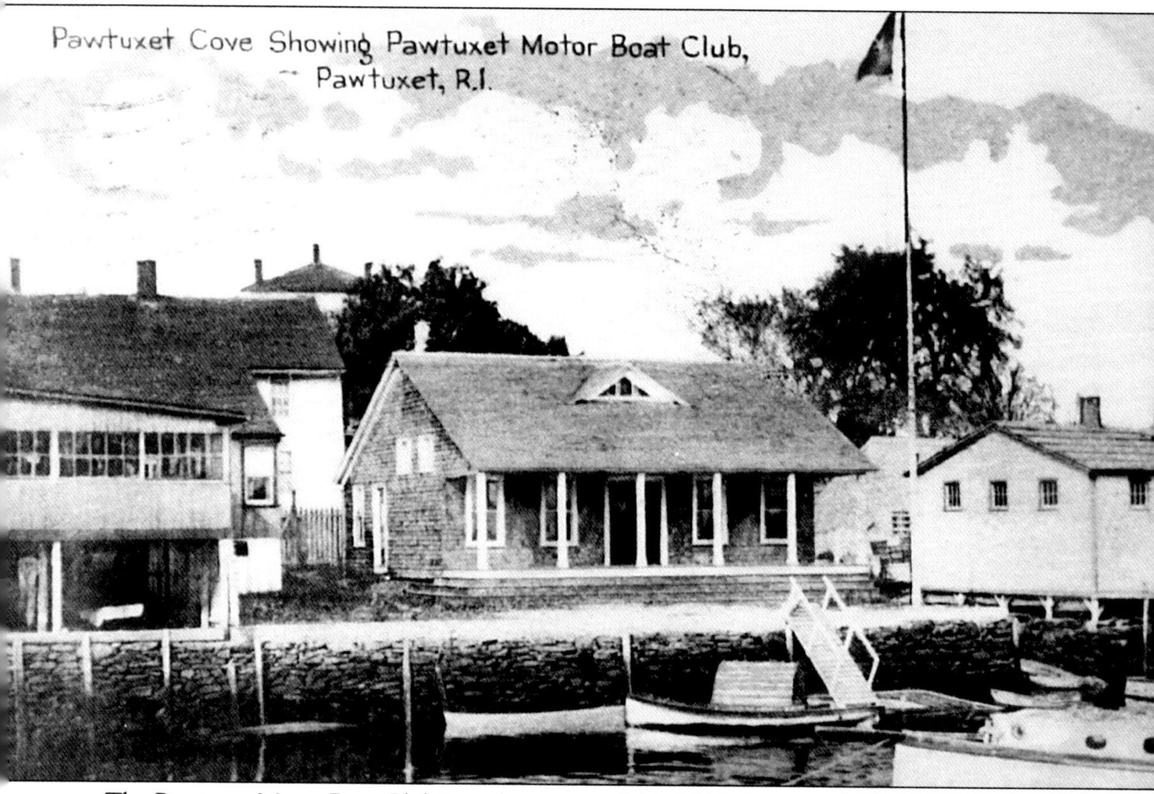

The Pawtuxet Motor Boat Club is at the center of this 1912 photograph. Slocum's famous bake house is to the left and the Pawtuxet Athletic Club (PAC) is to the far right. The flagpole is in front of the club. (Henry A.L. Brown Collection.)

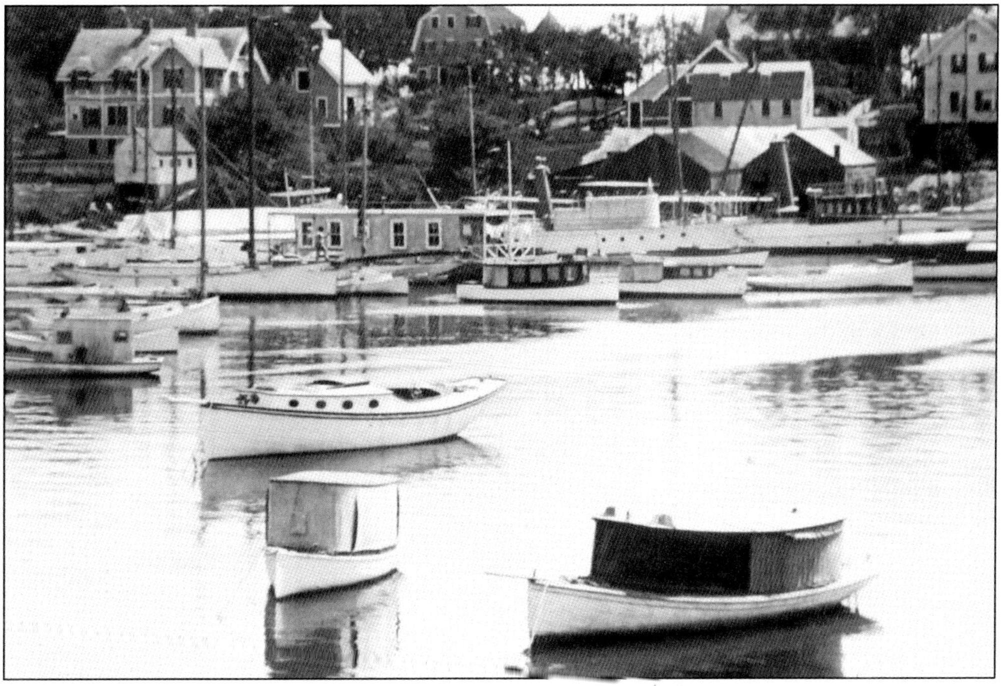

This idyllic scene, captured by a photographer looking toward the west side of Pawtuxet Neck in 1913, shows the many boats anchored in the cove. (Henry A.L. Brown Collection.)

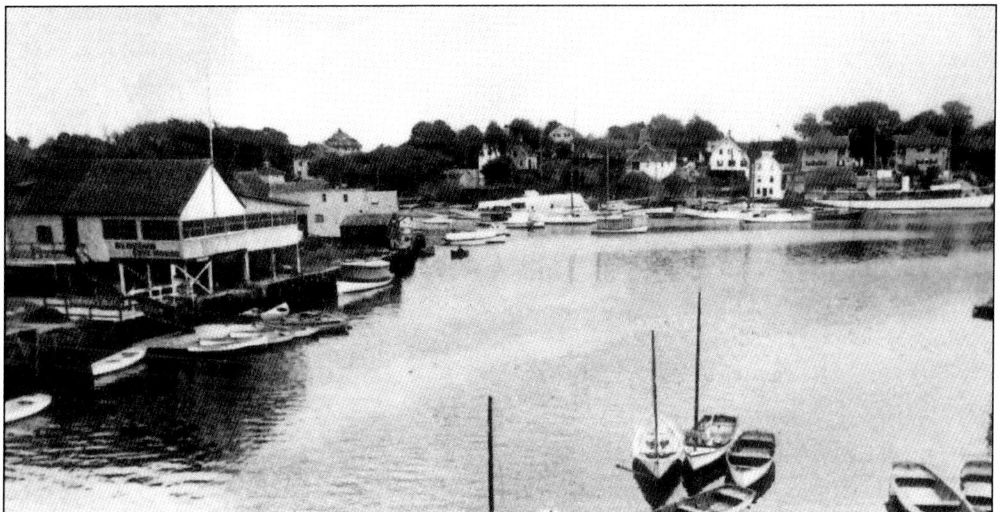

In 1915, John Austin's steam yacht could be seen here at the mouth of the Pawtuxet River. (Henry A.L. Brown Collection.)

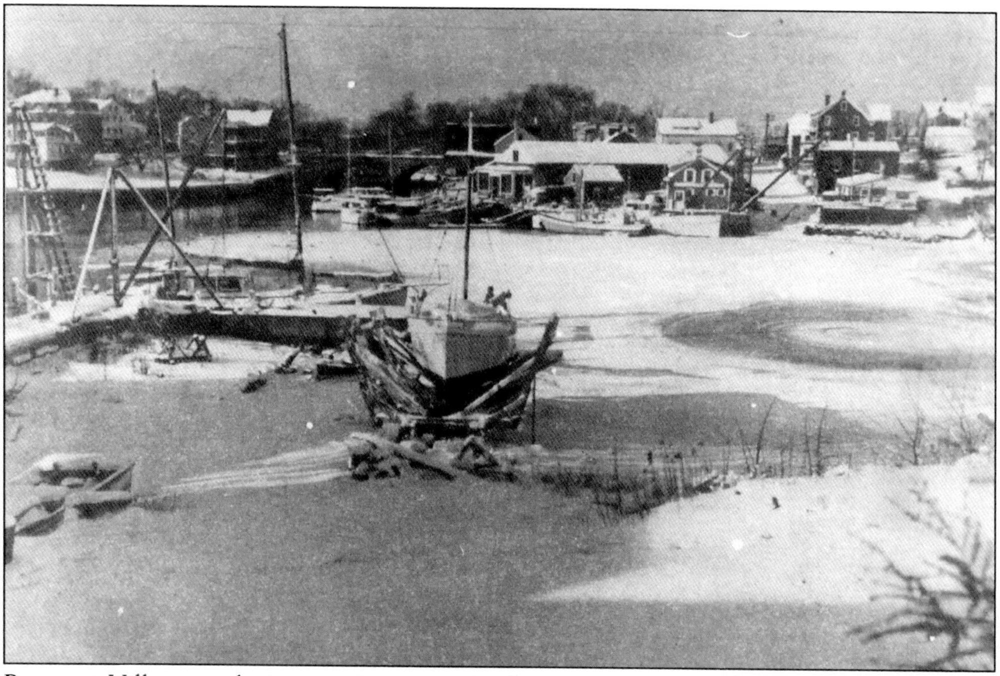

Pawtuxet Village can be just as picturesque in the winter as it is in the summer, as this 1946 photograph indicates. The ice and snow on Pawtuxet Cove make it difficult to imagine the activity that the summer brings to the area. The photograph, looking toward the bridge and falls, was taken from the west side of the cove . (William Hall Library Collection.)

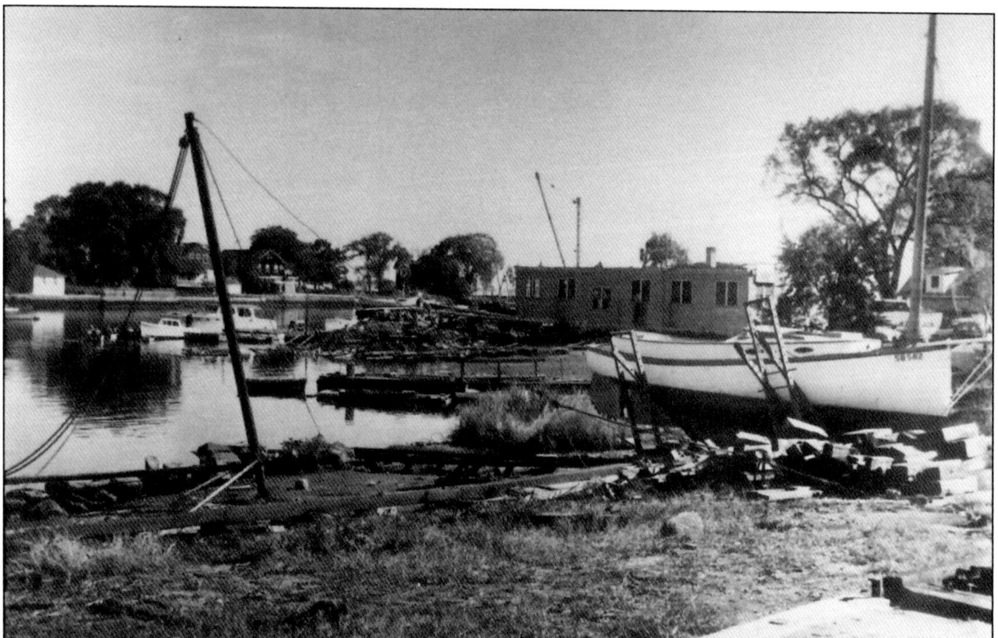

Dave and Mary Asprey's boatyard was an important part of the activity at Pawtuxet Cove in 1946. (William Hall Library Collection.)

The little building in this 1904 photograph is the Pawtuxet Athletic Clubhouse (PAC) at the foot of Bridge Street. Now in a new building, the association is still part of Pawtuxet's social life. (Henry A.L. Brown Collection.)

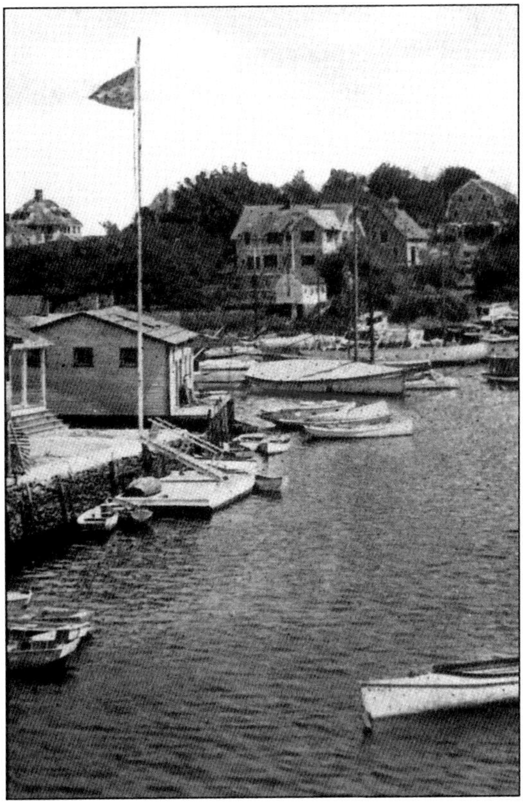

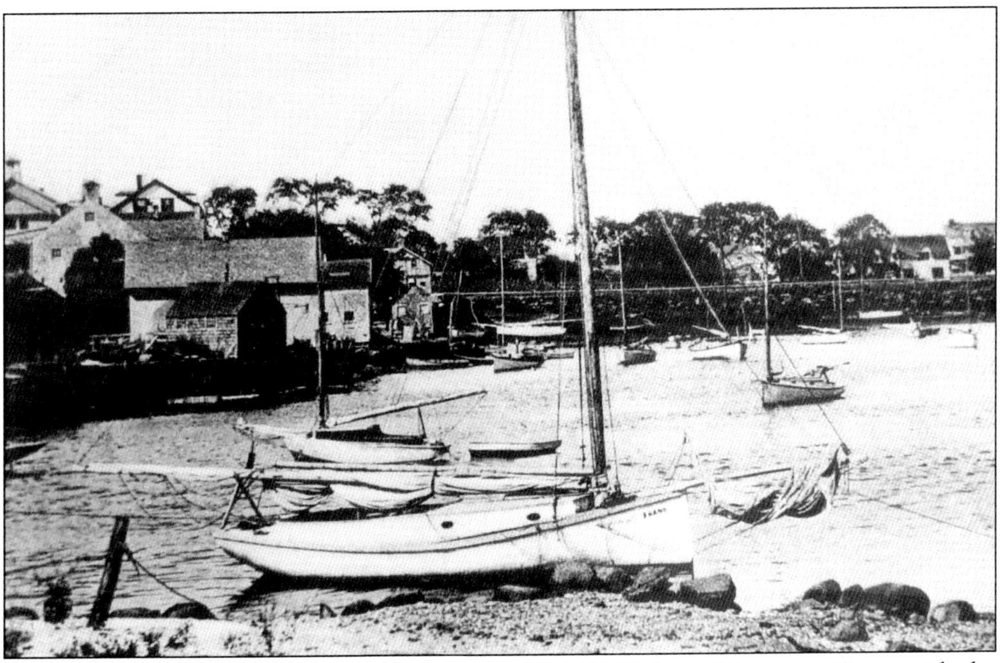

The ever-popular catboat is in the foreground of this 1907 shot of Pawtuxet Cove, with the Cranston shore in the background. The Pawtuxet Volunteer Fire Company #1 Station can be seen on the far left. (Henry A.L. Brown Collection.)

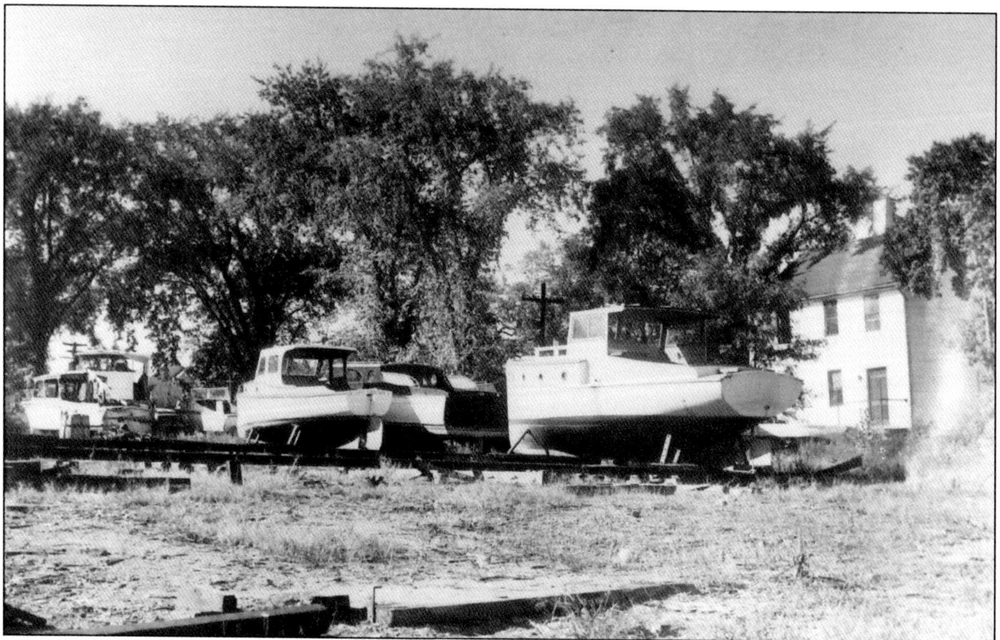

The nineteenth-century house shown near Asprey's Boat Yard on Emmons Avenue *c.* 1946 was most likely built by Lebbeus Bennett. (William Hall Library Collection.)

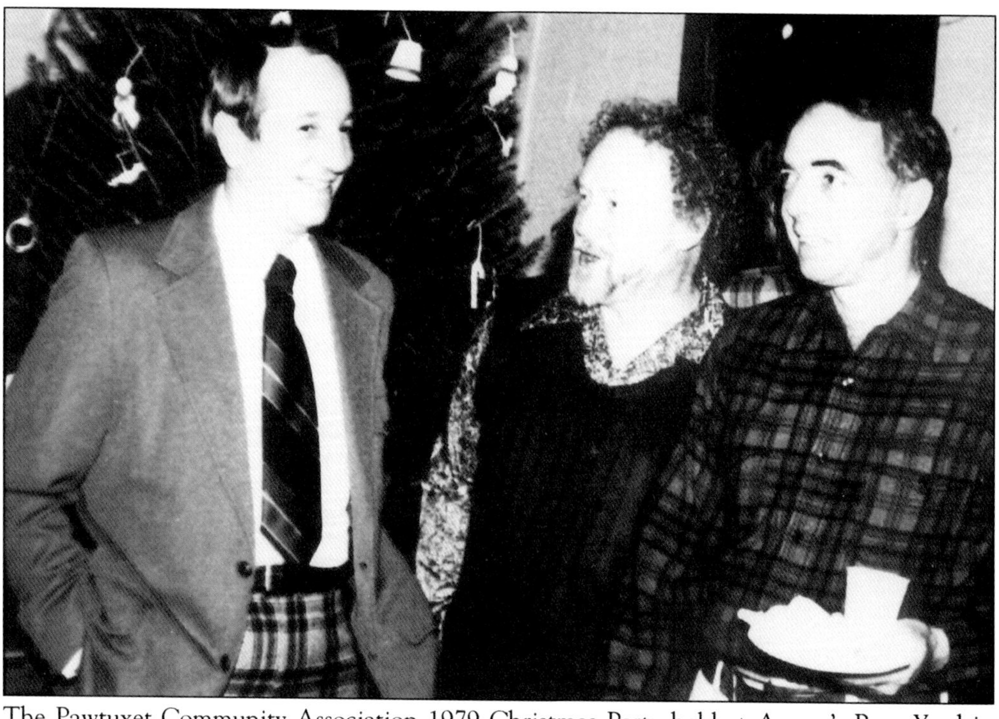

The Pawtuxet Community Association 1979 Christmas Party held at Asprey's Boat Yard in Pawtuxet brought many good friends together to share holiday festivities. Here, from left to right, we have Leo Perrone, Dick Asprey, and Henry A.L. Brown.

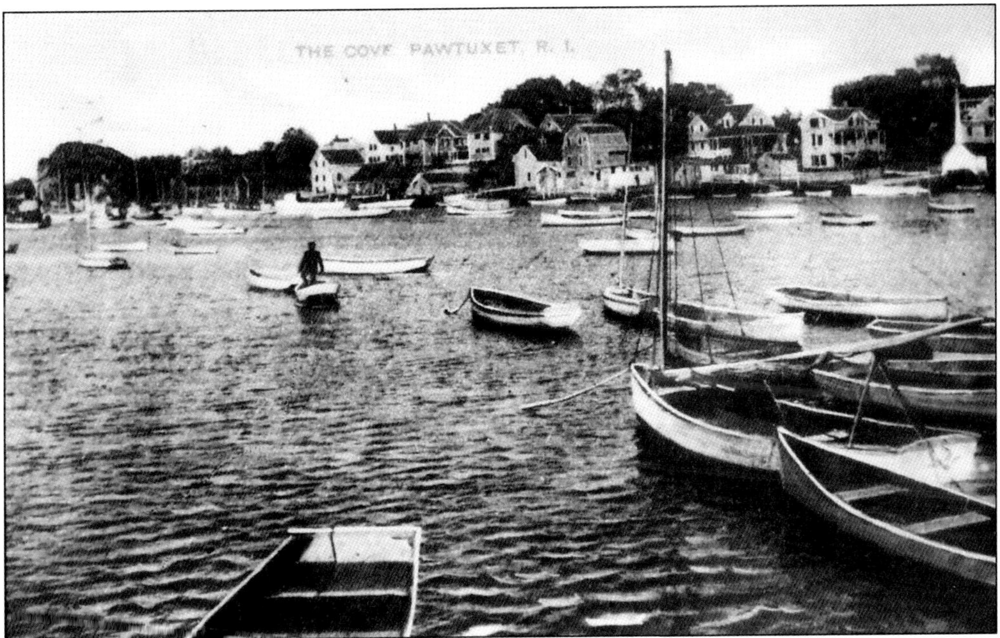

The Pawtuxet Cove in 1908, shown here looking at the west side of Pawtuxet Neck, was the milieu of many fishermen, quahogers, and oystermen. (Henry A.L. Brown Collection.)

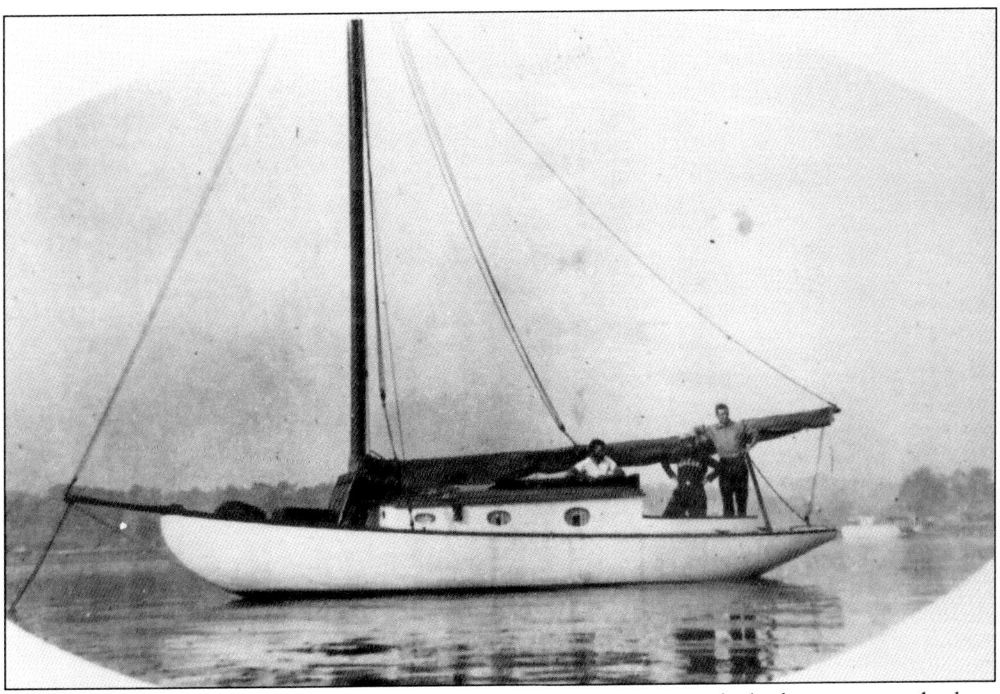

During the summer months in Pawtuxet, there was always a great deal of activity on the bay. This particular sailboat was travelling off Passeionqauis Cove near the Gaspee Point overview. (Henry A.L. Brown Collection.)

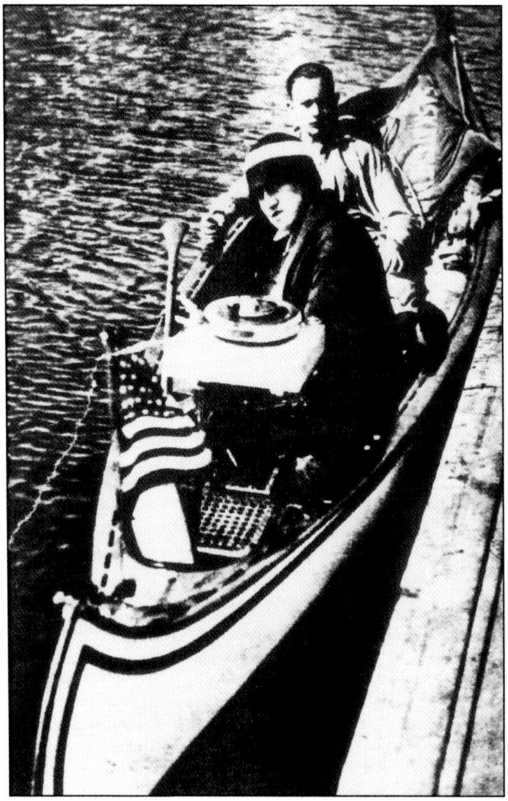

Everything changed in the twentieth century when the desire to get places faster and more efficiently was satisfied by the automobile. Eventually, the Pawtuxet River witnessed the motorized canoe as a form of transportation. The calm, romantic, old-fashioned canoe, however, never went out of fashion. (Henry A.L. Brown Collection.)

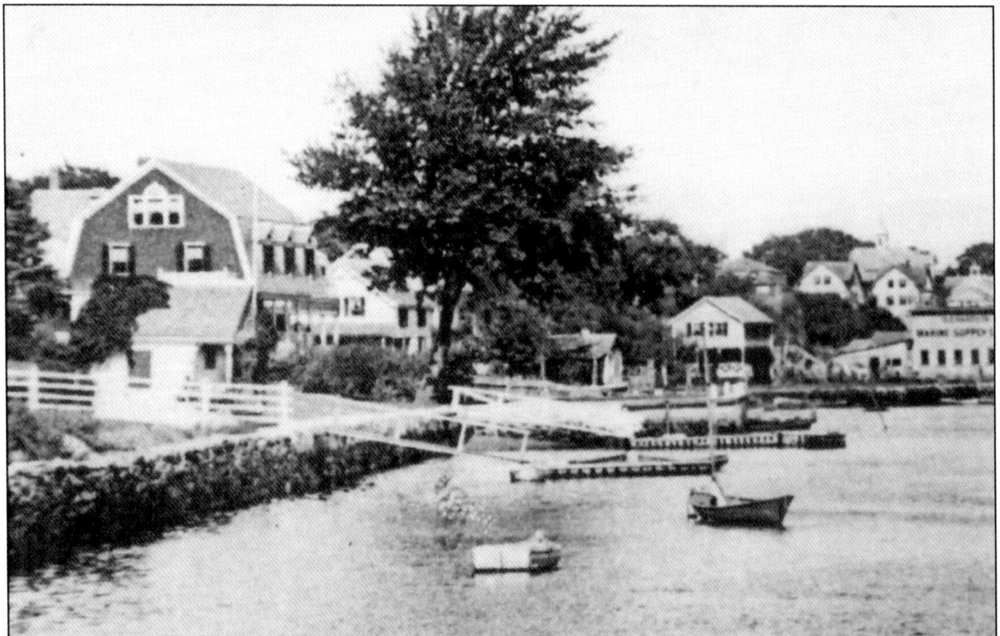

One of the nicest areas along the coast was this section of Pawtuxet Cove in 1905. (Henry A.L. Brown Collection.)

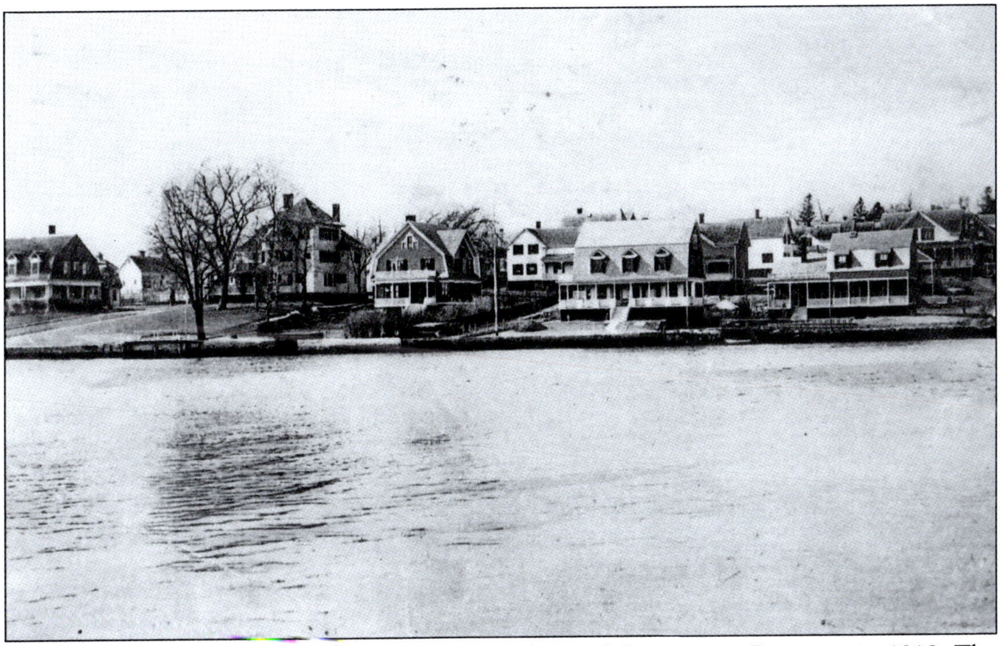

These homes looked majestically over the west shore of the cove in Pawtuxet in 1918. The flagpole, shown here at the center of the picture, is at the foot of Lawn Avenue in Warwick. (Henry A.L. Brown Collection.)

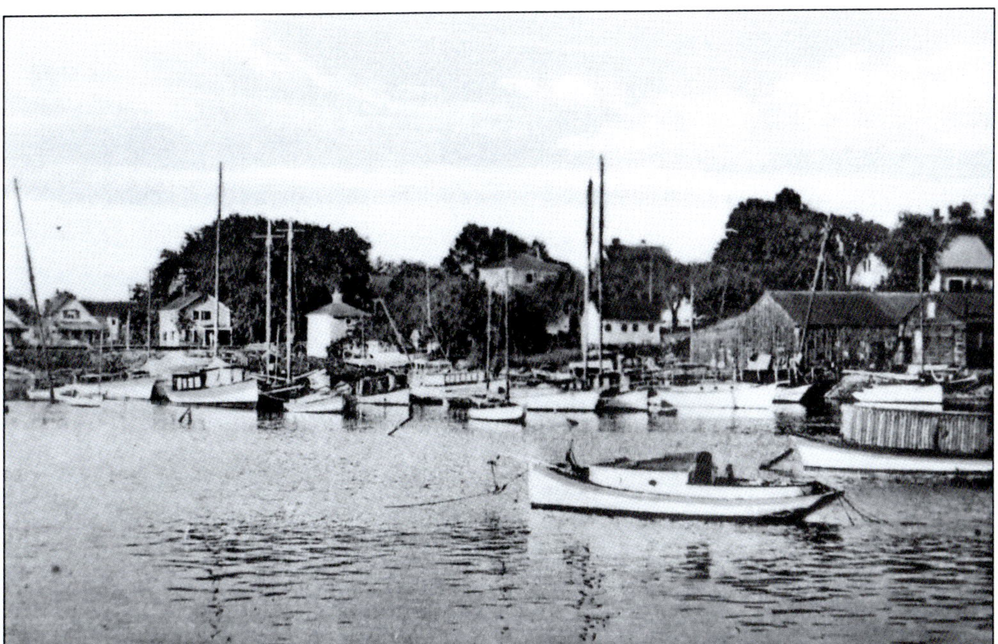

In 1905 the Pawtuxet Cove was home to catboats, rowboats, and quahog skiffs. (Henry A.L. Brown Collection.)

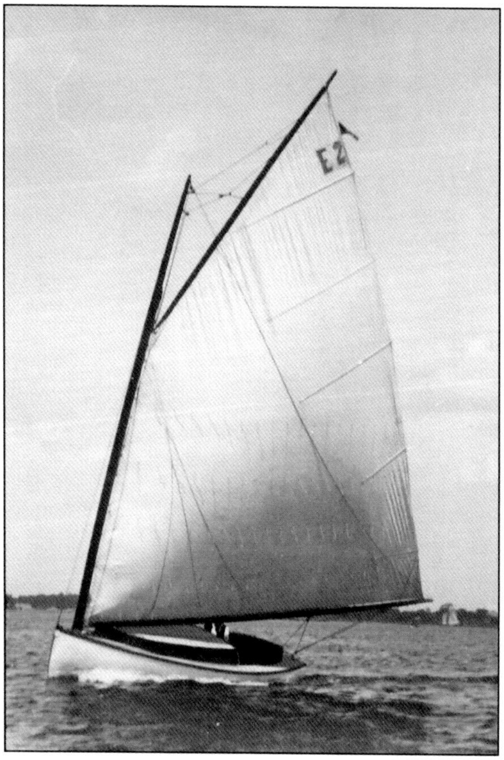

The majestic catboats, then and now, present a pretty picture of grace and nature as they capture the wind and glide toward their destination. This particular catboat was sailing near the Edgewood Yacht Club early in the twentieth century. (Henry A.L. Brown Collection.)

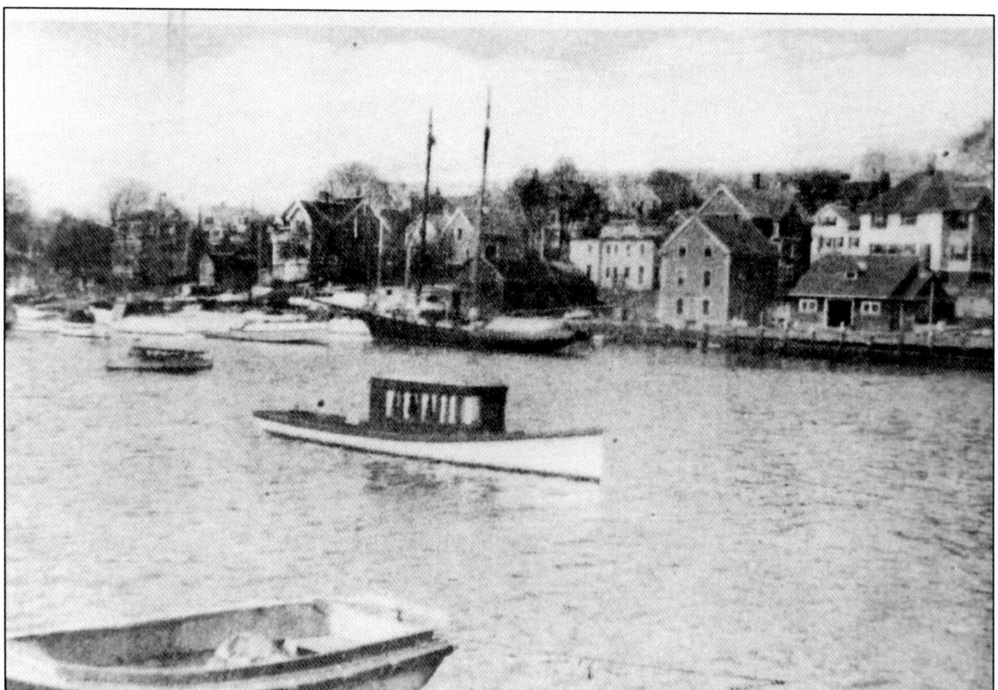

Eventually, more motorized craft came into the cove, and the day when sail reigned supreme was coming to an end. Here in 1913, we begin to see the inroads made by motorboats. (William Hall Library Collection.)

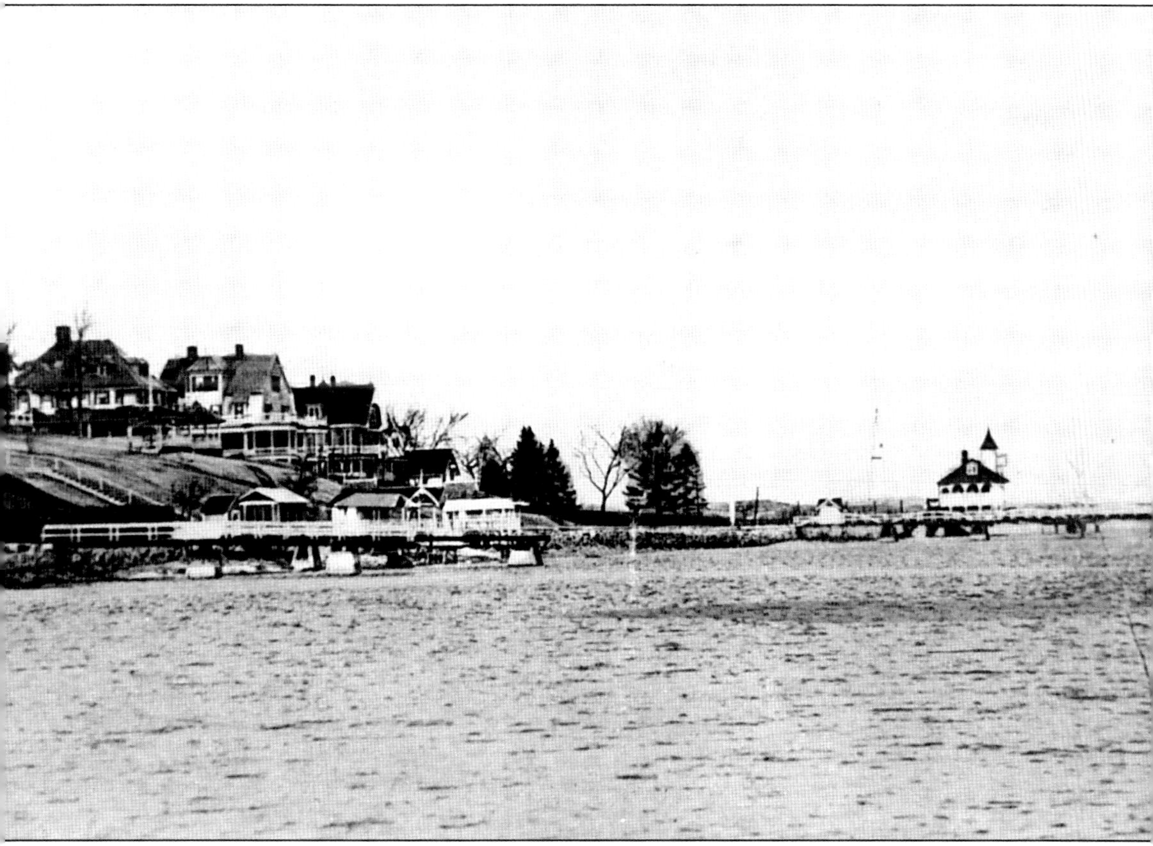

Pawtuxet Neck has always been important for its history and its beauty. Two of the houses on the neck are on the site of the Revolutionary War fort; the Rhode Island Yacht Club, as it was in 1908, is on the far right. (Henry A.L. Brown Collection.)

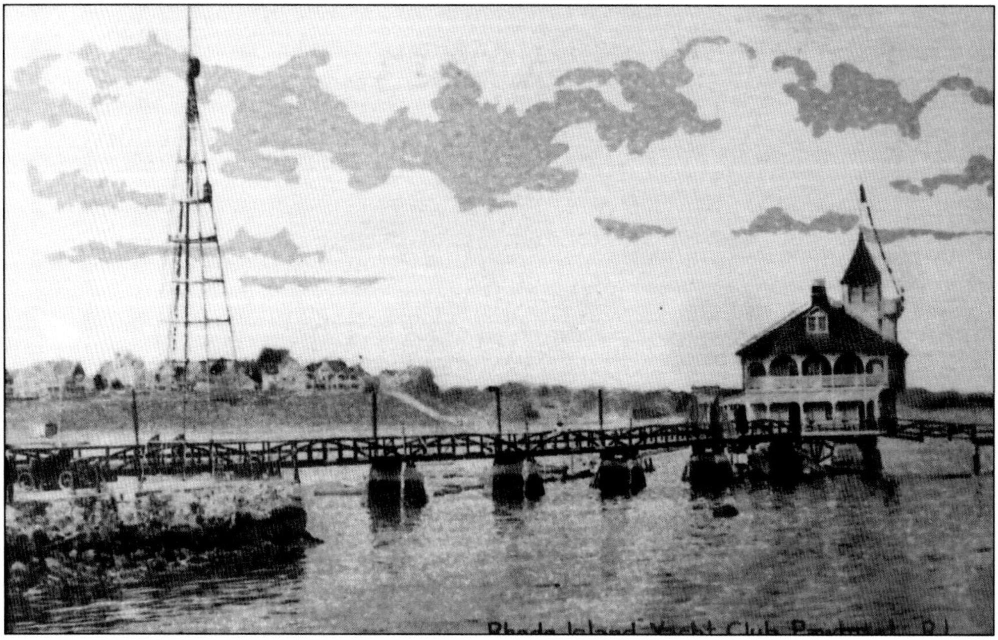

The receiver and radio transmission tower of the Rhode Island Yacht Club in Pawtuxet Neck was erected by Walter Massie, who was considered an eminent leader in radio technology. The club is shown here in 1913. (Henry A.L. Brown Collection.)

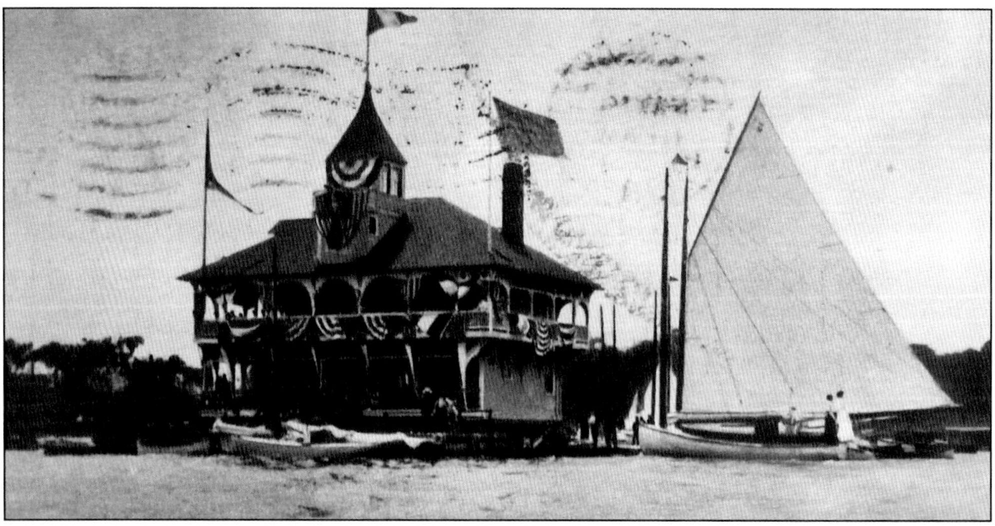

The Rhode Island Yacht Club was built in 1877. It was the second yacht club established in the United States and has a rich history in yachting circles. At about the time this picture was taken—*c.* 1910—the club was proudly displaying the cup that member Charles Tillinghast was given by Sir Thomas Lipton. Tillinghast won the longest ocean course race up to that time. (Henry A.L. Brown Collection.)

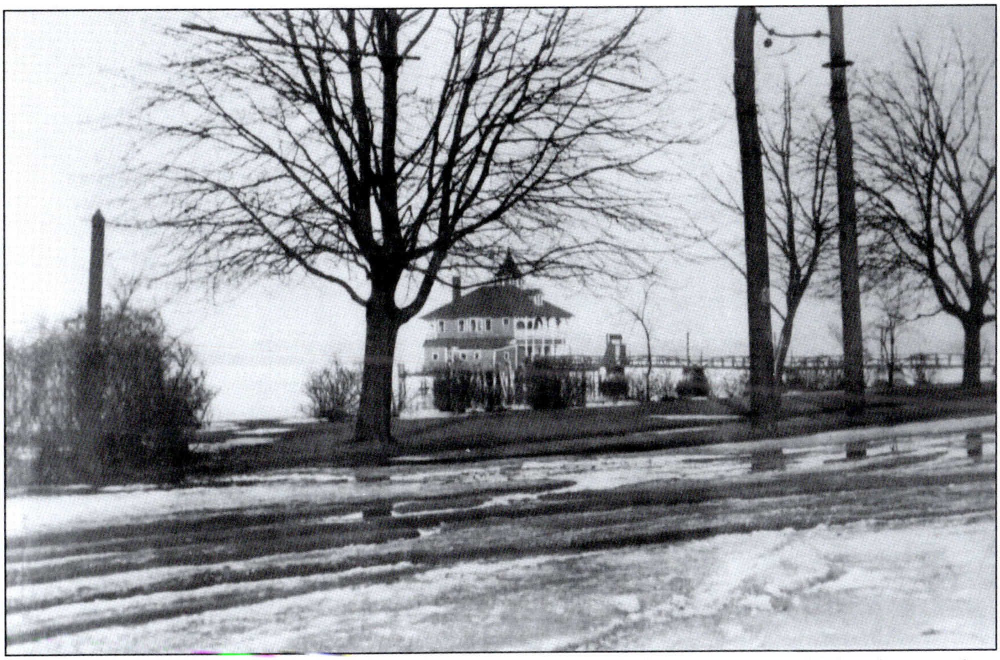

The Rhode Island Yacht Club was formed by a group of Providence men in 1875 and was at first called the Providence Yacht Club. This lovely building, shown here in 1915, was destroyed by the Hurricane of 1938. (Henry A.L. Brown Collection.)

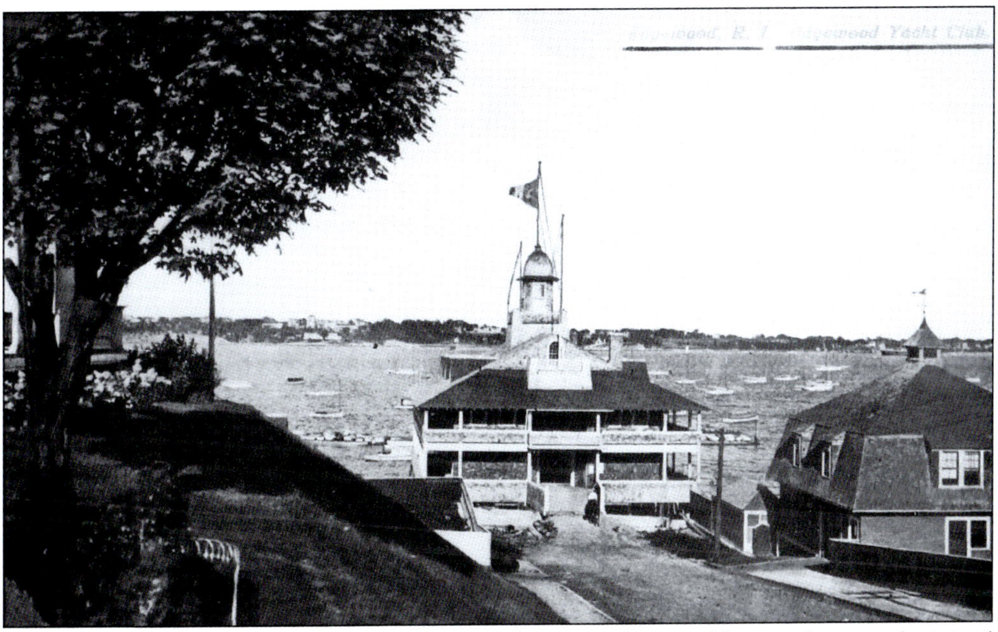

A lot of Pawtuxet residents, wanting a club of their own that would meet their needs, joined with a number of Edgewood residents to form the Edgewood Yacht Club. This building, like so many others along the shore, washed away in the Hurricane of 1938. It is shown here in 1914. (Cranston Historical Society Collection.)

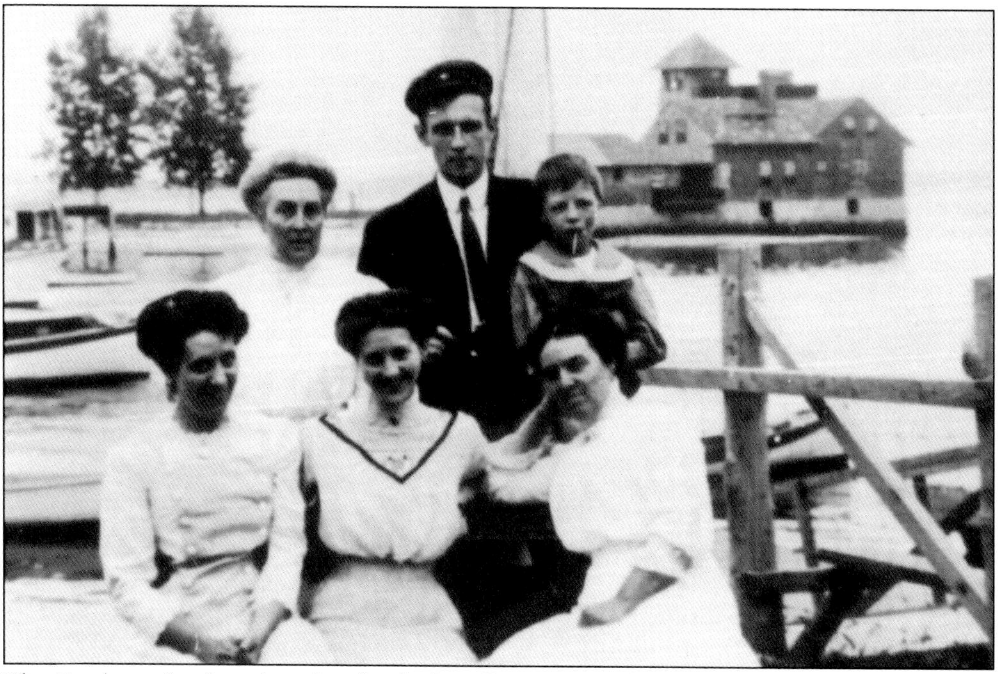

The Creelman family gathered at the dock on Pawtuxet Neck in 1910. The Robert Pettis house can be seen in the background. (Richard Harnedy Collection.)

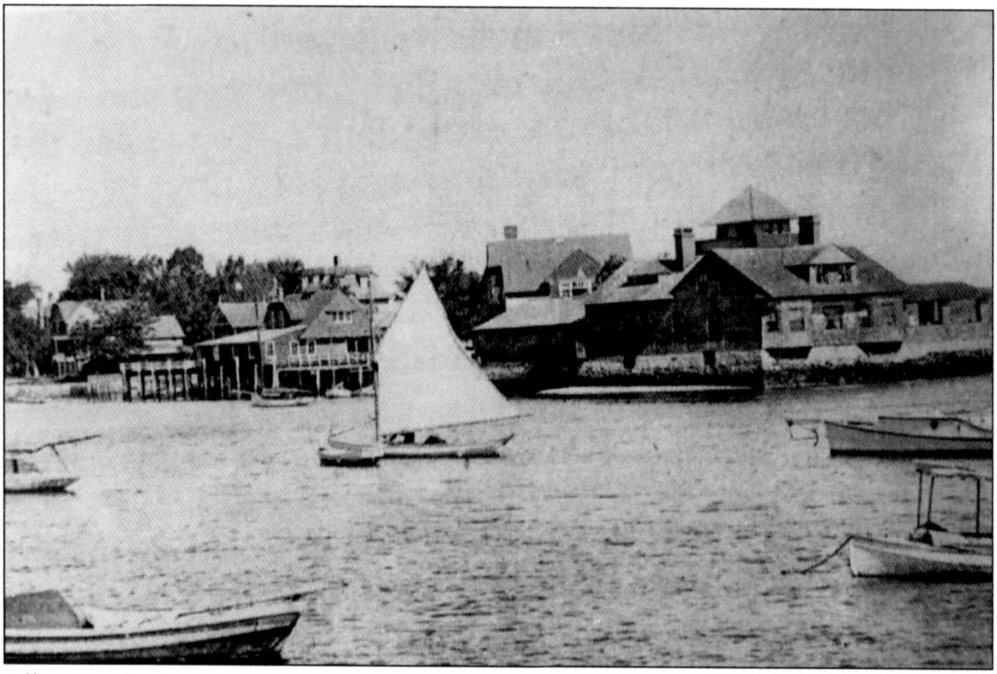

All types of sailing craft glided by the old Pettis Oyster House on Pawtuxet Neck in the early twentieth century. The seafood facility was erected in 1850 and remained on the point for over one hundred years. (Henry A.L. Brown Collection.)

Five

Pawtuxet's Pride

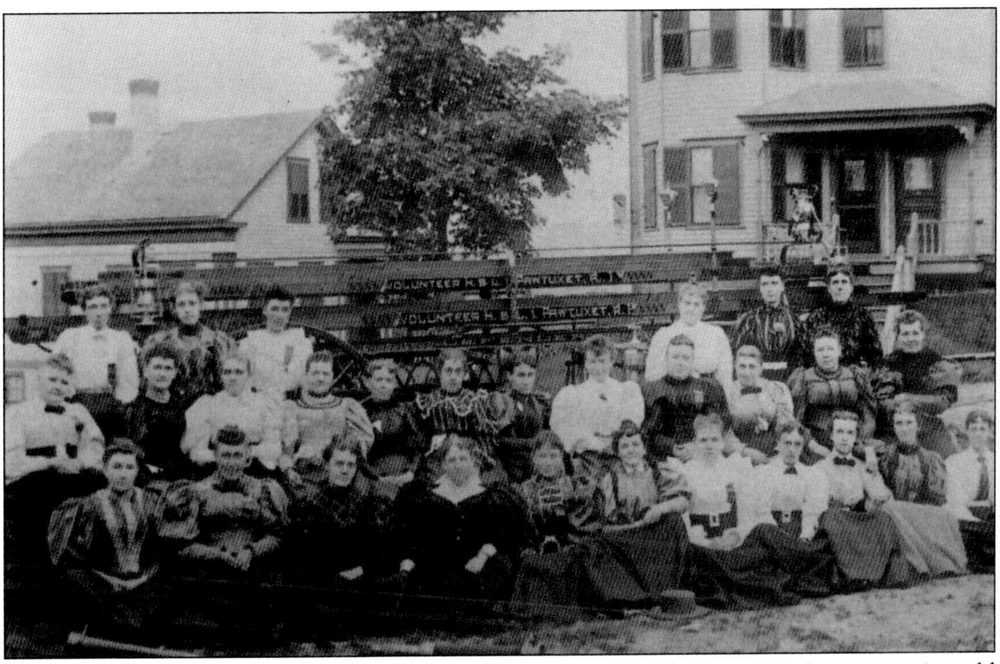

The key to the social and financial success of the Pawtuxet Volunteer Fire Company #1 could be found in the ladies' auxiliary. In 1895, the ladies' auxiliary was already organized and their support, approval, and enthusiasm were crucial in those early years. The ladies helped make the company an integral part of village life. (Pawtuxet Fire King Veterans Firemen's Association Collection.)

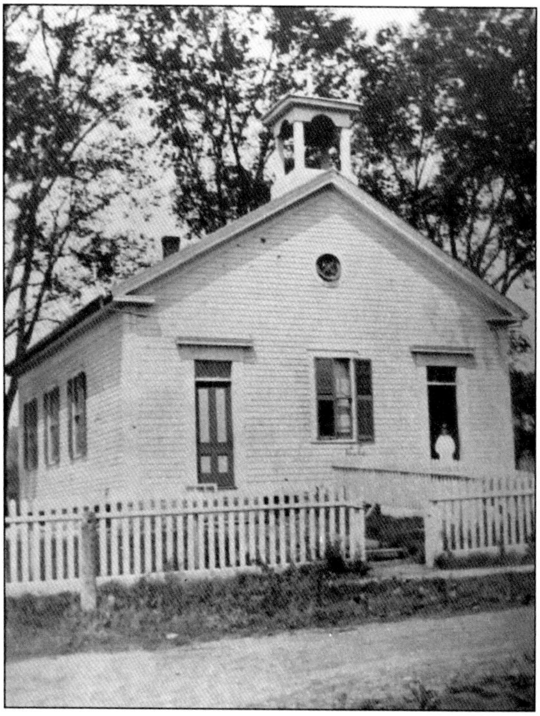

According to Mrs. Ida Lee, whose mother attended the Commercial Street School (shown here *c.* 1889), it was built in 1830. Civil War hero Elisha Rhodes attended class here. Once, when speaking to a group in Pawtuxet, Rhodes said the floors in the school were made from molasses packing crates, and on hot days molasses oozed out, drawing clouds of flies. (Cranston Historical Society Collection.)

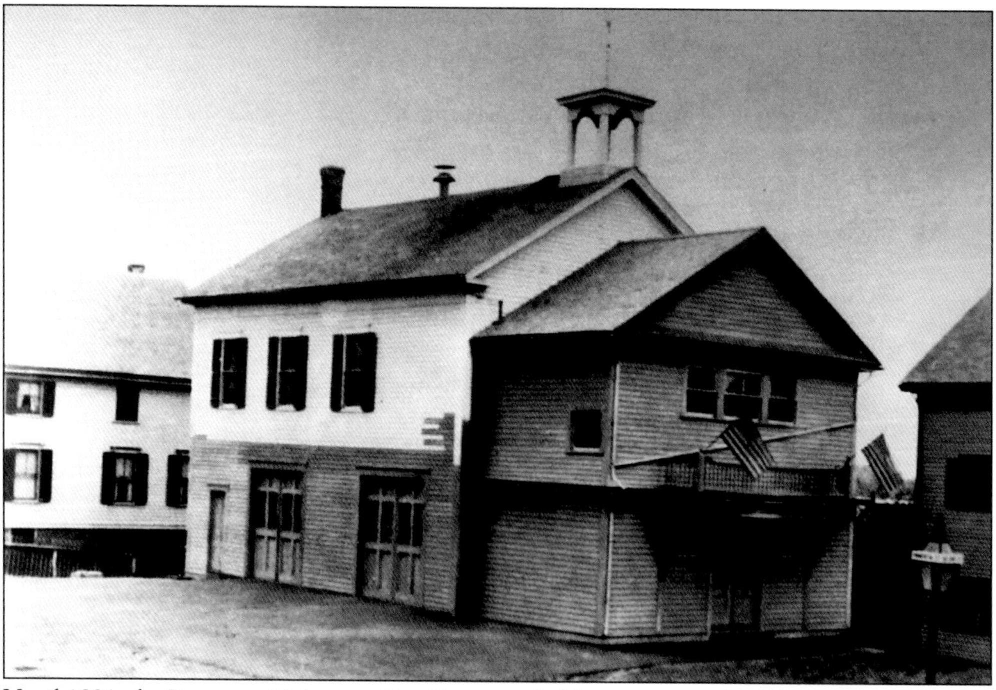

Until 1891, the Pawtuxet Volunteer Fire Company held meetings at the old Commercial Street (Red) School, built in 1835–40. When the company purchased the lot on Commercial Street, they bought the red school building for $50 and moved it across Commercial Street in July 1897. It was raised and a fire station was built underneath. This picture was taken *c.* 1899. (Cranston Historical Society Collection.)

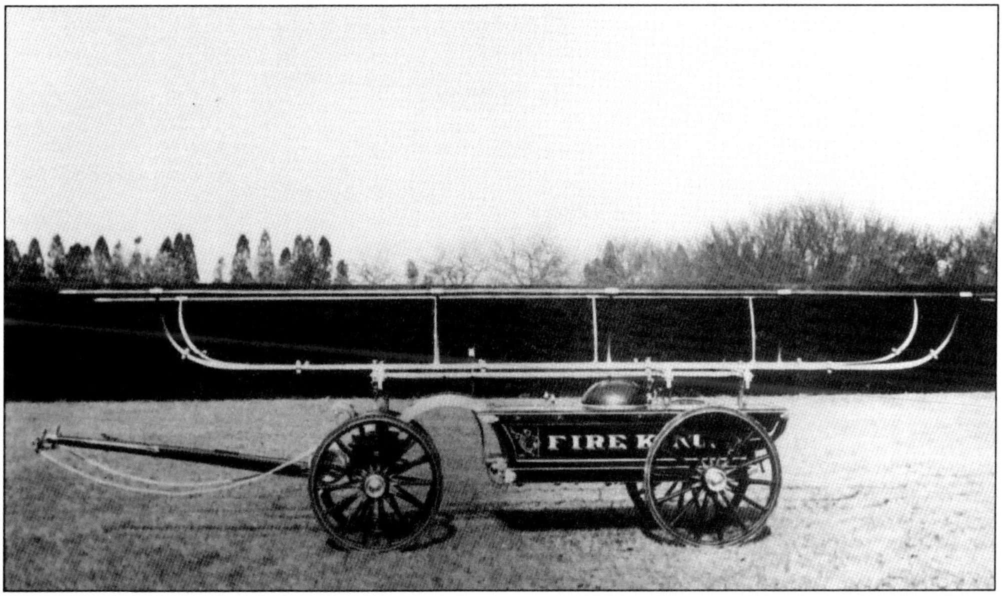

Pawtuxet's pride and joy was the Fire King, the early tub-pumper of the Pawtuxet Volunteer Fire Company. The tub was built in 1855 by James Smith, and was acquired by the Pawtuxet volunteers in 1892. The Fire King won the Rhode Island State Championship and the New England State Championship in 1906 and 1916. It was sold in 1946 and came back to Pawtuxet in 1974. (Cranston Historical Society Collection.)

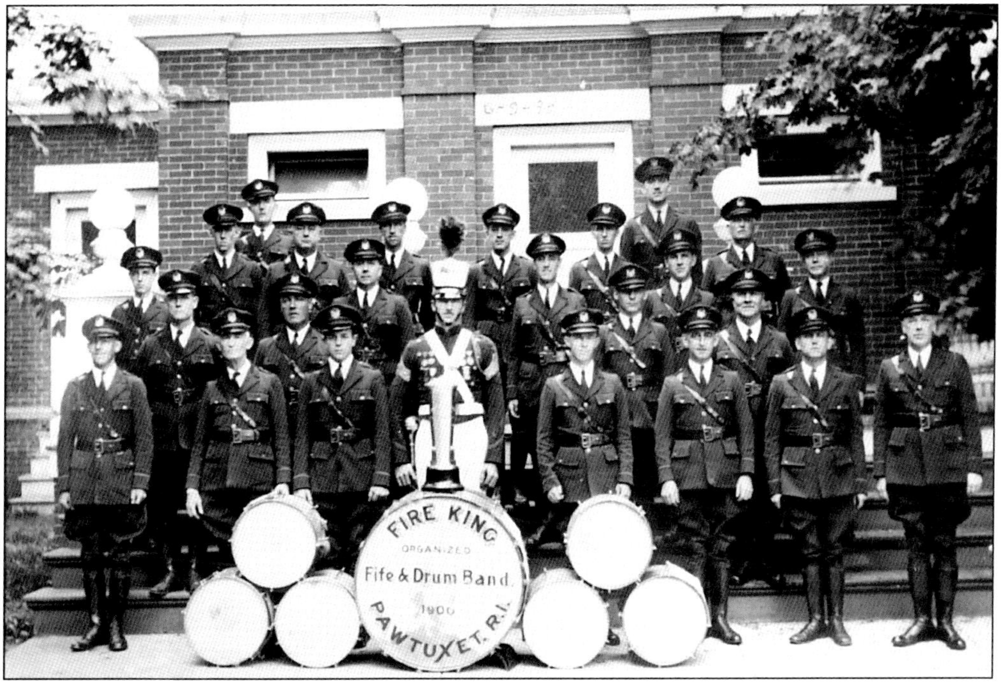

The popular and talented Fire King Fife and Drum Corps Band was in demand throughout Rhode Island. The group enhanced just about any celebration and was a source of pride to the village. This photograph was taken in front of Harmony Lodge next to Trinity Church *c.* 1930. (Henry A.L. Brown Collection.)

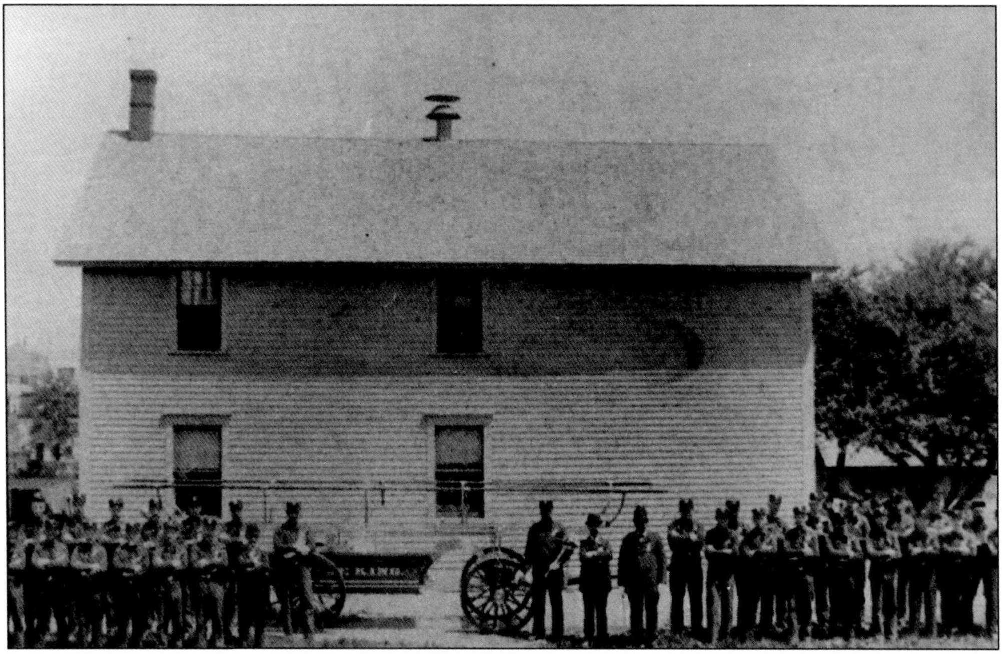

Prior to the purchase and removal of the Commercial Street (Red) School, this building stood on the present site of the Pawtuxet Volunteer Company building. The building was inadequate for the company's purposes and was torn down and replaced by the transported school. While the building was still in use, the company stored some of their equipment at the nearby Pawtuxet Armory. (Pawtuxet Fire King Veterans Firemen's Association Collection.)

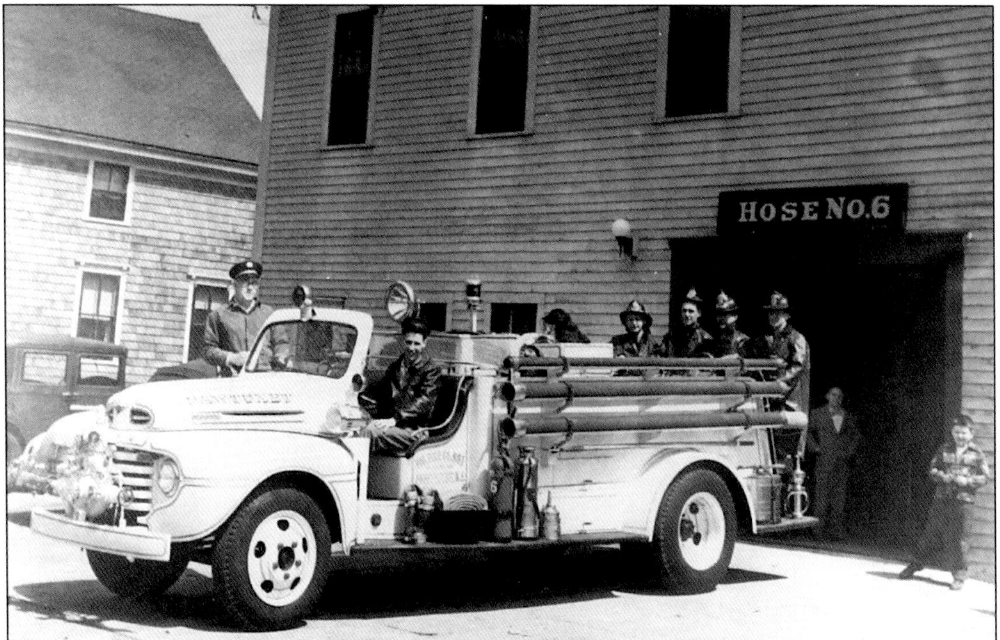

The Pawtuxet Volunteer Fire Company's 1949 Ford was painted all-white as opposed to the traditional red of other companies. (William Hall Library Collection.)

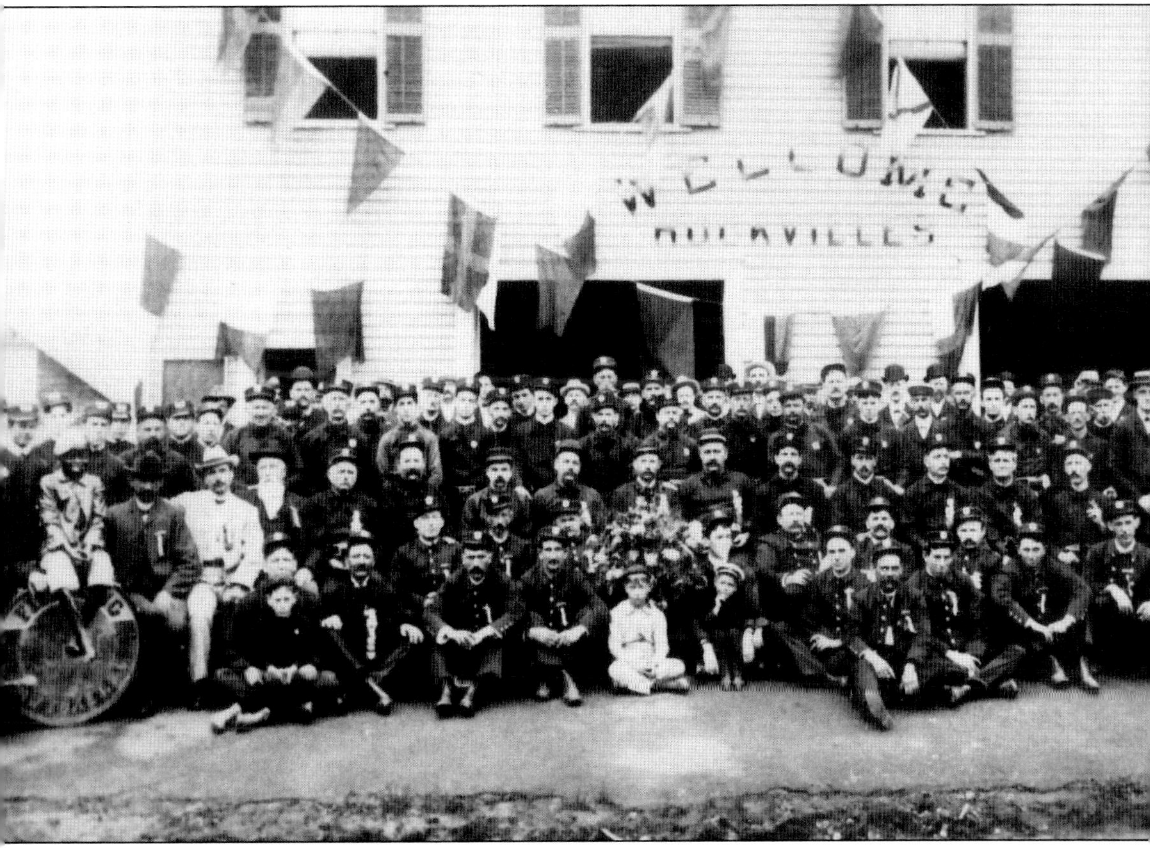

During the early twentieth century, close friendships were developed among members of volunteer fire companies who vied for honors at firemen's musters. In 1910, the Pawtuxet Volunteer Fire Company and its friends welcome a similar group from Rockville, Connecticut. (Pawtuxet Fire King Veterans Firemen's Association.)

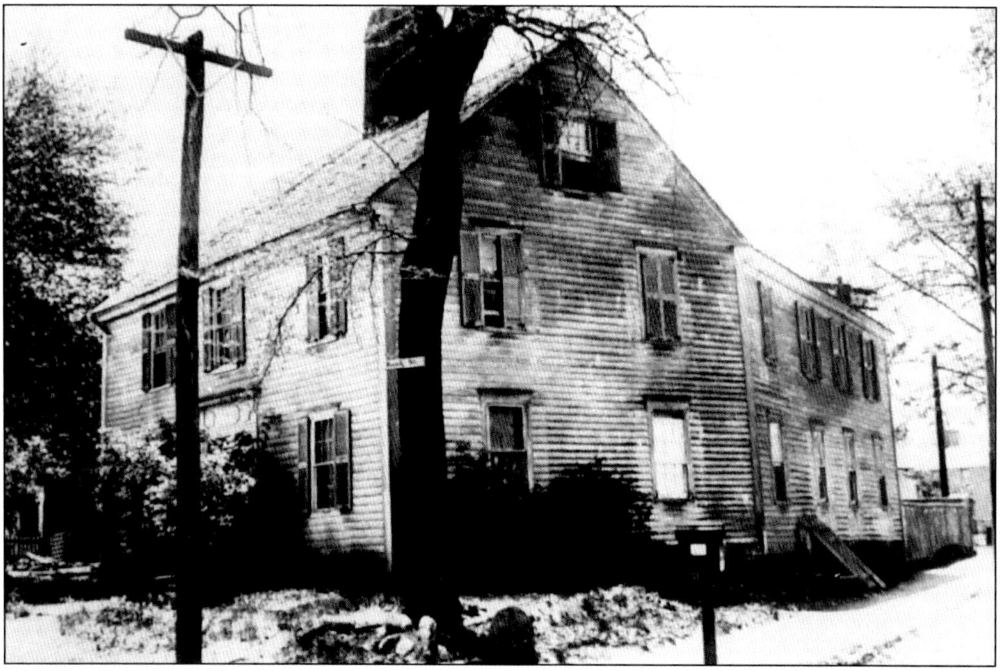

The first meeting place for Pawtuxet's Harmony Lodge was in the Mitchell Tavern, located on the corner of Bank Street and Post Road (then called Main Street) with the front door on Bank Street. The tavern was demolished in 1960 when Post Road was widened. (Cranston Historical Society Collection.)

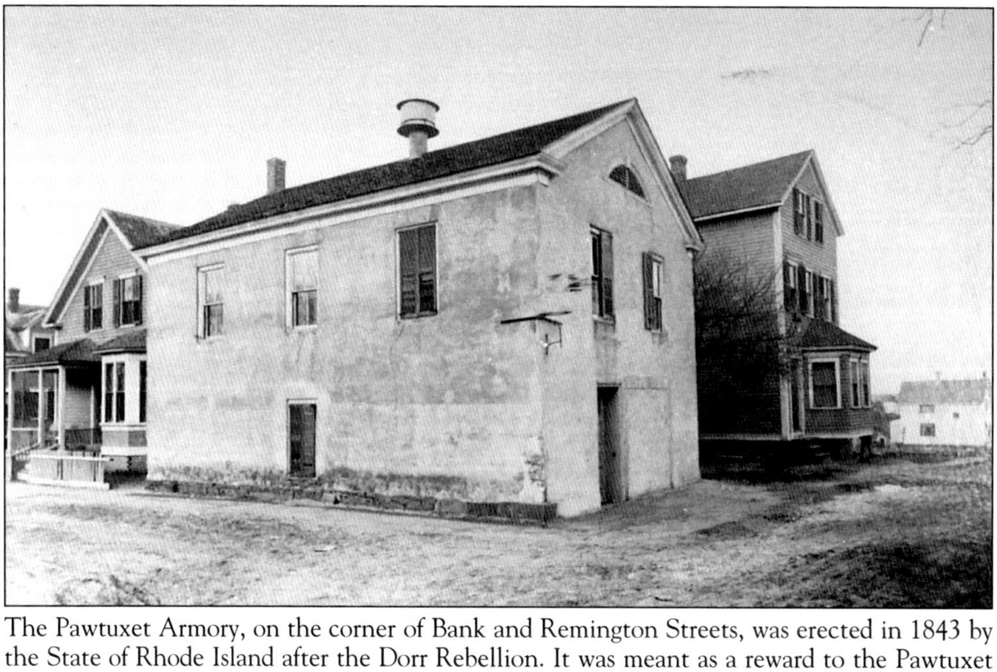

The Pawtuxet Armory, on the corner of Bank and Remington Streets, was erected in 1843 by the State of Rhode Island after the Dorr Rebellion. It was meant as a reward to the Pawtuxet Artillery for remaining loyal to the Law and Order Party. The armory was also the second Temple of Harmony Lodge, and meetings were held there for fifty-seven years. (Robert H. Rhodes Collection.)

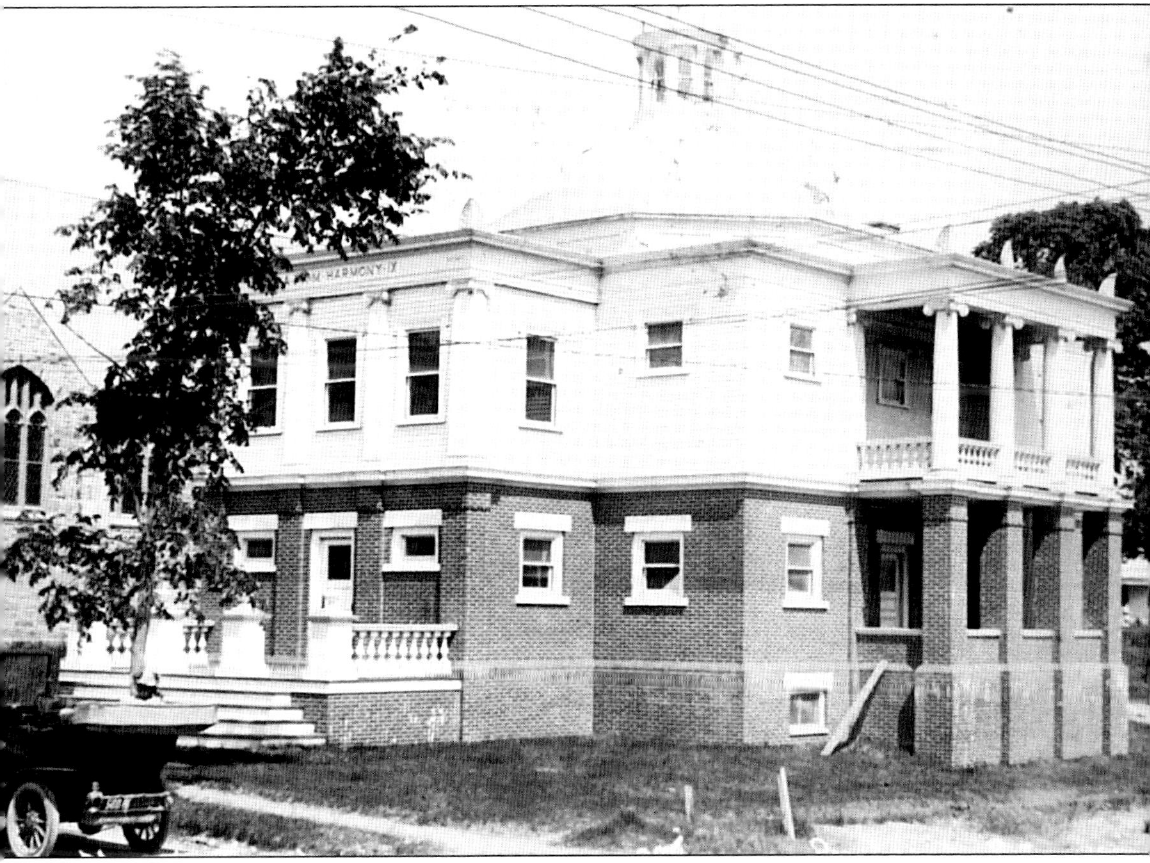

The Masonic temple was built on the site of Joseph Rhodes's distillery. (That enterprise predated the Revolutionary War, and Rhodes is reported to have drowned in one of his large distillery tanks.) The temple stood at the corner of Ocean Avenue and Circuit Drive. Harmony Lodge, which appears here in 1913, held its first meeting in this temple on November 27, 1906. When the Masons purchased the castle on Narragansett Boulevard in 1942, the temple building was purchased by the Trinity Episcopal Church, which was located next to it. The Masonic temple burned in 1946. (Henry A.L. Brown Collection.)

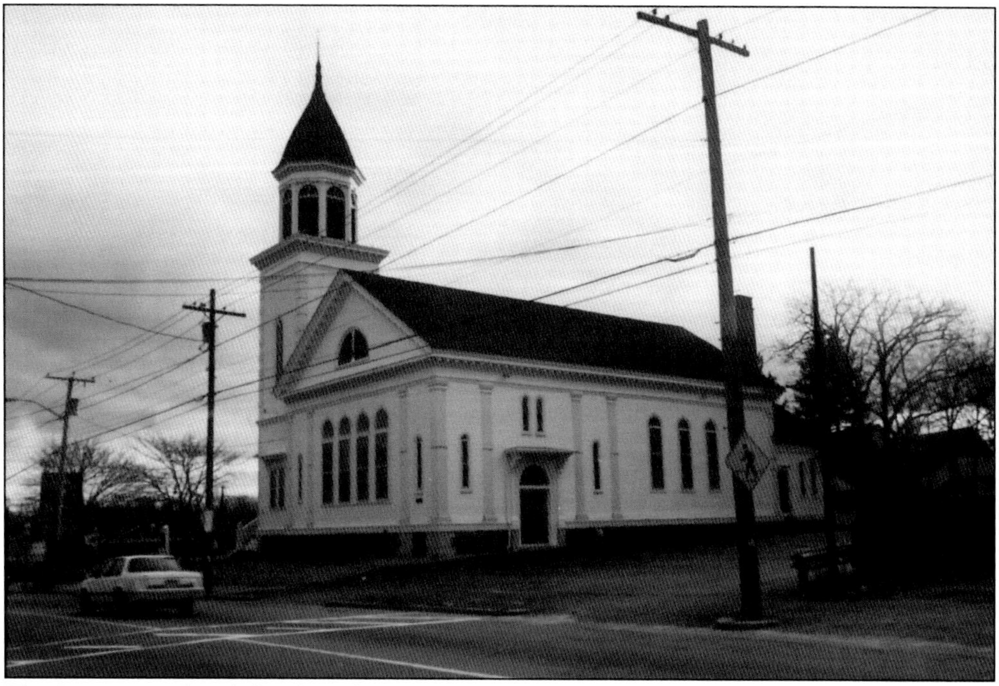

The Pawtuxet Church has long been one of the village's most well-known landmarks. It is renown for its great May breakfasts—1997's was a sellout. (Don D'Amato Collection.)

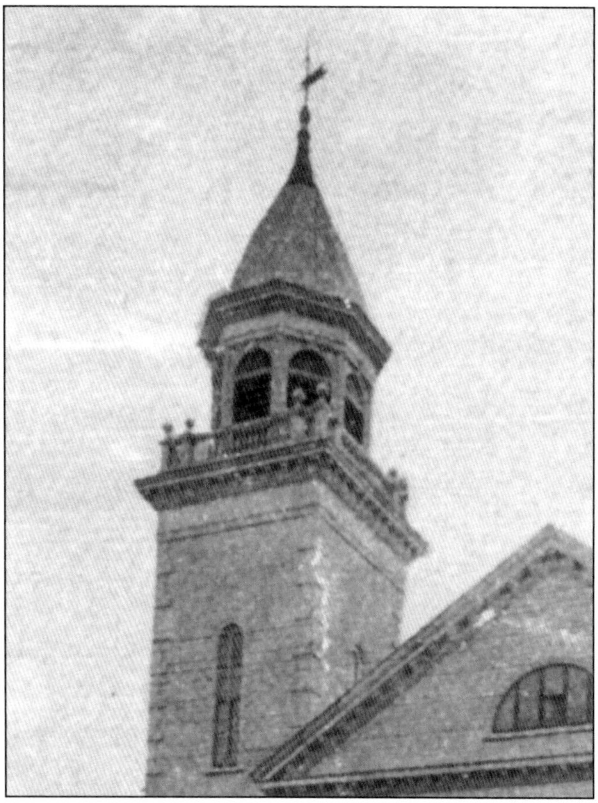

The Pawtuxet Baptist Church was designed by architect Frank W. Angell. It is the third church on the site and was built when Broad Street was widened in 1895. The 1906 photograph was a gift of R.F. Weller. (Cranston Historical Society Collection.)

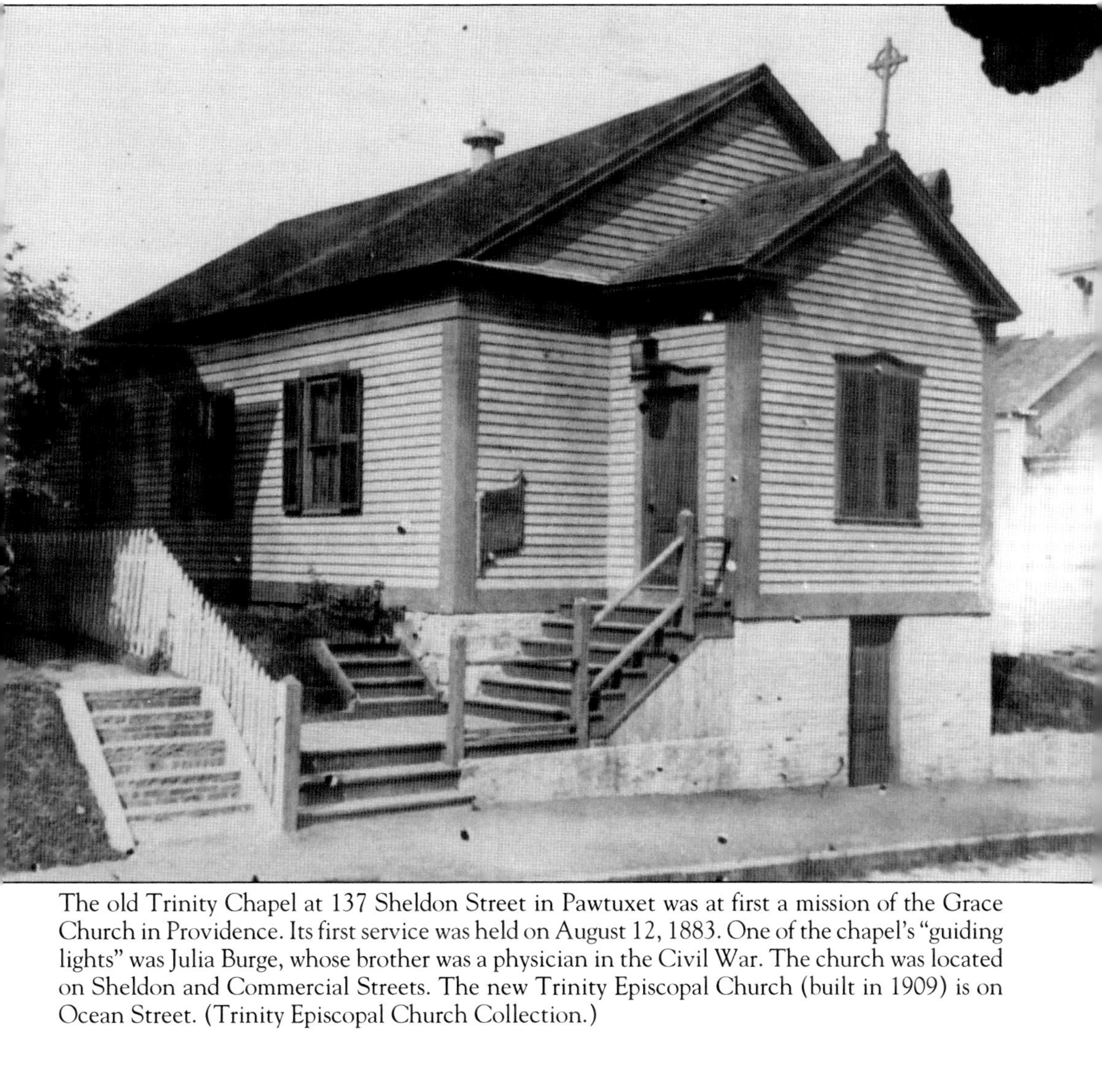

The old Trinity Chapel at 137 Sheldon Street in Pawtuxet was at first a mission of the Grace Church in Providence. Its first service was held on August 12, 1883. One of the chapel's "guiding lights" was Julia Burge, whose brother was a physician in the Civil War. The church was located on Sheldon and Commercial Streets. The new Trinity Episcopal Church (built in 1909) is on Ocean Street. (Trinity Episcopal Church Collection.)

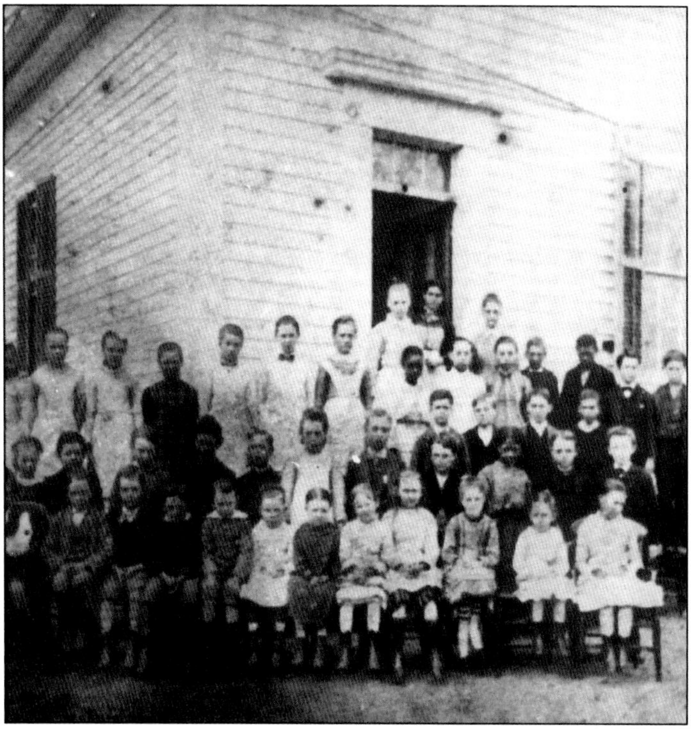

The Commercial Street School was a one-room school with students ranging from age six to thirteen. In 1870, the class was large and the age difference was obvious, as evidenced by the varying height of the students. This photograph was a gift of Betty Budlong Briggs. (Cranston Historical Society Collection.)

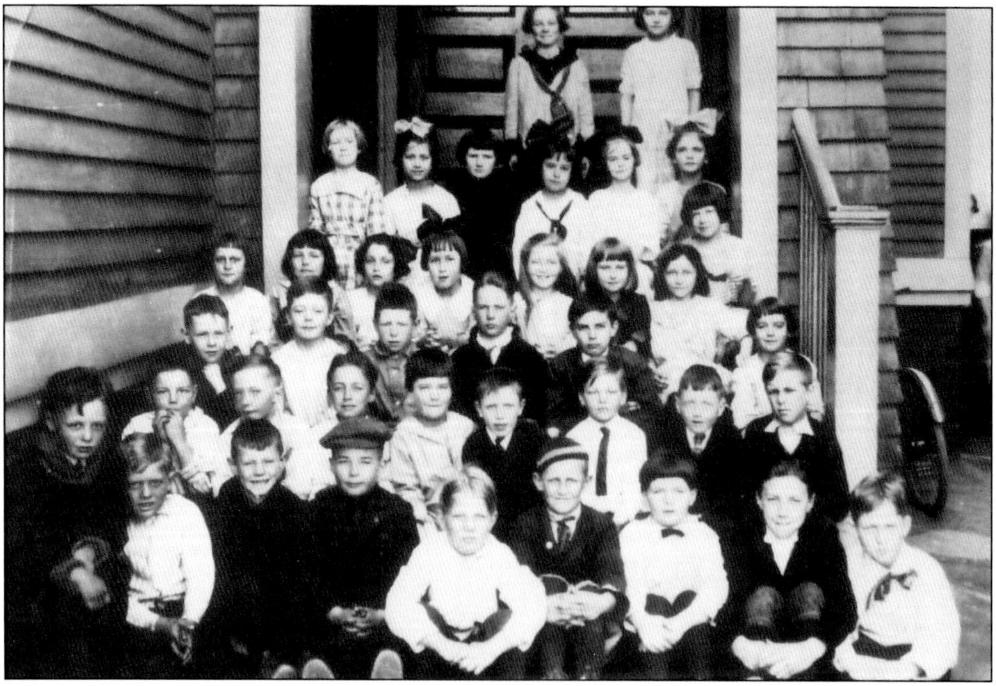

This handsome group of young scholars at the Pawtuxet Grammar School in 1915 had Olive Faguland as their teacher. The school on South Atlantic Avenue served the community well until it was demolished in 1938. This photograph was a gift of Olive Faguland. (Henry A.L. Brown Collection.)

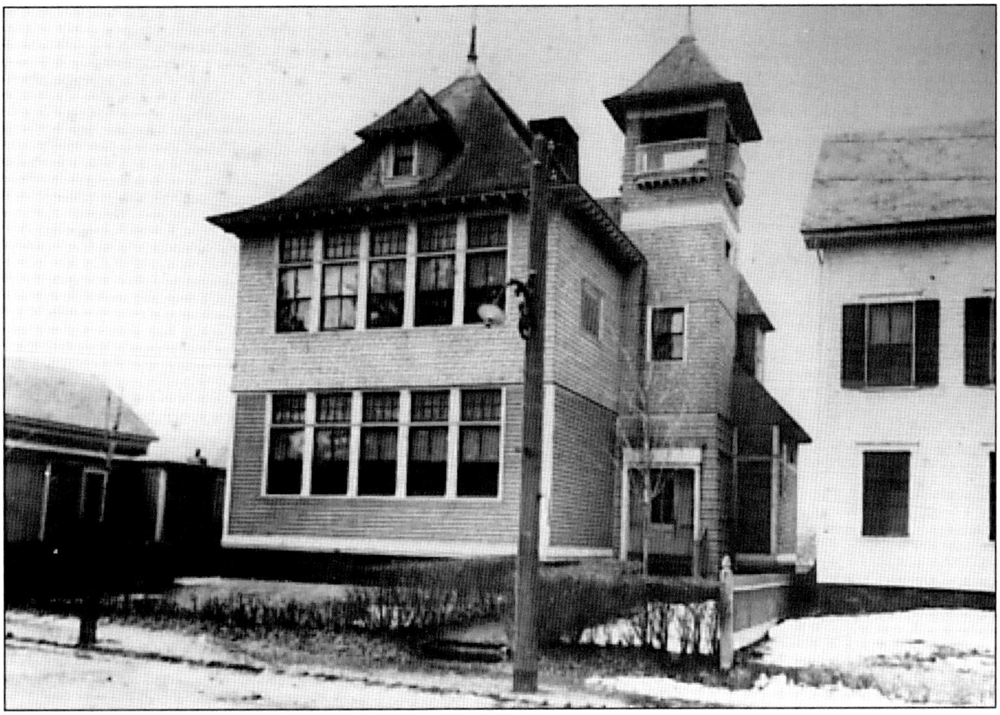

The Pawtuxet Grammar School on South Atlantic Avenue, nearly opposite North Fair Street, was built to replace a building that had burned. The school looked like this in 1920. It was demolished in 1938. (Henry A.L. Brown Collection.)

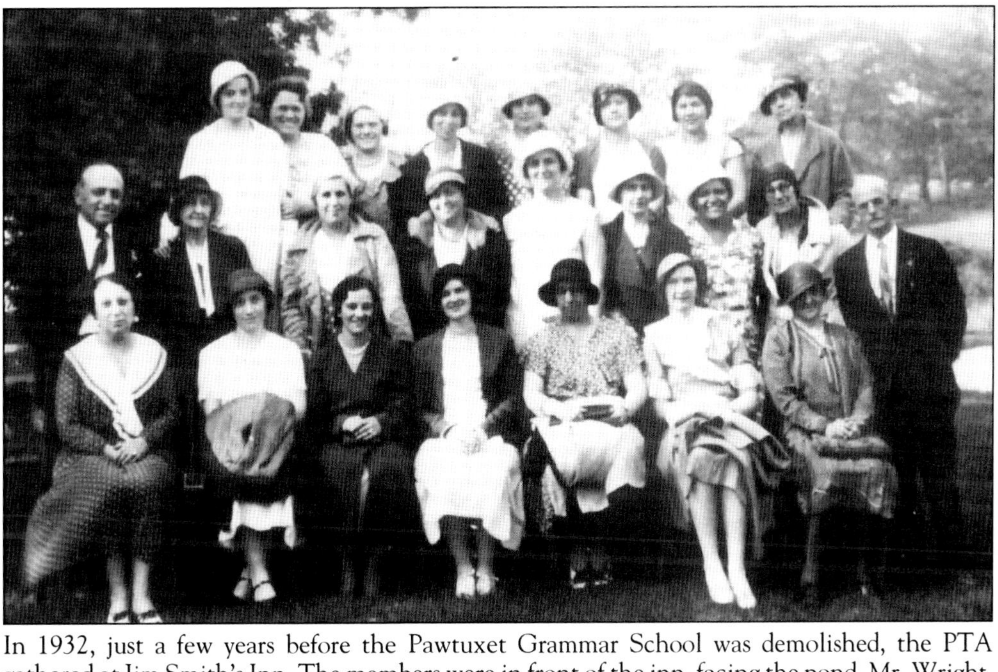

In 1932, just a few years before the Pawtuxet Grammar School was demolished, the PTA gathered at Jim Smith's Inn. The members were in front of the inn, facing the pond. Mr. Wright, the principal, is on the far right and Miss Edna Shanley, a well-known Pawtuxet teacher, is in the front row. (Henry A.L. Brown Collection.)

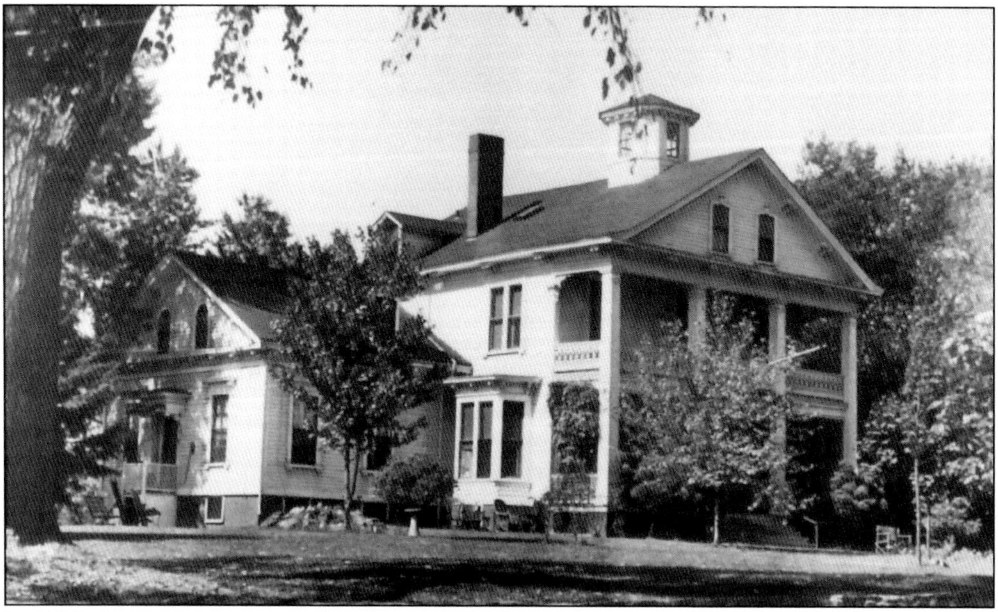

In 1830, the meetinghouse and headquarters for the Rhode Island Society for the Encouragement of Domestic Industries was located in this lovely building. When this picture was taken in 1940, the King's Daughters and Sons occupied the building. Now it is the Gaspee Mansion Limited, a nursing facility. (William Hall Library Collection.)

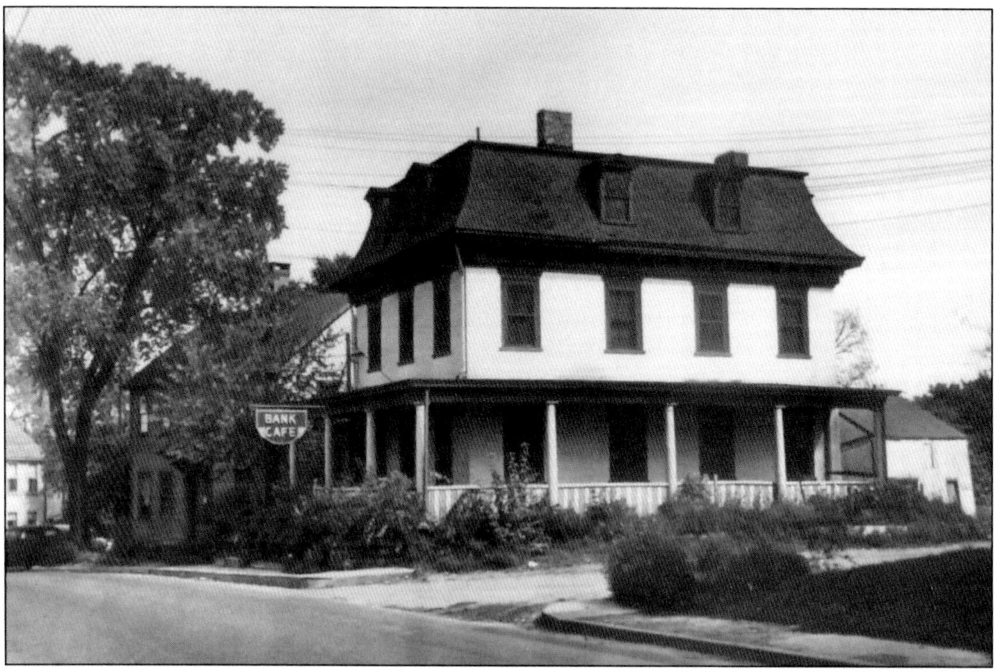

The Bank Cafe has long been a Pawtuxet landmark. It began its existence in 1814, when it was chartered as a bank. James Tinker established a hotel and restaurant there in 1874, and the enterprise operated in that capacity for nearly one hundred years. The cafe has had a number of owners since Frank and Pauline LaCasio sold the building in 1984. (William Hall Library Collection.)

Six

Warwick Village Views

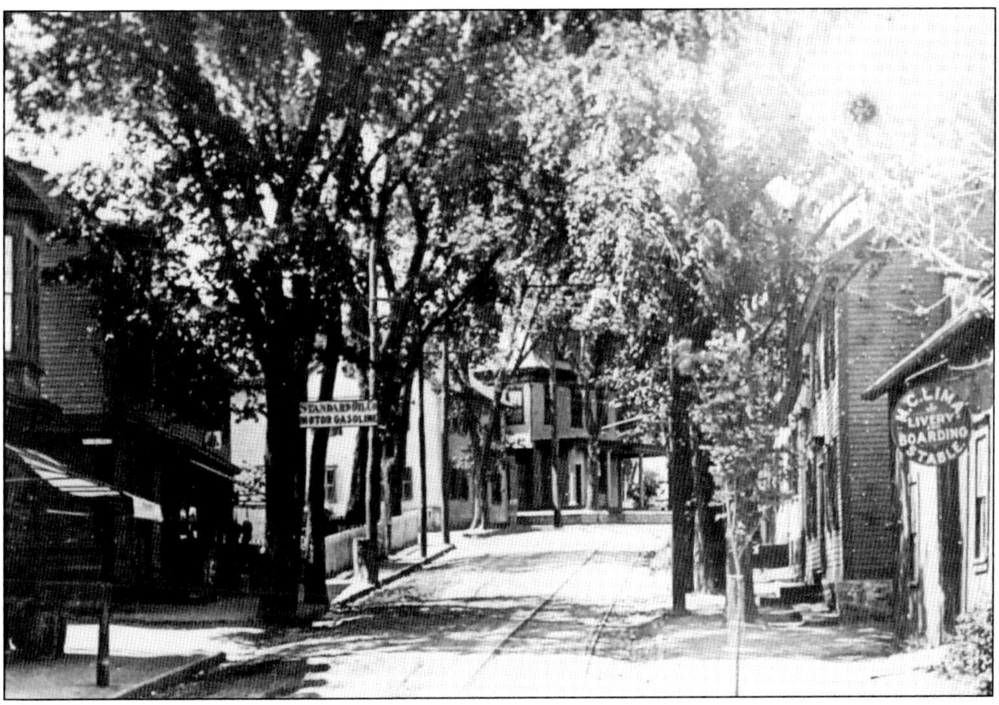

In 1918, the Standard Oil Company gas station, Lima's stable, and the Bumble Bee trolley all vied for Pawtuxet customers. For a while, the trolley, whose tracks can be seen here, seemed to be the winner as it sped up the road past the Bank Cafe and on to Lakewood. (Cranston Historical Society Collection.)

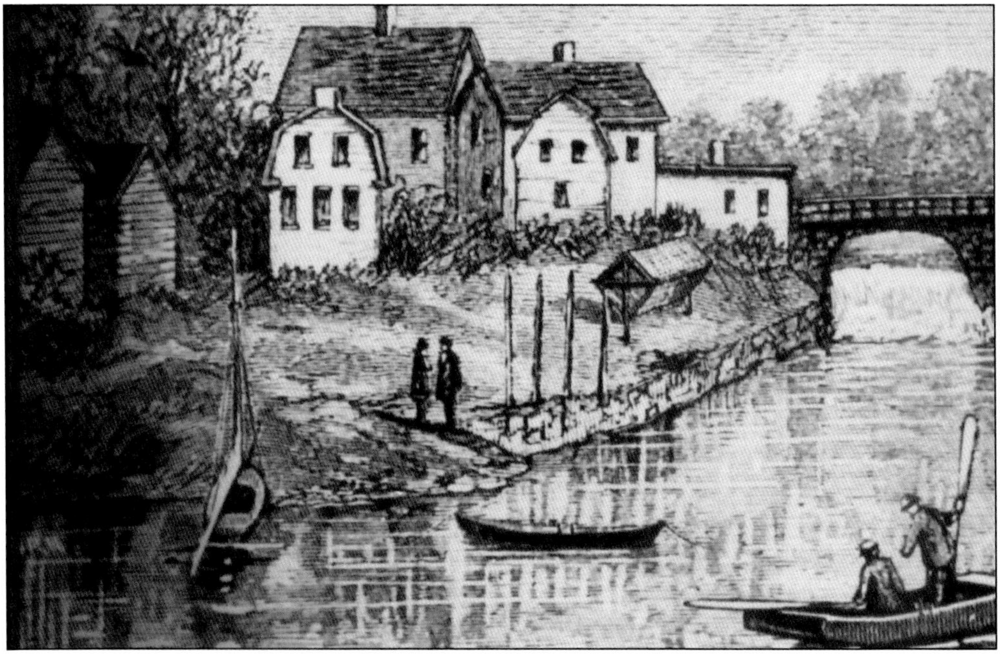

The three houses near the bridge seen on the Warwick side of Pawtuxet Falls in this c. 1870 sketch were built before the Revolutionary War. The house nearest the bridge was operated as a saloon by Constable Charles Gorton. The small house located in back, off the road, was occupied by the Harris family. Harris was an expressman whose route ran from Pawtuxet to Providence. Instead of horses pulling his wagon, he used two mules. (Henry A.L. Brown Collection.)

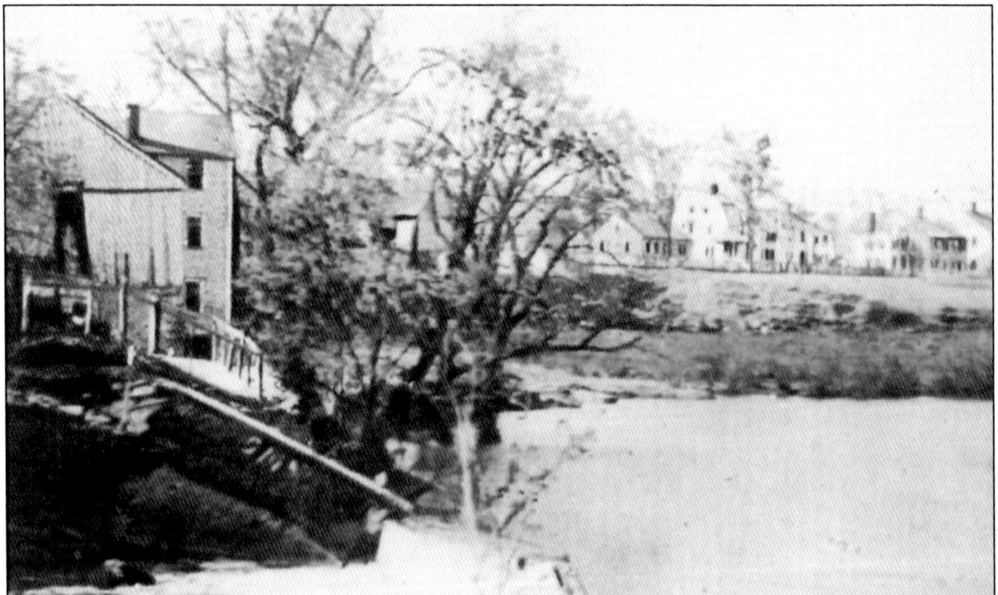

Part of the old mill complex can be seen to the left in this 1910 photograph of the Warwick side of Pawtuxet Falls. The houses seen here are on Post Road and include the Carder Tavern, the Wrightman house, and the Sherman house. (William Hall Library Collection.)

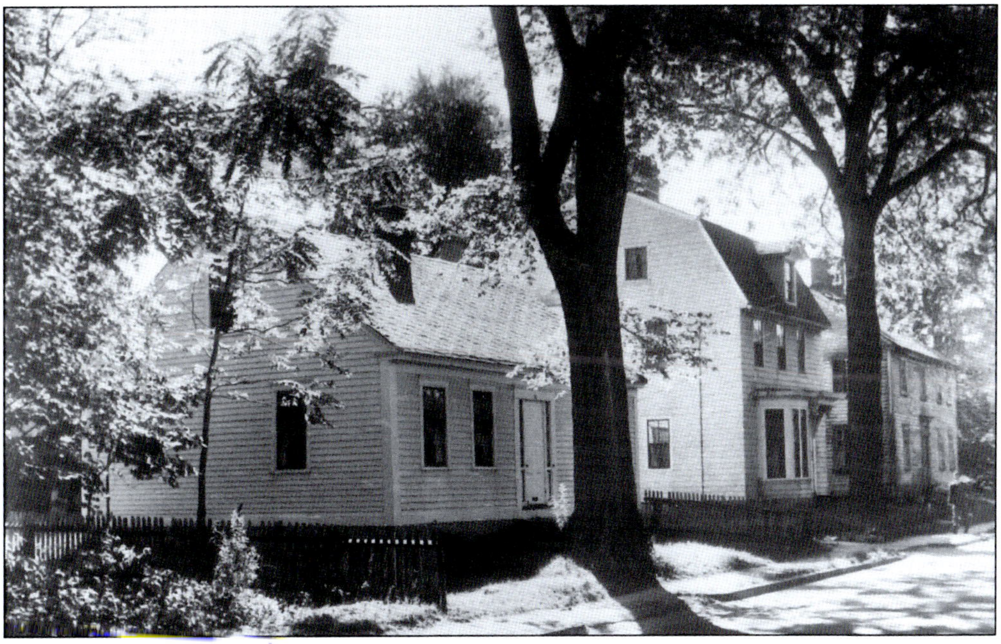

Fortunately, a number of eighteenth-century houses have survived on old Main Street (Post Road) in the Warwick section of Pawtuxet. The first one shown here on the left is the Jeremiah Randall house (built in 1785). Next to it is the gambrel-roofed Wrightman house (built in 1760 with nineteenth-century additions). The third residence is the Sherman family house (built in 1740). (William Hall Library Collection.)

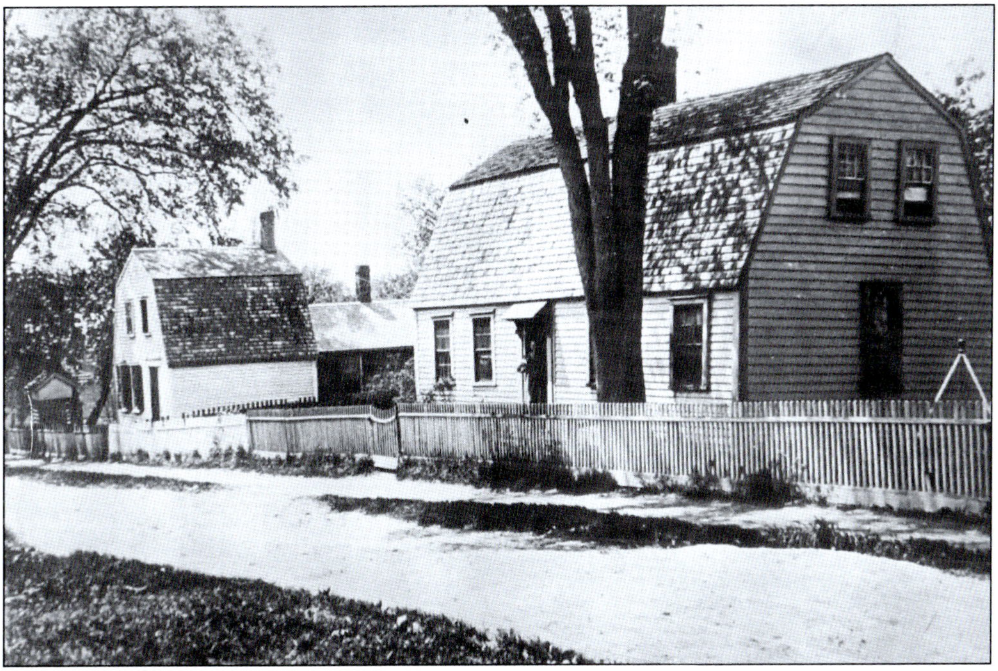

Before 1915, North Fair Street was still a dirt road. Then, as now, two of the most impressive and historical residences were the Captain Crandall house and, to its left, the Ephraim Bowen Still house. (Susan Totten Currie Collection.)

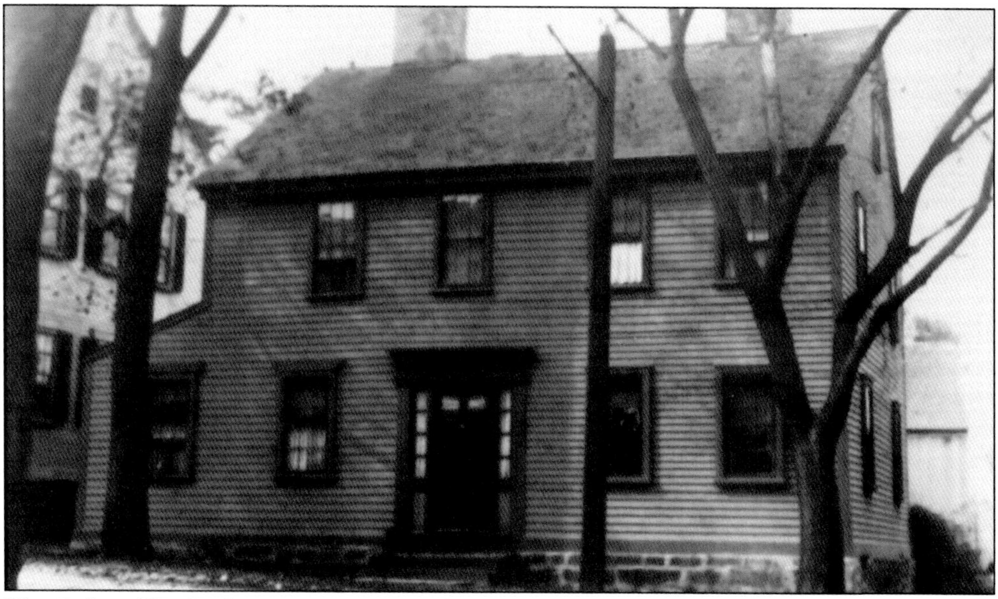

The Robert Rhodes house was next to the H.L. Johnson Blacksmith Shop c. 1915. Robert Rhodes was the oldest captain in the Battle of Rhode Island. His son, Captain Elisha Hunt Rhodes, and his bride, Eliza Chase Rhodes, set up housekeeping here. The house in later years was used as a stable by Manuel Lima and was later demolished in 1934. (Henry A.L. Brown Collection.)

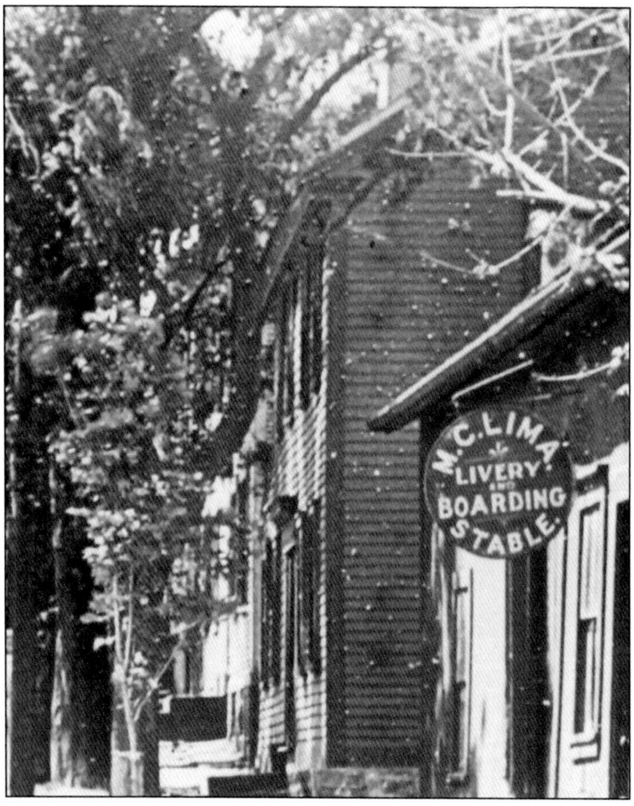

Manuel Lima, an immigrant from the island of Pico in the Azores, leased the old Robert Rhodes house on Main Street (now Post Road) on the Warwick side of Pawtuxet Village. Lima used part of the dwelling as a stable and ran a successful dairy business from there in the early twentieth century. He drove his cows up Main Street to the Cole Farm for pasturage. (Cranston Historical Society Collection.)

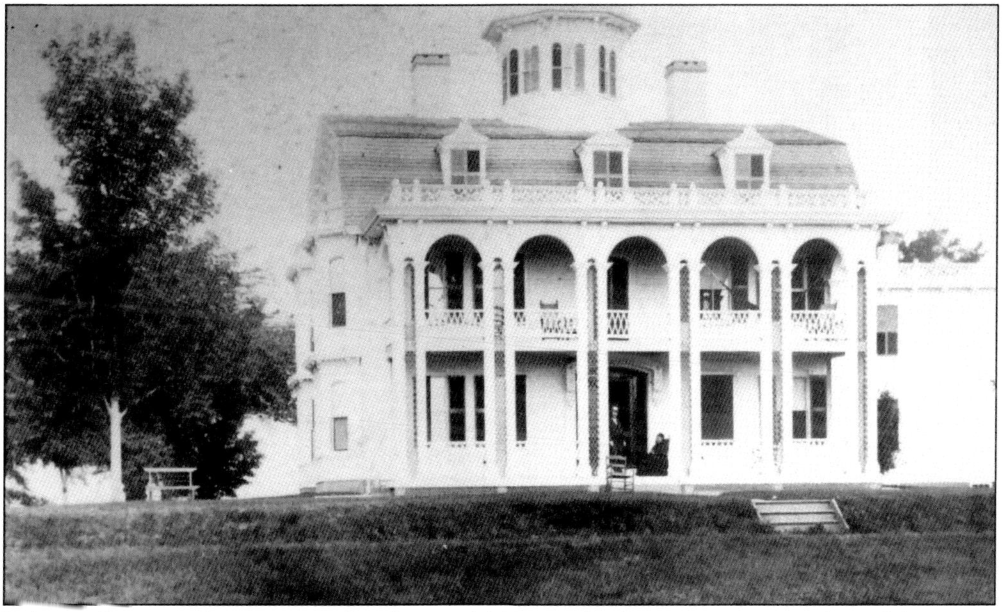

Ephraim Bowen, who at age eighty-four in 1840 was the last surviving member of the group that burned the *Gaspee*, built this house in 1779. The house was acquired by Joseph Butler, a Providence merchant, who commissioned Italianate renovations in 1860. In 1881, John and Ellen Brown owned the home. They can be seen here in the doorway of their charming home at 130 Fair Street in Pawtuxet. (Henry A.L. Brown Collection.)

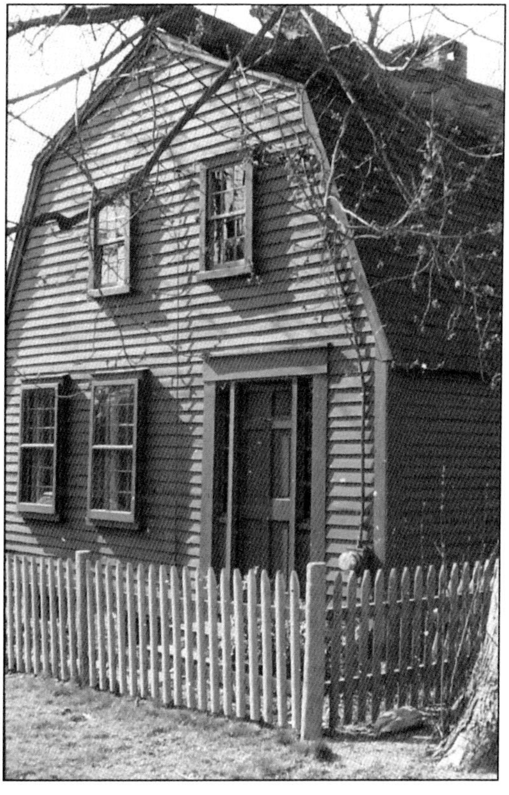

The Ephraim Bowen Still house had been used to distill West Indies molasses into rum. The building was moved from Bowen's wharf and placed on North Fair Street c. 1850. (Don D'Amato Collection.)

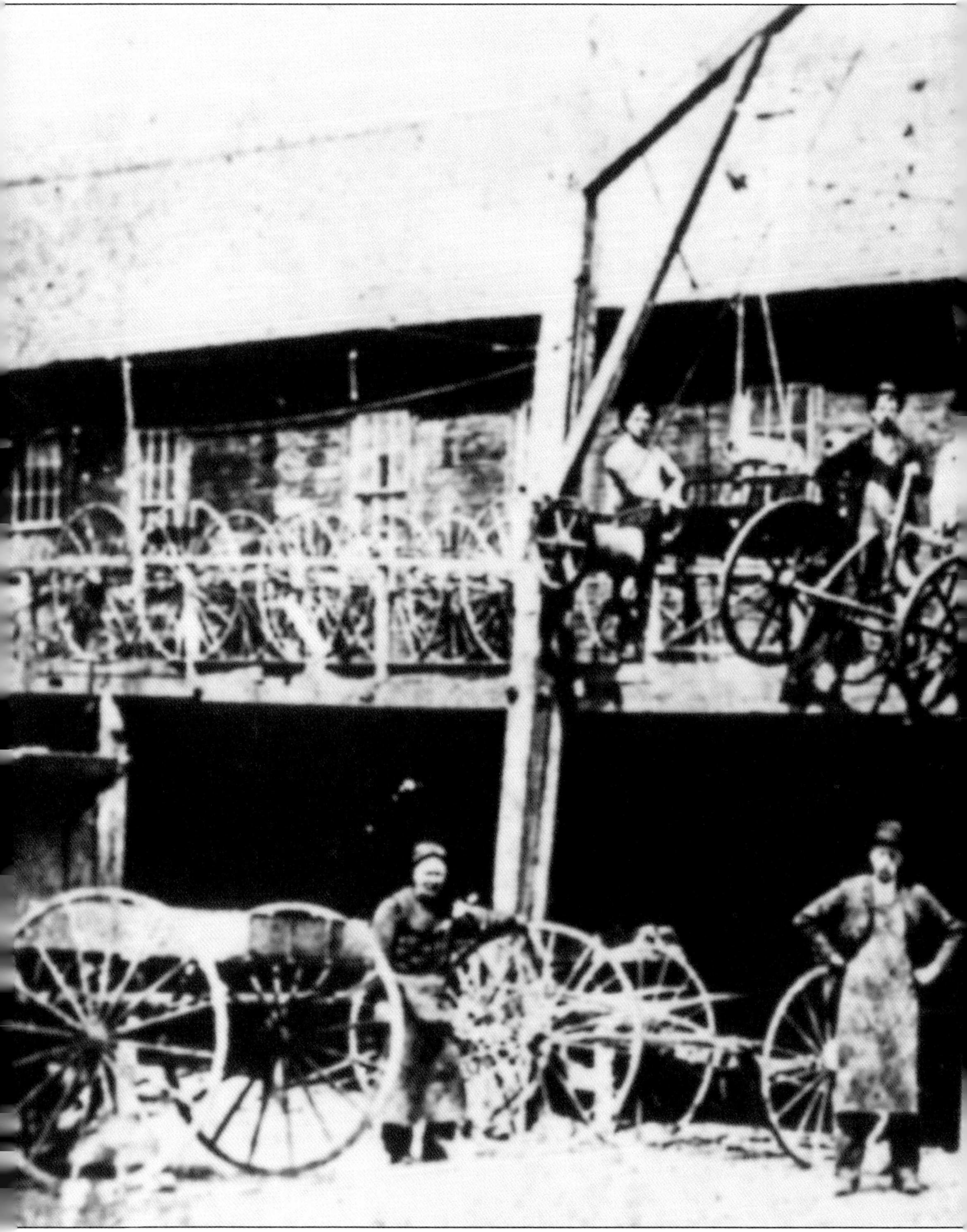

The H.L. Johnson Blacksmith Shop was built in 1860 and quickly became one of the most important businesses in the village. It grew rapidly and became such a large, sprawling enterprise

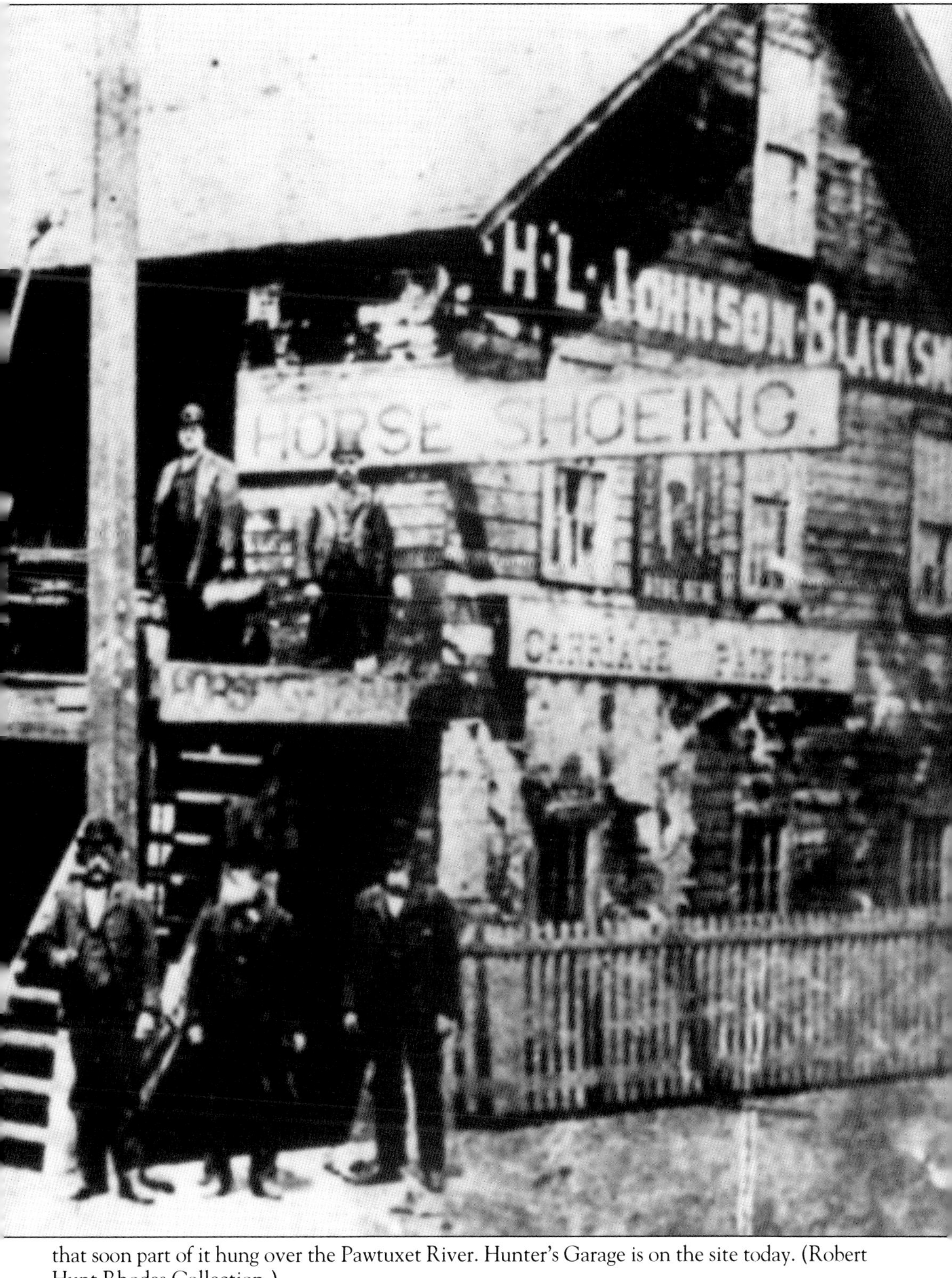

that soon part of it hung over the Pawtuxet River. Hunter's Garage is on the site today. (Robert Hunt Rhodes Collection.)

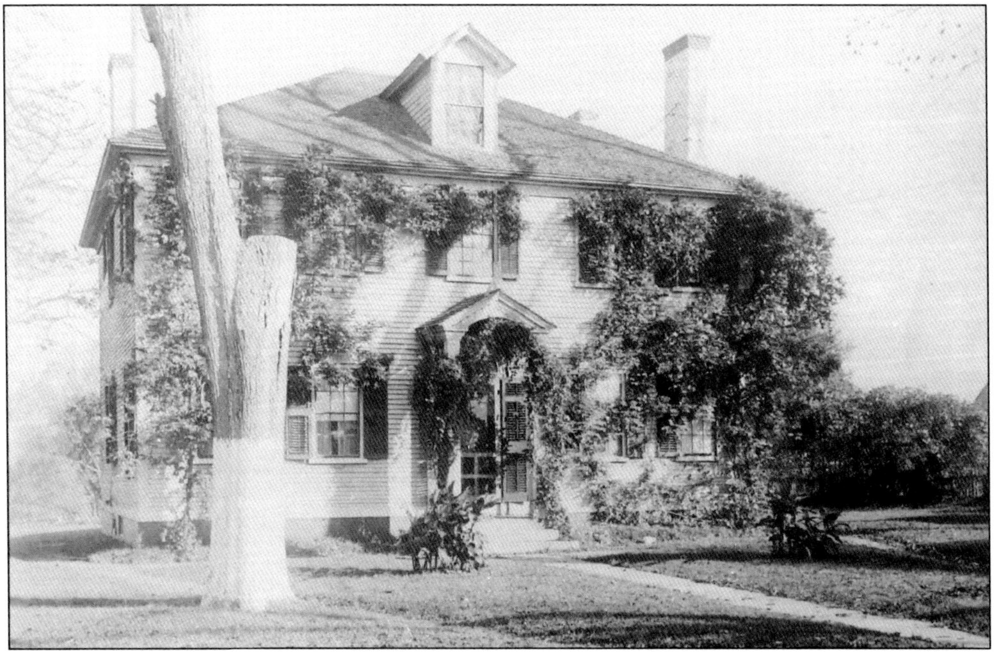

William Rhodes built this fine house as his residence around 1800. William was one of three Rhodes Brothers who were successful merchants at the end of the eighteenth century. In the early nineteenth century, Christopher and William formed the C & W Rhodes Mfg. Co. and the Pawtuxet Bank. It is believed that Pawtuxet historian Horace Belcher took this photograph in the early twentieth century. (Henry A.L. Brown Collection.)

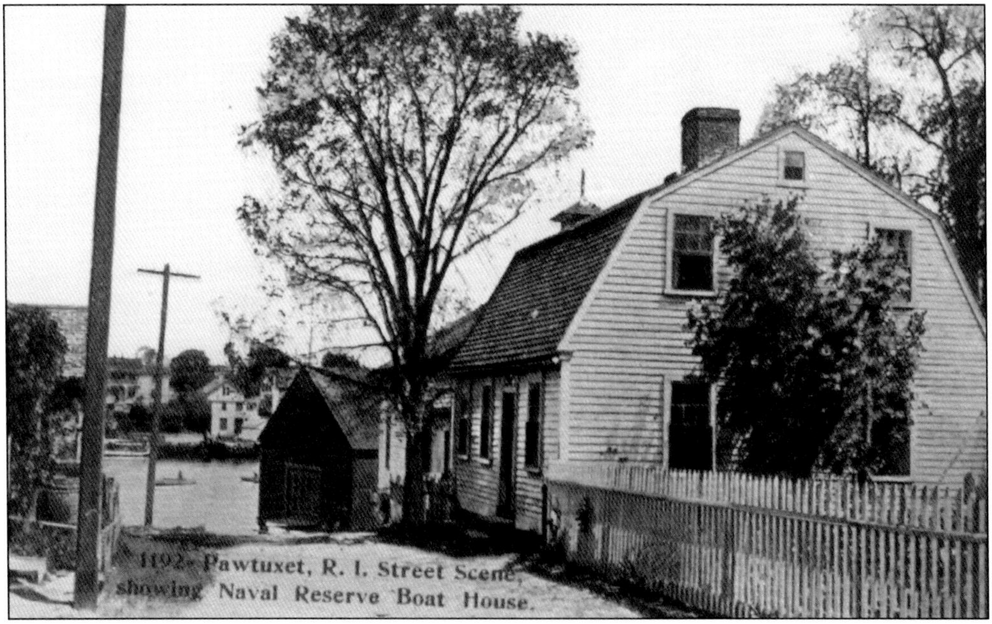

Peck Lane is one of the oldest streets in Pawtuxet. It was laid out in 1734. Tradition says that the captured crewmen from the *Gaspee* were brought ashore at the foot of the street and marched to a nearby farmhouse. The boathouse was built in the nineteenth century and was used by the naval reserve. (Henry A.L. Brown Collection.)

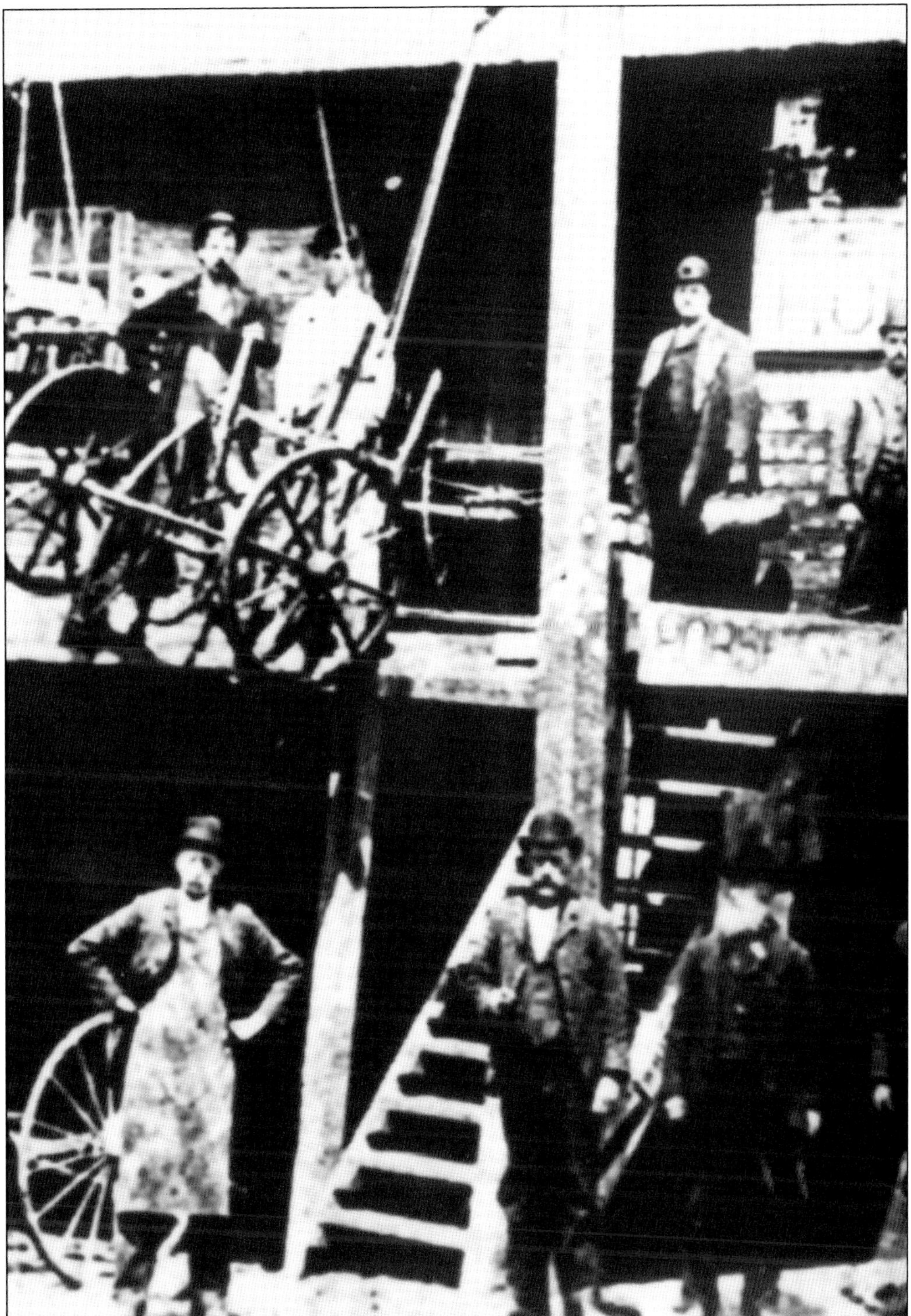

The man with the apron in this 1912 photograph is H.L. Johnson, the blacksmith. On the second story of the building is the then-famous veterinarian, R. Arnold, with his doctor's bag and derby hat. (Robert Hunt Rhodes Collection.)

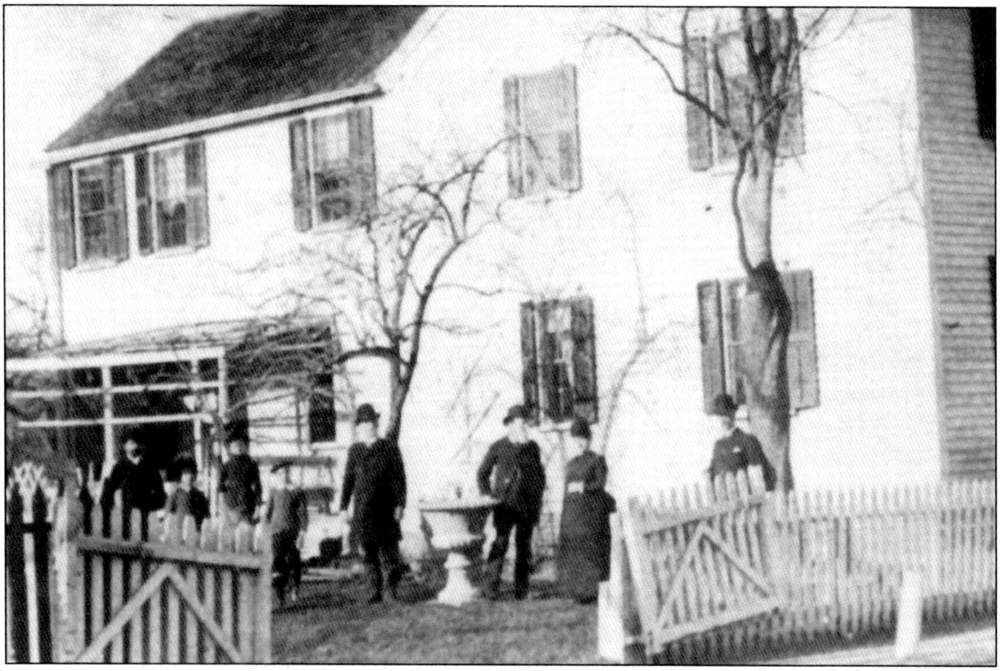

One of the well-known families in Pawtuxet in the late nineteenth century was the Hawkins family. A number of family members have gathered at the homestead at 25 Fair Street in 1886. (Gladys Dyer/Henry A.L. Brown Collection.)

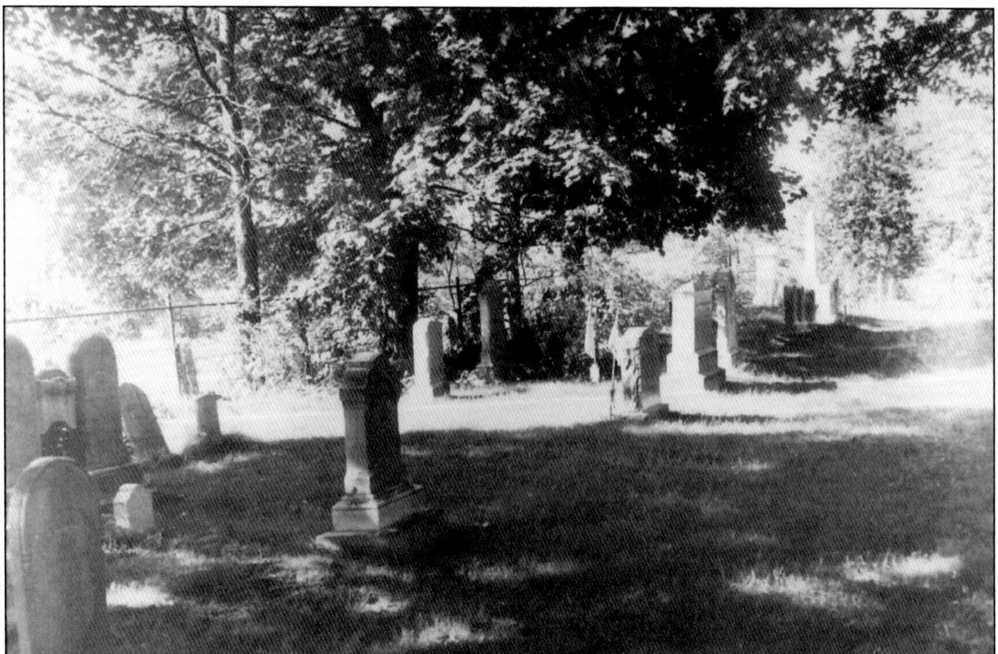

Many times, the only visual reminders we have of past heroes are found in cemeteries. Warwick Historical Cemetery #3, on the corner of Post Road, is a treasure trove of old graves. Often called the Sea Captains' Cemetery or the Greene Cemetery, it contains the graves of many early Pawtuxet residents. (Henry A.L. Brown Collection.)

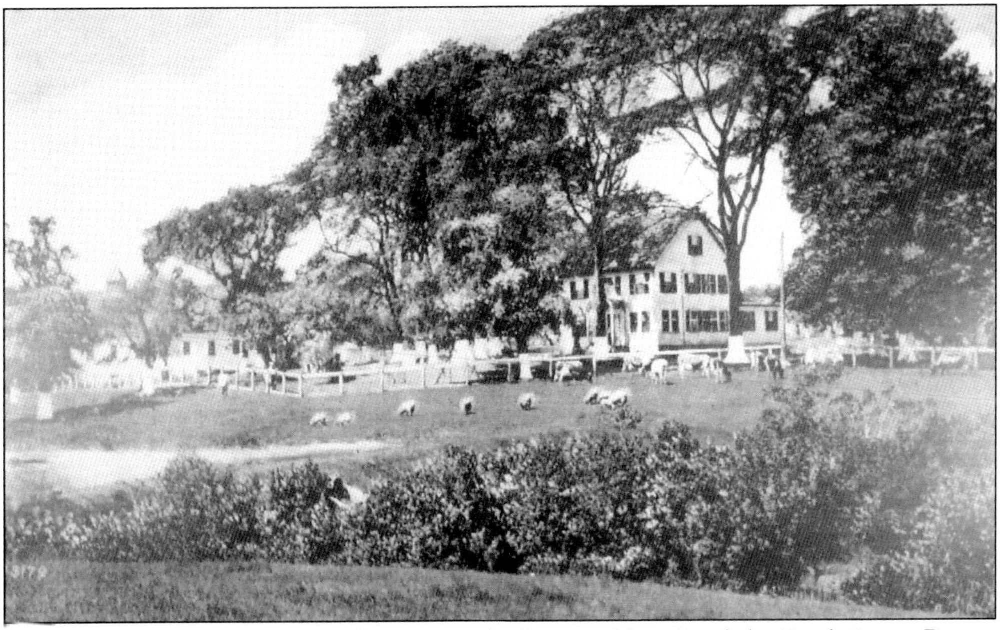

The property on which Jim Smith's Inn was built was sold to Smith by Frank Pettis. During the Revolution there was a salt works on the site, where salt was extracted from seawater. John Notte, who managed the inn, purchased the property from Smith and called it The New Farm Supper Club. The club was destroyed by fire in 1937. (Edward Lawrence Collection.)

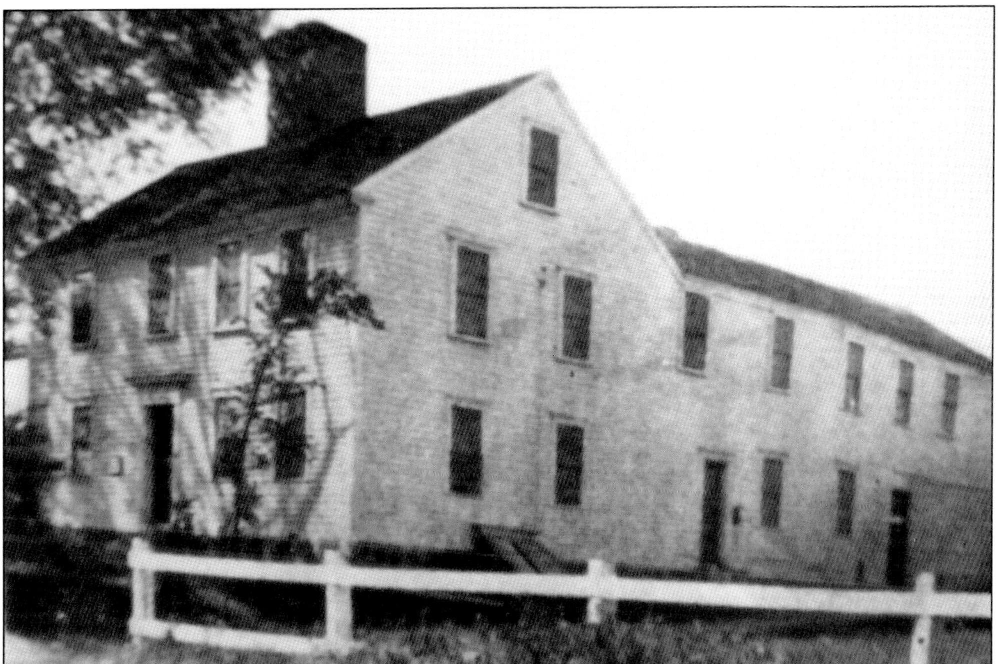

The Golden Ball Inn on the north side of Main Street, built c. 1799, was a very well-patronized, early-nineteenth-century establishment. For many years it was the residence of Mr. and Mrs. Frank Cole. It was demolished in 1951. (E. Lockwood, *Episodes in Warwick History*.)

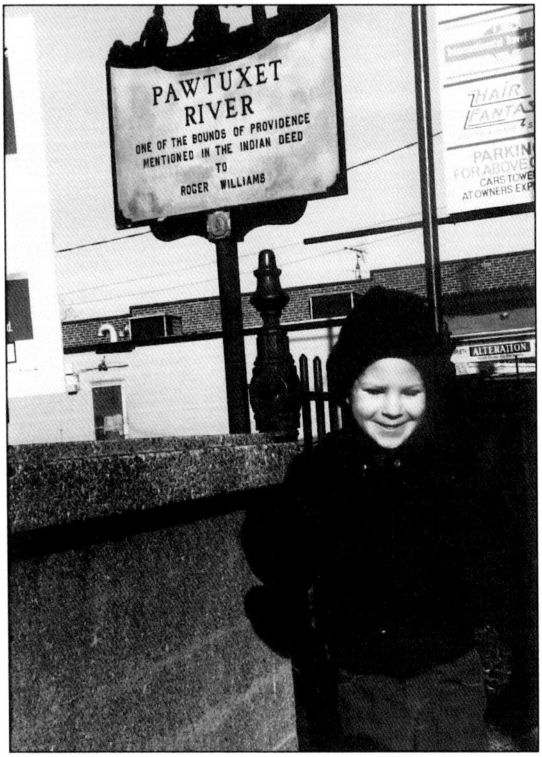

Six-year-old Charles Heinig from nearby Apponaug gets his first look at Pawtuxet Village from under the commemorative sign at the bridge in 1987. The sign depicts Roger Williams and the Native Americans, indicating that the Pawtuxet River was "one of the bounds of Providence mentioned in the Indian Deed." (Don D'Amato Collection.)

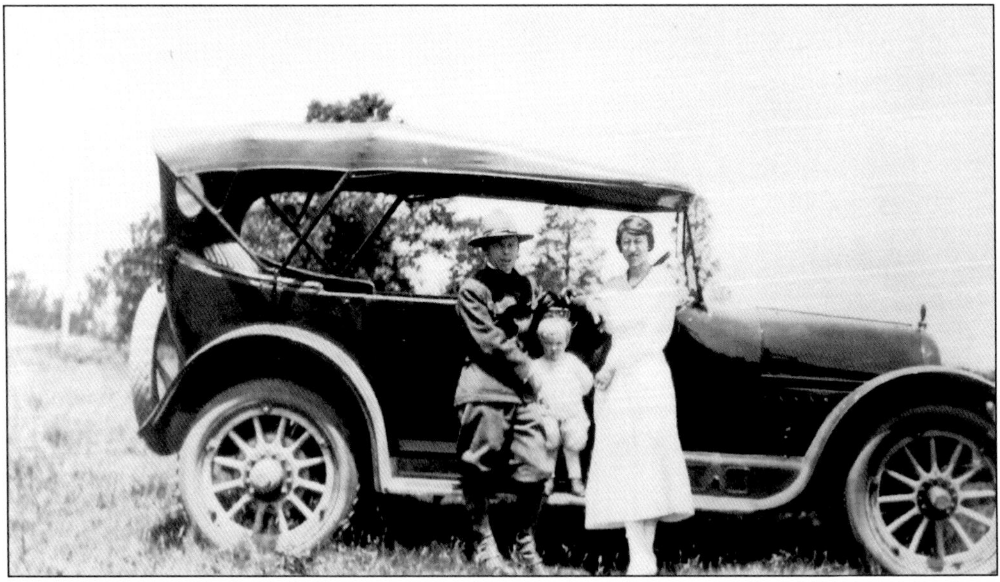

In 1917, patriotic fever ran high as we were about to enter the "War to End All Wars." On June 5 of that year, all male citizens in Rhode Island aged twenty-one to thirty had to register for the draft. Soon after, Robert Poole was called to arms. His wife, Louise Rheinhardt Poole, and their baby join him for a photograph in Pawtuxet. (Henry A.L. Brown Collection.)

A very significant part of the summer activities of the Swedish Covenant Evangelical Lutheran Church was the picnic at Warwick Downs. These men were the church elders in 1909. (Henry A.L. Brown Collection.)

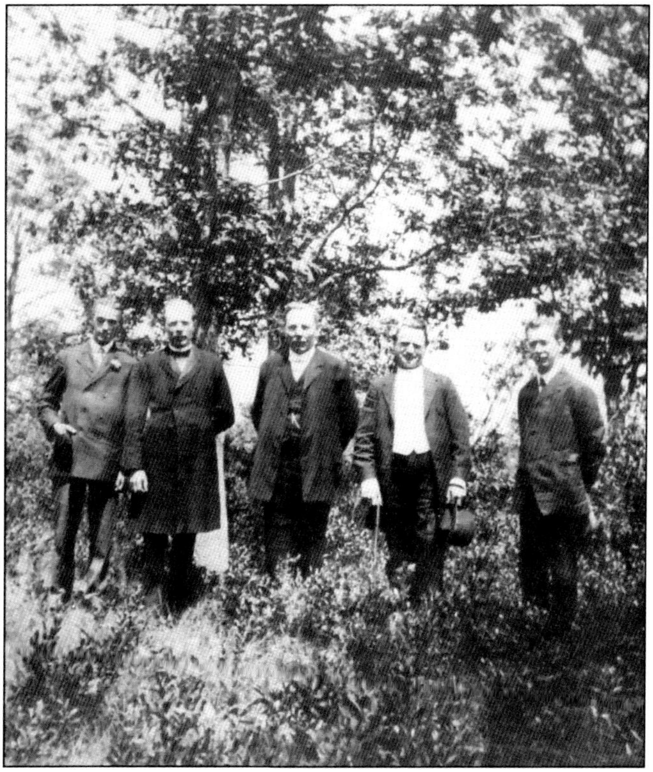

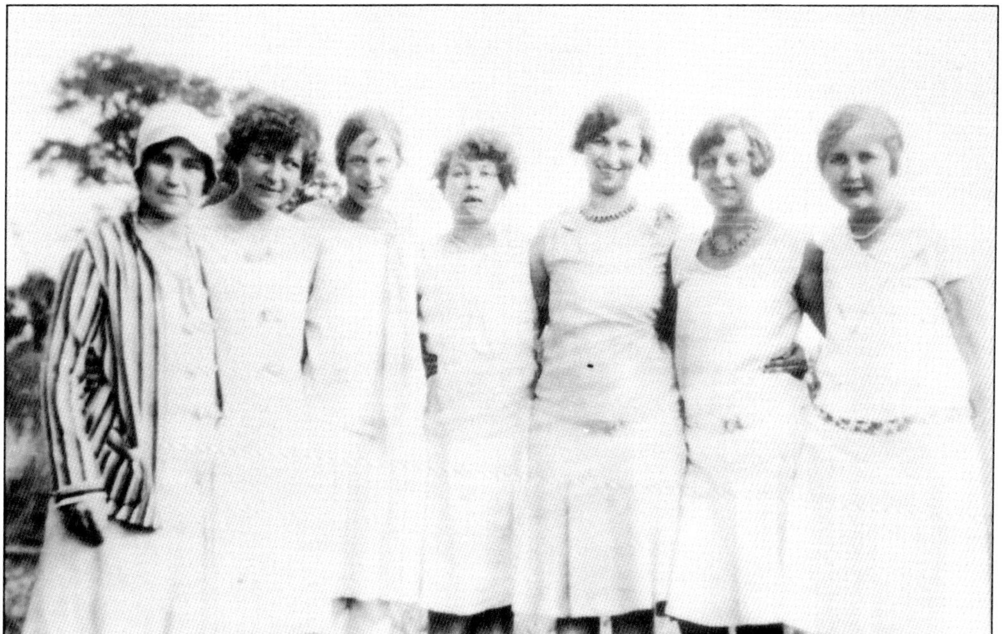

Over the years, Pawtuxet and Warwick Downs have been comfortable places to relax in the summer. Bessie Nye and her lady friends, dressed in cool summer attire, make the most of the summer season in 1925. (Henry A.L. Brown Collection.)

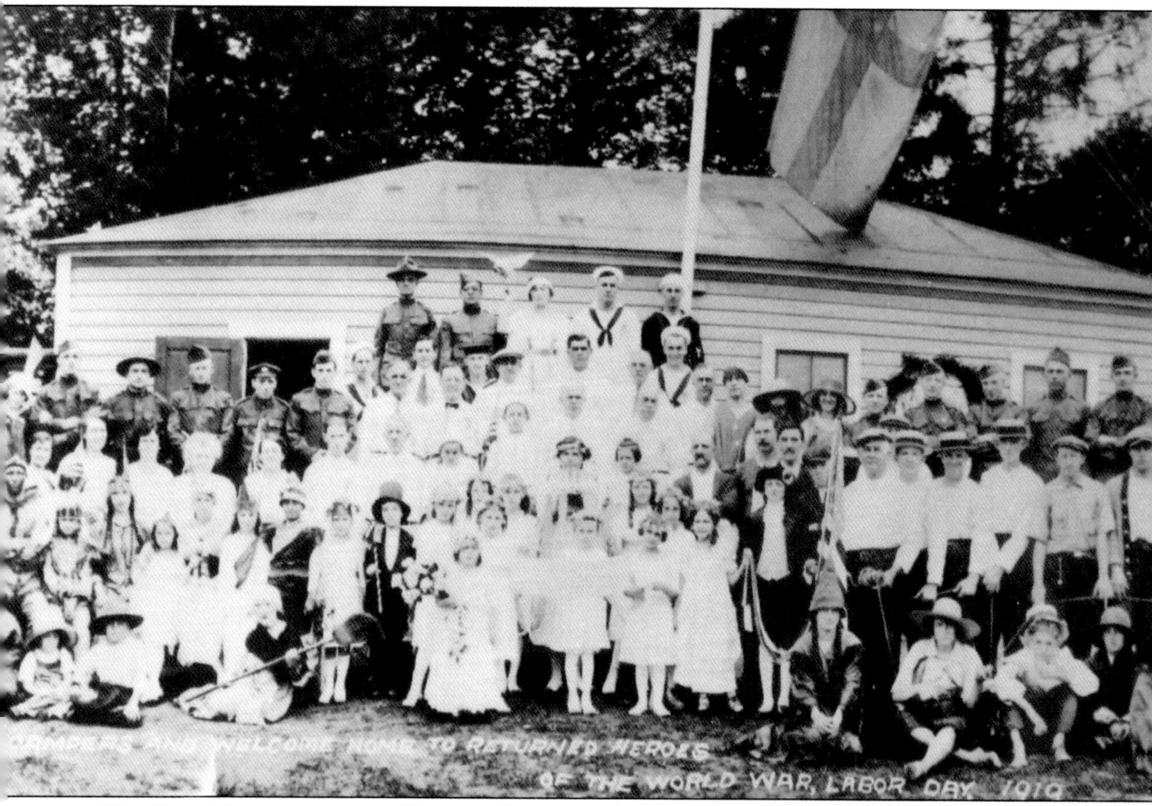

The Swedish community at Warwick Downs turned out to honor the returning veterans of the First World War on Labor Day in 1919. (Warwick Historical Society Collection.)

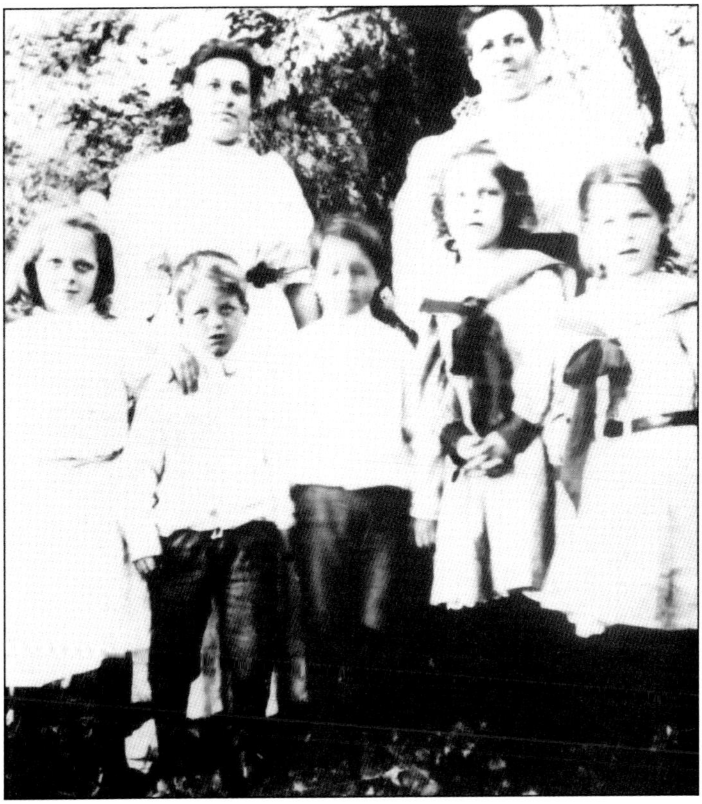

One of the rewards for diligent study at the Swedish Covenant Evangelical Lutheran Sunday School in 1905 was the Sunday school picnic at Warwick Downs. (Henry A.L. Brown Collection.)

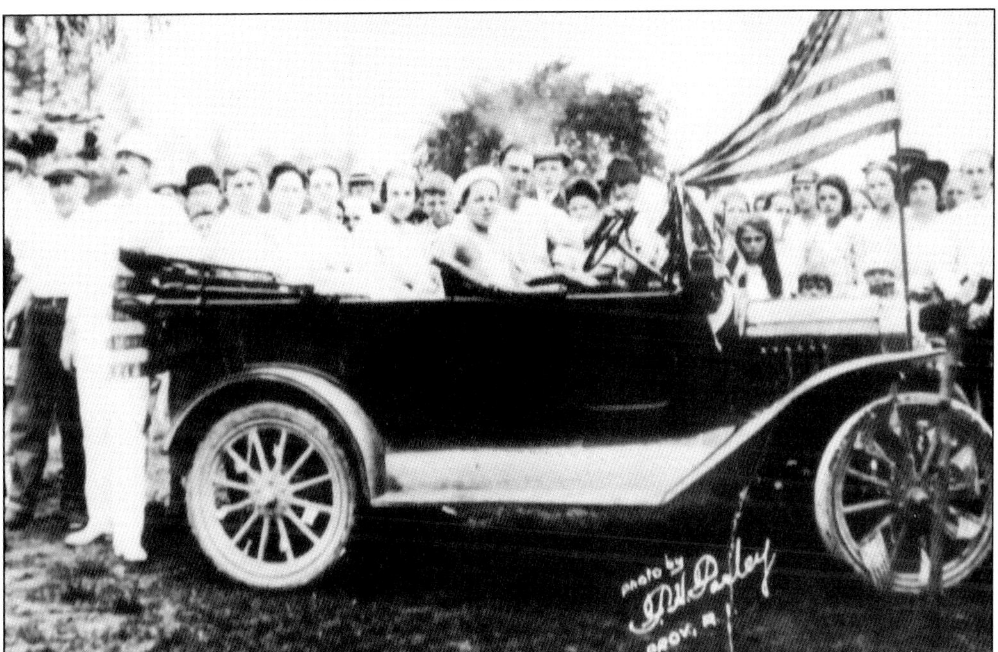

This patriotic display of cars and flags conveyed the feelings of the Swedish group at Warwick Downs in 1919. (Warwick Historical Society Collection.)

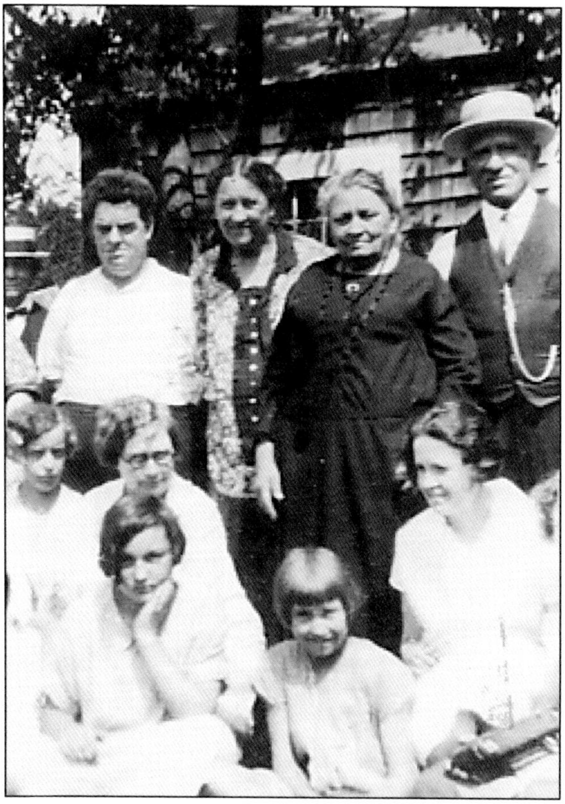

The Rheinhardt family picnic, c. 1922, was a happy summer event. Rheinhardt, a prominent jewelry manufacturer, and his wife are the two on the far right. (Henry A.L. Brown Collection.)

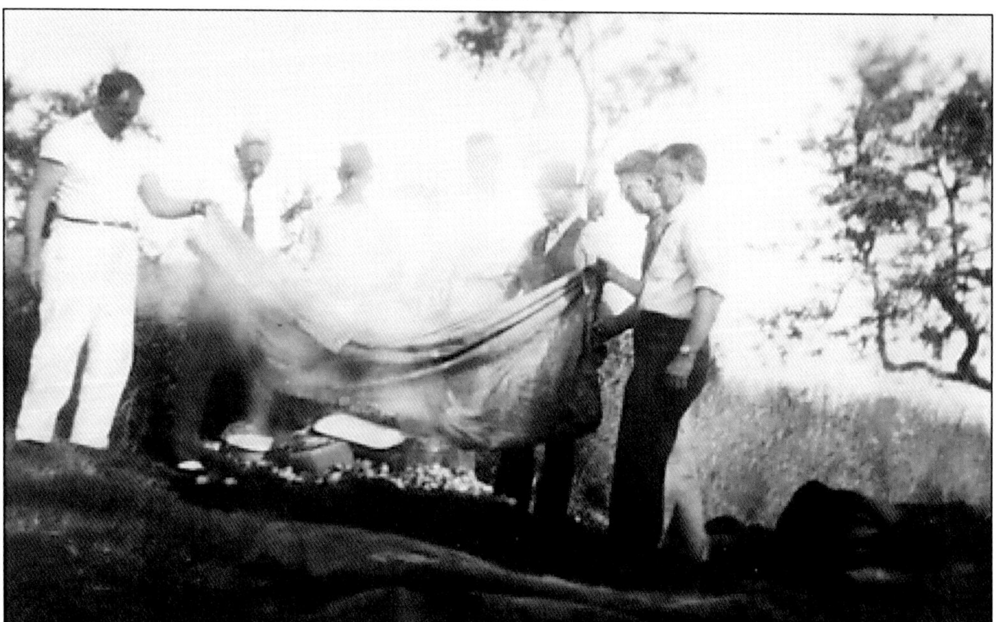

For years Pawtuxet was synonymous with clambakes to many families. In 1920, on North Fair Street, the Rheinhardt, Smith, and Hauser families gathered to enjoy one of Rhode Island's favorite feasts. (Henry A.L. Brown Collection.)

Pawtuxet stable owner Manuel Lima (on the far left) joins members of the Rheinhardt family for summer fun at a clambake in Pawtuxet in the early twentieth century. (Henry A.L. Brown Collection.)

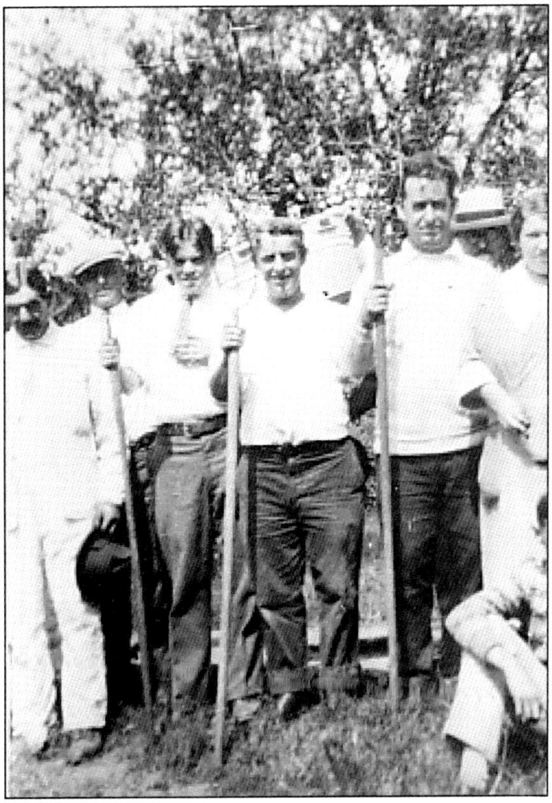

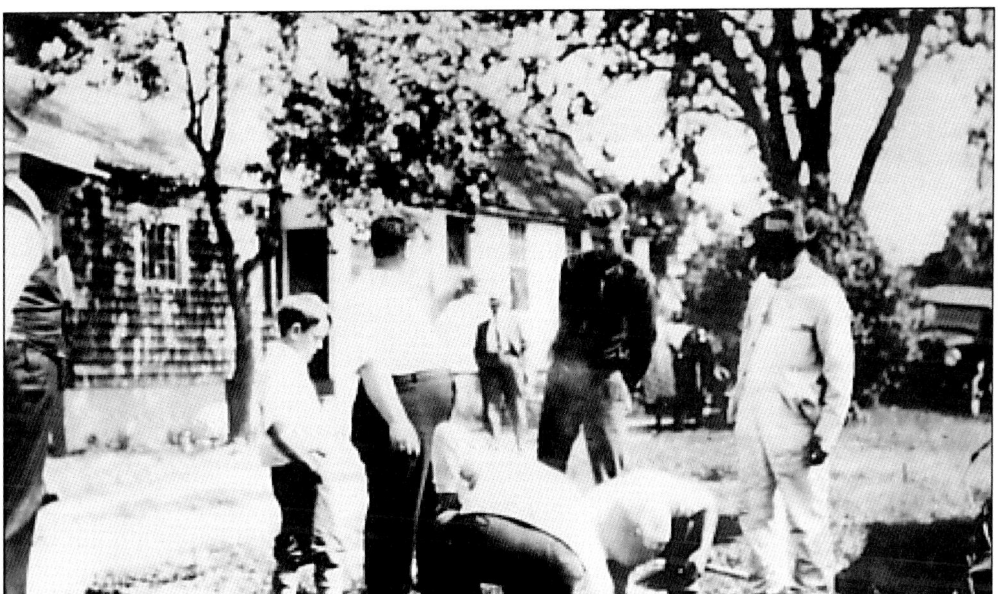

Just about everyone took part in the clambakes at Pawtuxet in the early twentieth century. The gentleman in the white overalls on the far right at this clambake is Manuel C. Lima, whose stable on Main Street (Post Road) was located in the old Robert Rhodes house. (Henry A.L. Brown Collection.)

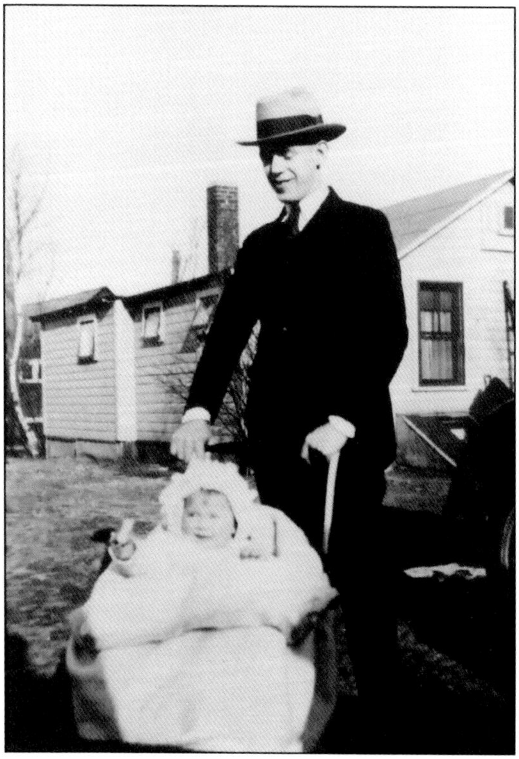

Ossian Anderson, in his Sunday best, takes great pride in pushing his daughter Elsie in her carriage at Warwick Downs in 1925. (Elsie Anderson Drew Collection.)

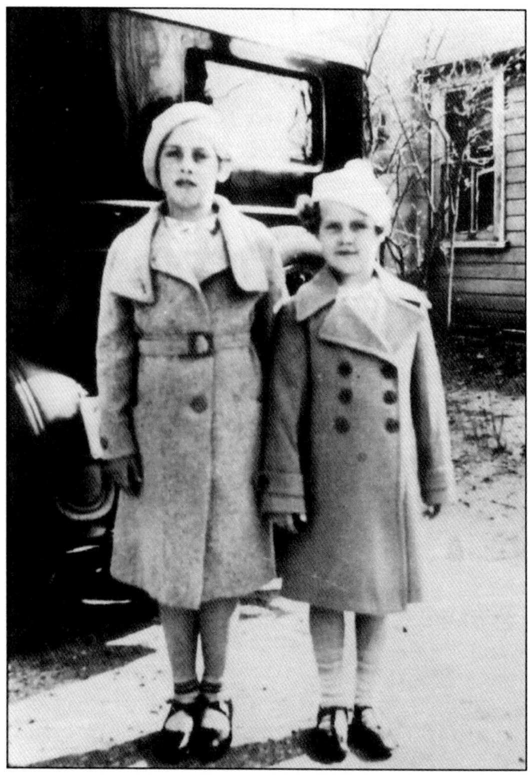

Today, Elsie and Doris Anderson have a clear memory of helping to polish their father's car c. 1932. Ossian, their father, owned a 1928 Buick, which was the family's pride in that era when automobiles were still a luxury. (Elsie Anderson Drew Collection.)

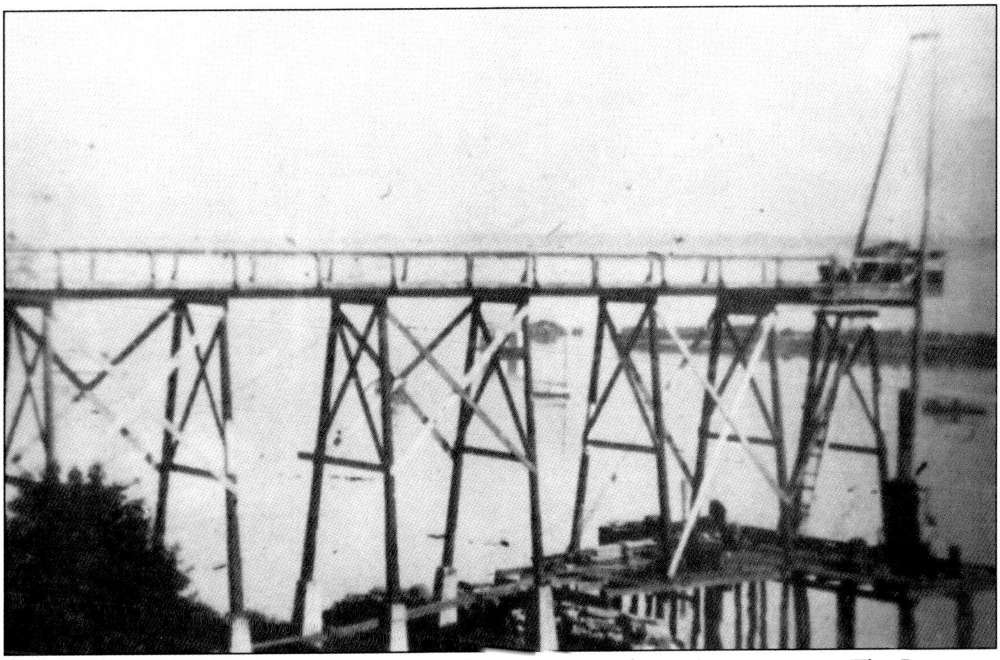

At the turn of the century, coal was the fuel most commonly used in Pawtuxet. The Pawtuxet Coal Dock at the George Upper & Son yard at the foot of Canonchet Avenue in Pawtuxet was a busy depot in 1901. (Malcolm Hinchcliff Collection.)

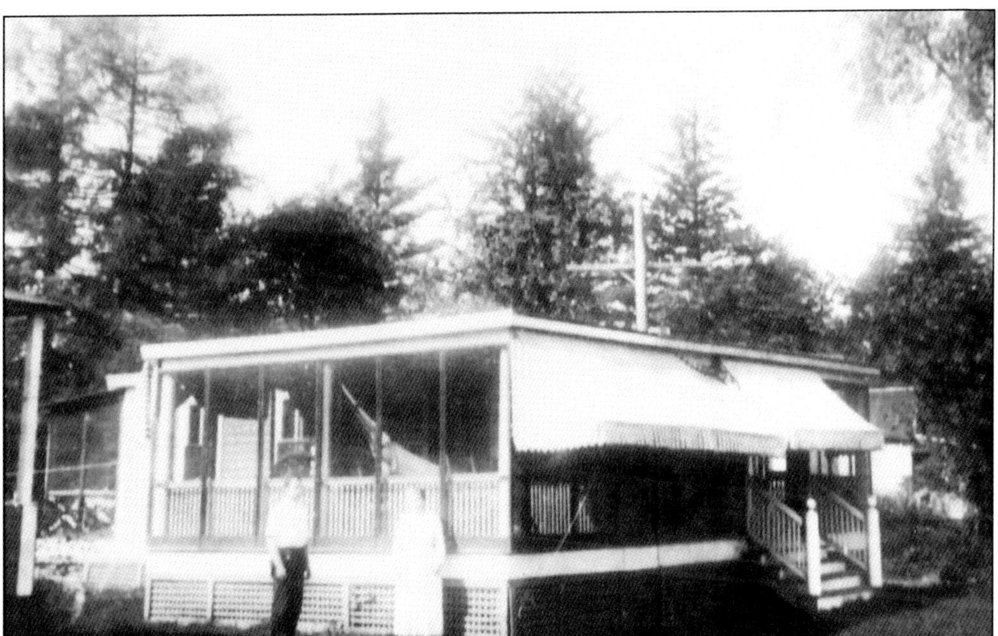

Spending the summer at a cottage at any of the beach resorts around Pawtuxet was a getaway much anticipated throughout the winter months. This Warwick Downs cottage belonged to George and Myrtle Potter *c.* 1916. (Ralph Potter Collection.)

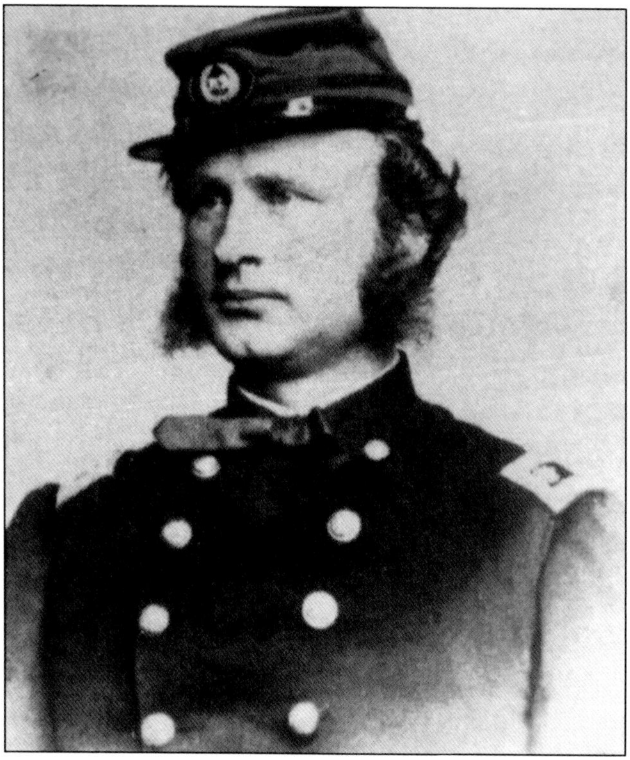

Pawtuxet men acquitted themselves well during the Civil War. One of the village's most upstanding citizens, Surgeon George W. Carr, served with distinction along with Elisha Hunt Rhodes. At one time, Carr owned the famous Pawtuxet landmark, the Bank Cafe. (Robert Hunt Rhodes Collection.)

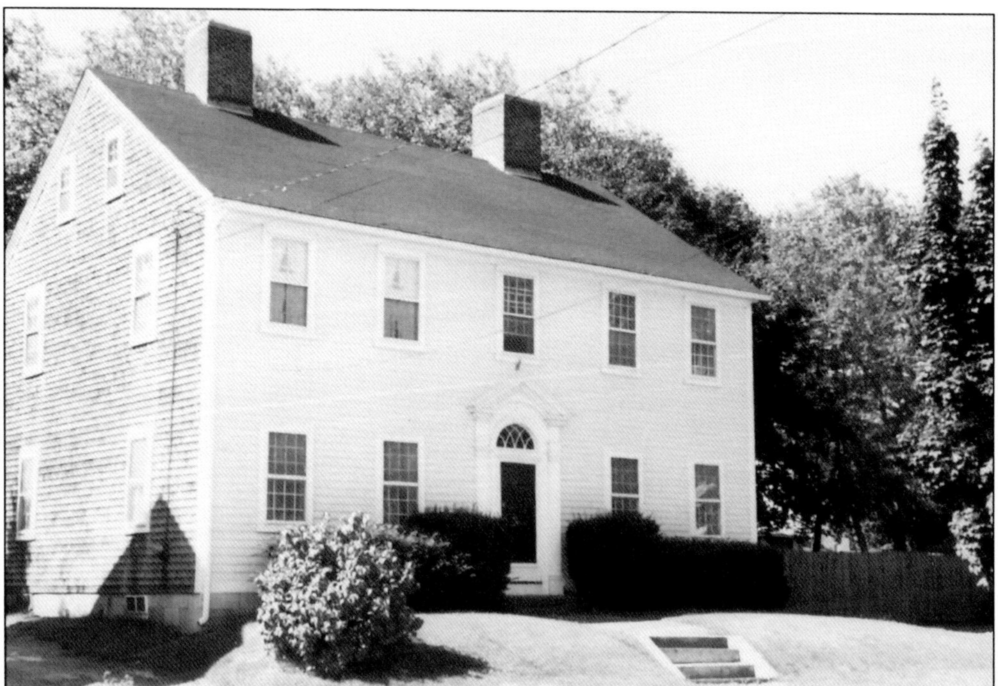

The Carder Tavern was built by Malachi Rhodes III c. 1740, and it has always been owned by family members. The late L. Hazard Knowles was proud of his home and the part it played in Pawtuxet's history. (Don D'Amato Collection.)

Seven

Cranston Village Views

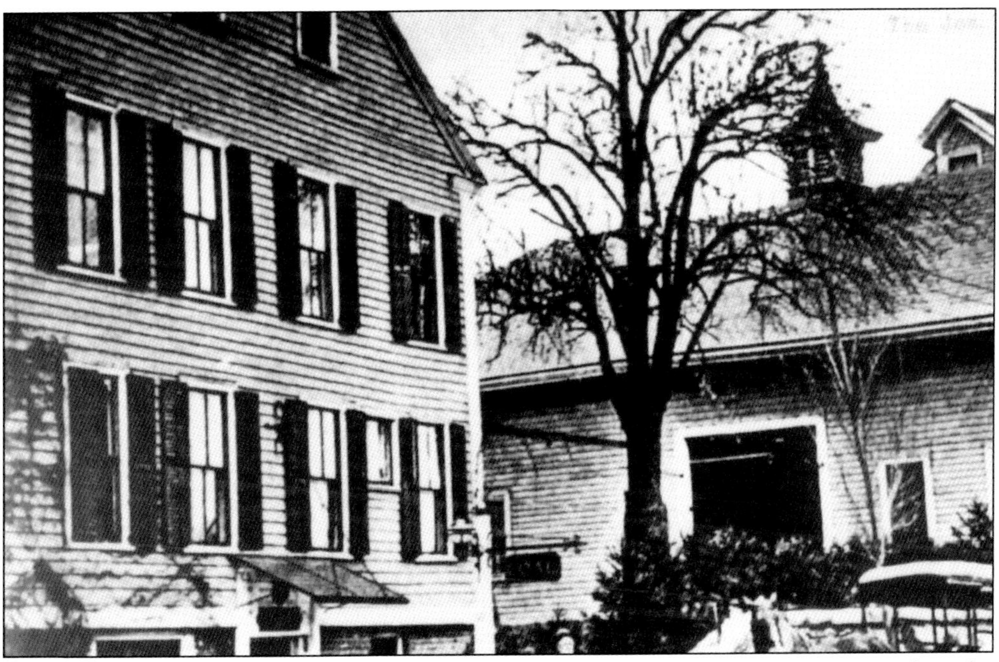

At the end of the first decade of the twentieth century, much of the area surrounding the Pawtuxet Bridge was still agrarian, and the Joseph B. Hayward Grain Co. did a thriving business. The building was on Broad Street, north of the Watson Pharmacy. Hayward stored bags of coal for the convenience of Pawtuxet residents in the days before oil, gas, and electric heat. (Cranston Historical Society Collection.)

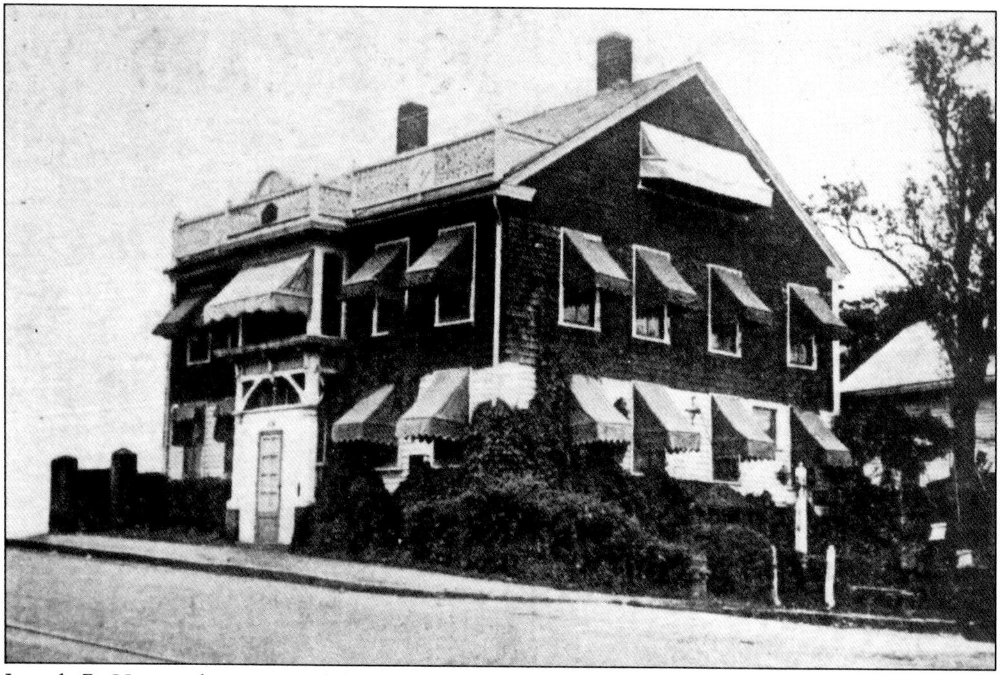

Joseph B. Hayward was one of the village's leading citizens. He operated a grain store in the village and lived in this beautiful residence on Broad Street. Murray S. Upham purchased the property in 1924 and created a commercial block on the site. The Hayward house was demolished *c*. 1930, and the new buildings were erected to house several Upham family enterprises, including Upham's Pawtuxet Paint and Hardware and Henry F. Upham, Real Estate. (Henry A.L. Brown Collection.)

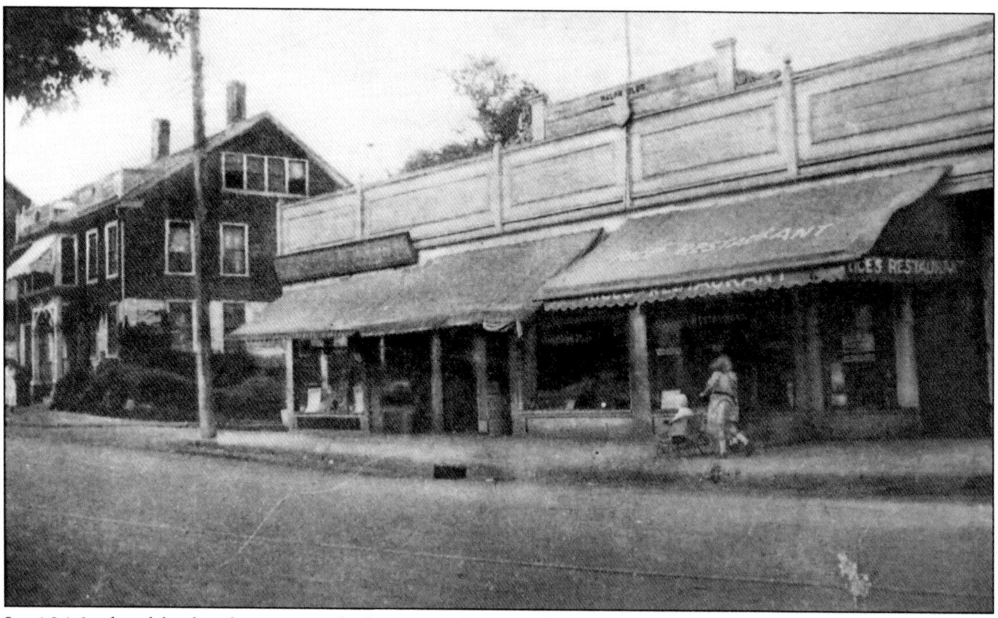

In 1916, this block of stores included a market on the corner of Bridge Street and also Rice's (later Seven Seas) Restaurant. At one time it was known as the Ralph Block. (Henry A.L. Brown Collection.)

Andrew Lindsay, the owner of Lindsay's Market, was a Highlander soldier in World War I. He is shown here in his dress uniform c. 1919. In 1932, Lindsay settled in Pawtuxet and opened his market in the Odd Fellows Hall at 2178–84 Broad Street. He is fondly remembered as being exceptionally kind during the Depression, when he helped many people through the difficult years. The market is now run by his two sons, Bill and Jack. (Bill and Jack Lindsay Collection.)

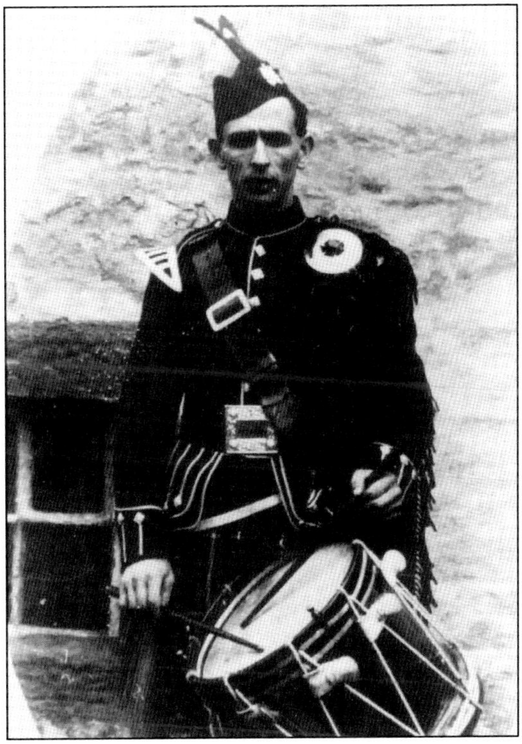

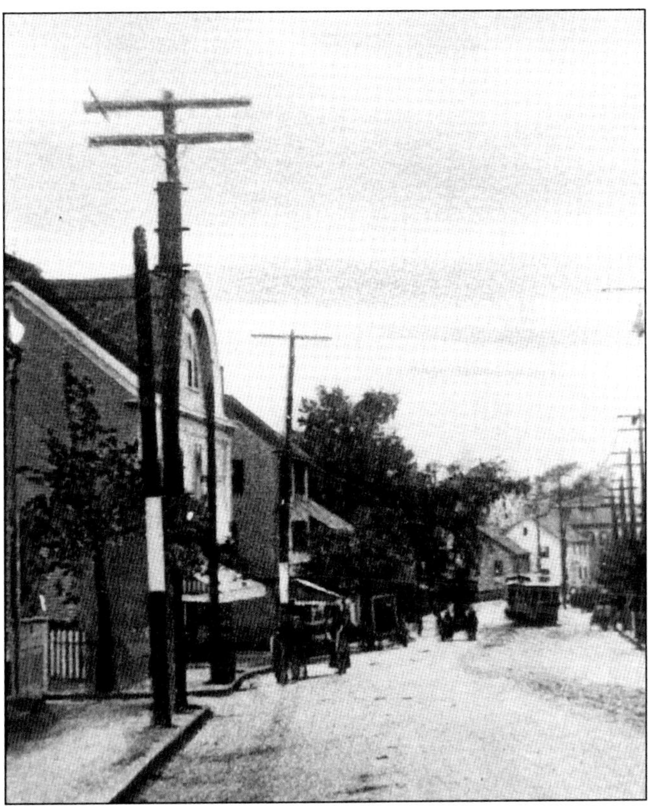

Broad Street in 1910 was a far cry from the busy thoroughfare of the 1990s. Here the Odd Fellows Hall, which was later purchased by Thomas Lindsay for a market, and the Hayward house seem serene and quiet. (Henry A.L. Brown Collection.)

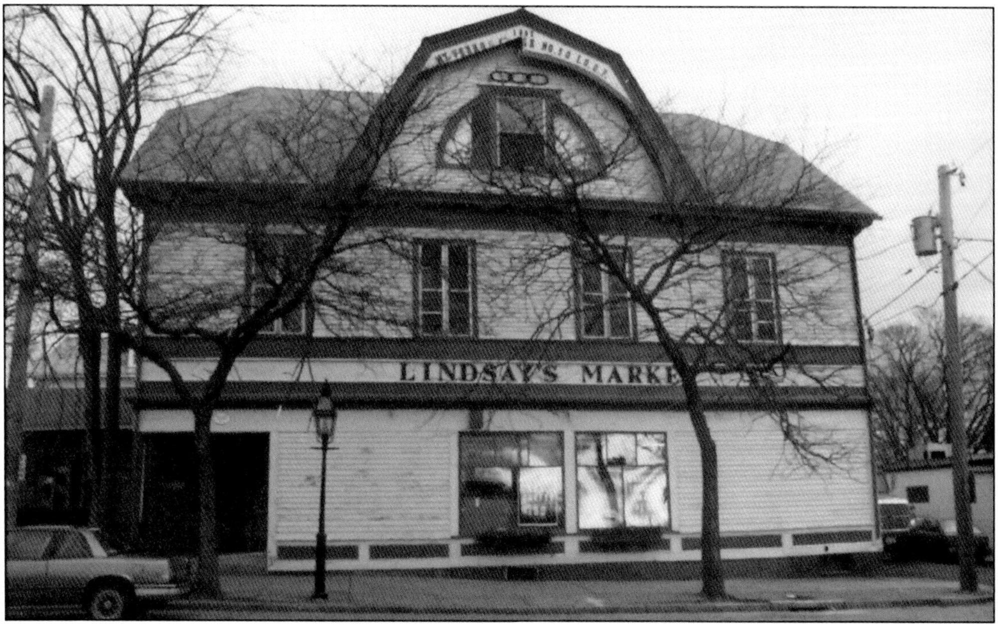

Lindsay's Market was the Odd Fellows Hall, Vernon Lodge #50 in 1893. Today, it is one of Pawtuxet's most cherished old buildings and a place where neighbors often meet to share the news of the day. (Don D'Amato Collection.).

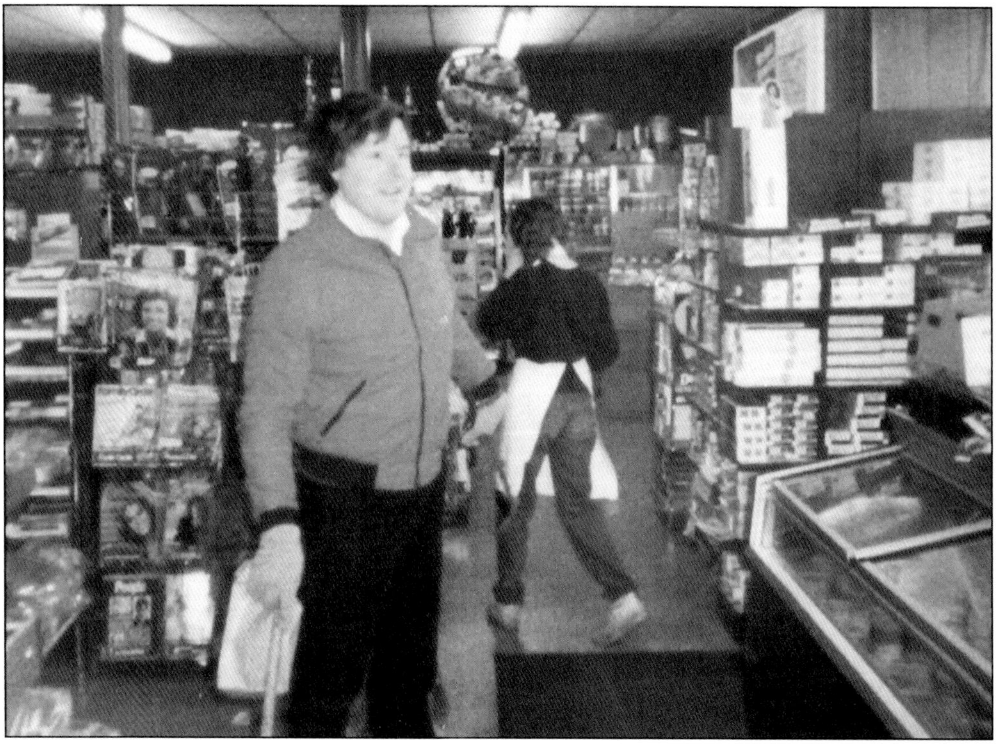

Walter Brokaw was well known in the village as a person who did a lot with the kids of the area. He was especially active in the YMCA and with handicapped persons and was a frequent visitor to Lindsay's Market. This photograph was taken *c.* 1990. (Henry A.L. Brown Collection.)

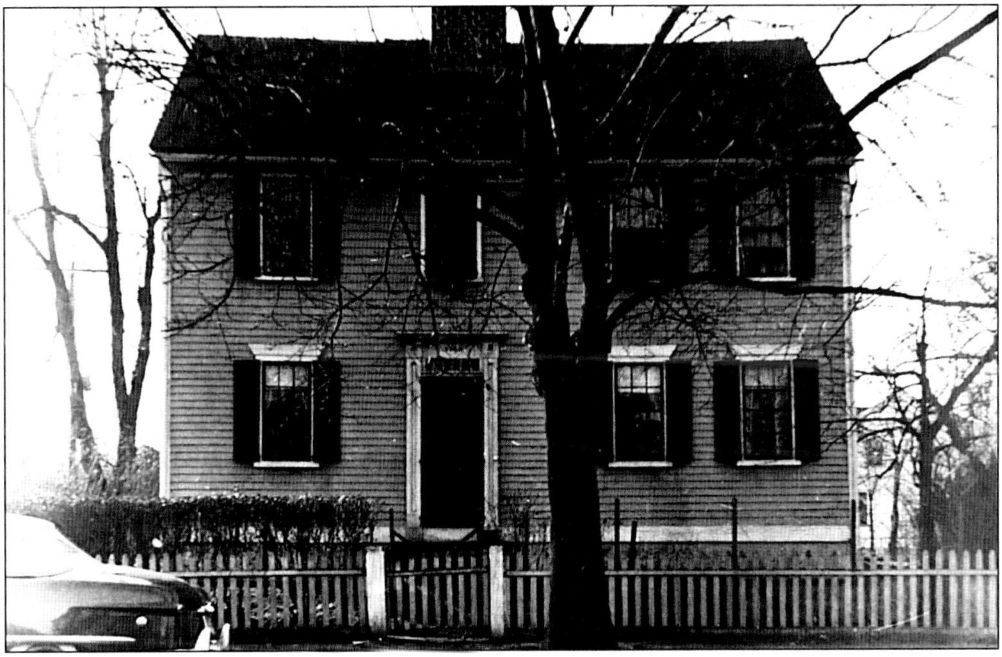

The Dr. Comfort A. Carpenter house (built *c.* 1760) was the home of Eliza D. Gardiner in 1952, when this picture was taken. Carpenter was the village doctor in 1790 and resided here at 2139 Broad Street until his death in 1830. This residence is often regarded as the northern limit of Pawtuxet Village. (Cranston Historical Society Collection.)

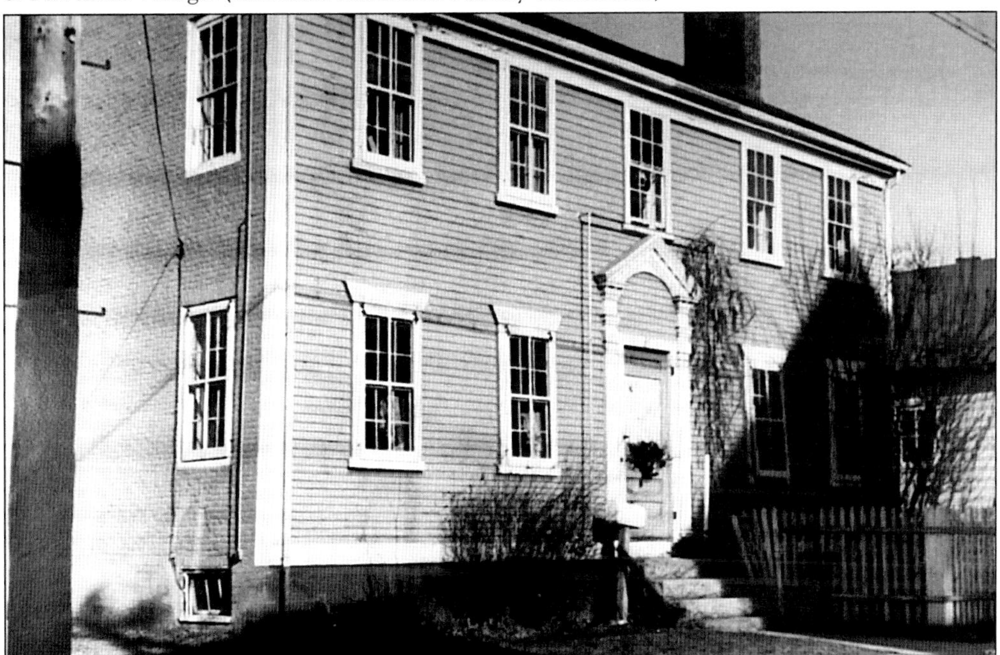

George L. Tucker was a dentist when Broad Street was widened in 1896. At that time his house was moved to 27 Tucker Avenue, where this picture was taken in 1951 by Betty Budlong Briggs. (Cranston Historical Society Collection.)

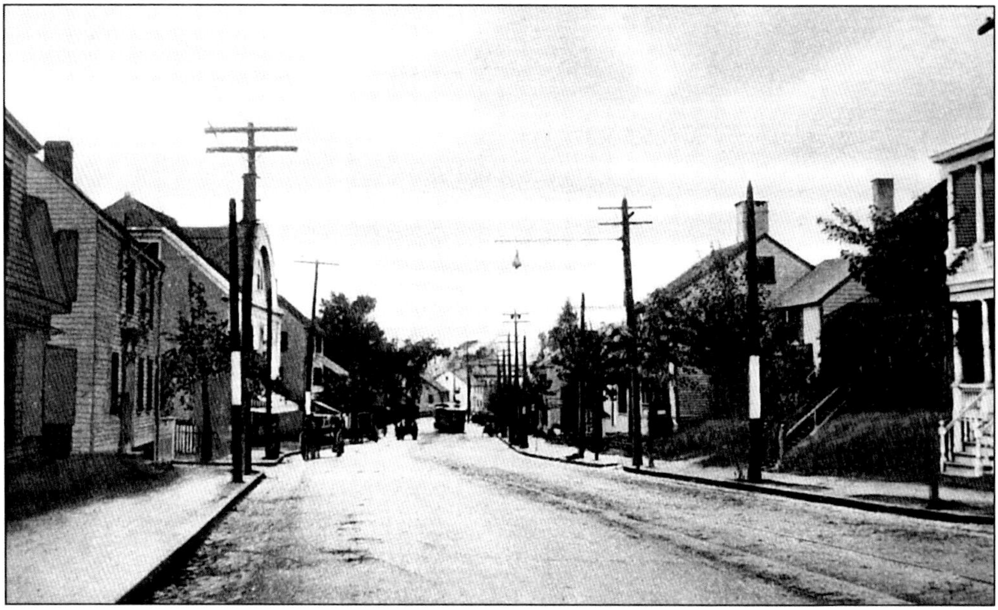

In 1905, Broad Street in Pawtuxet (sans streetlights) looked more like a country lane than the modern, busy thoroughfare it is today. The Elisha H. Rhodes house is where the Sunoco Gas Station is now. The present-day Lindsay's Market was still the Odd Fellow's Hall, and the Charles Gorton saloon was doing a thriving business at the Warwick end of the bridge. (Henry A.L. Brown Collection.)

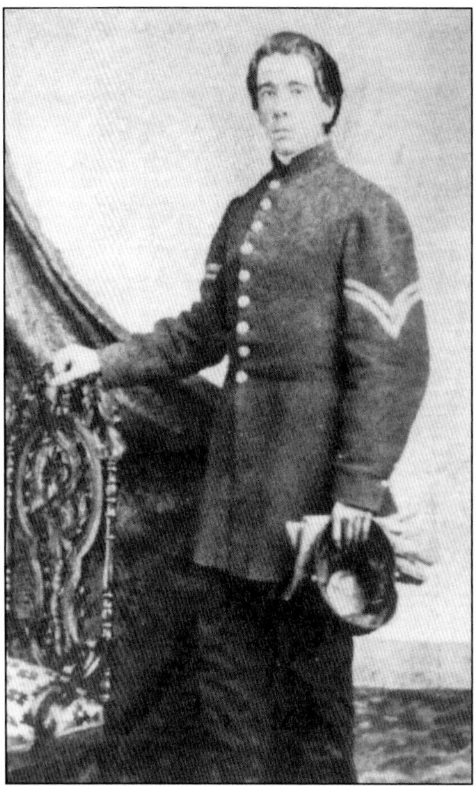

Elisha Hunt Rhodes, an intelligent and articulate soldier during the Civil War, kept a diary that Ken Burns turned into a prize-winning TV show. At age nineteen, shortly after joining the army in 1861, Rhodes was promoted to 8th corporal of Company D. (Robert Hunt Rhodes Collection.)

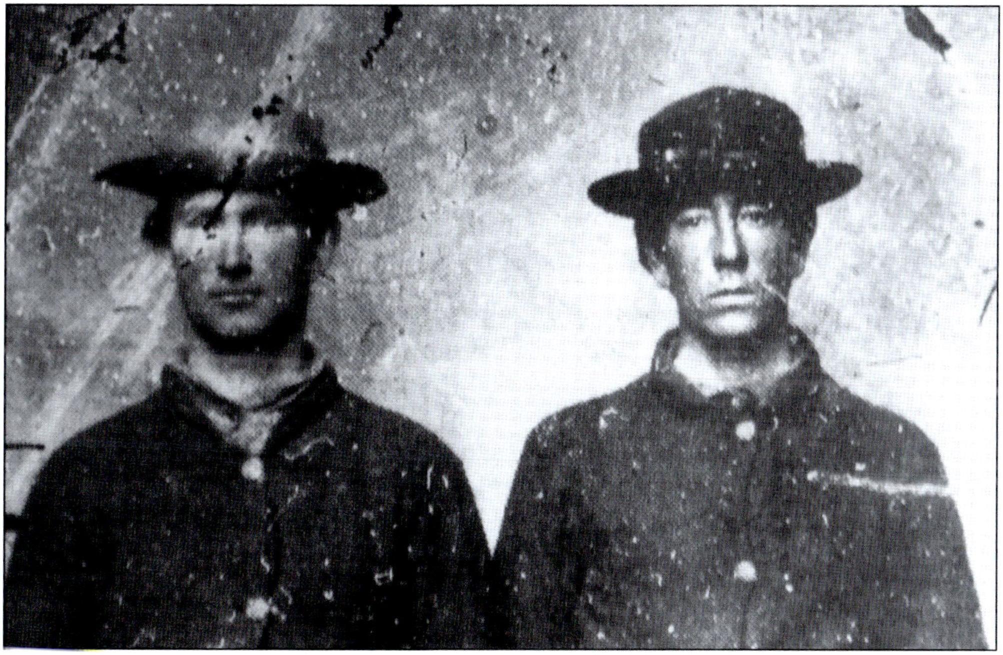

By age twenty, Elisha Hunt Rhodes (right) had reached the rank of sergeant major. He is shown here in 1863 with his friend, Levi Carr, also of Pawtuxet. (Robert Hunt Rhodes Collection.)

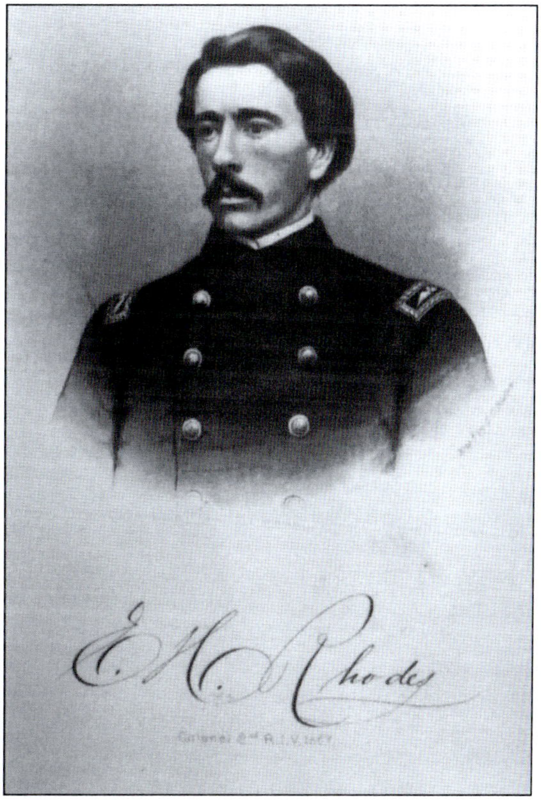

Colonel Elisha Hunt Rhodes was one of Rhode Island's most celebrated Civil War heroes. He joined Company D, Rhode Island 2nd Regiment as a private in 1861 and left the army in 1865 with the rank of colonel. (Robert Hunt Rhodes Collection.)

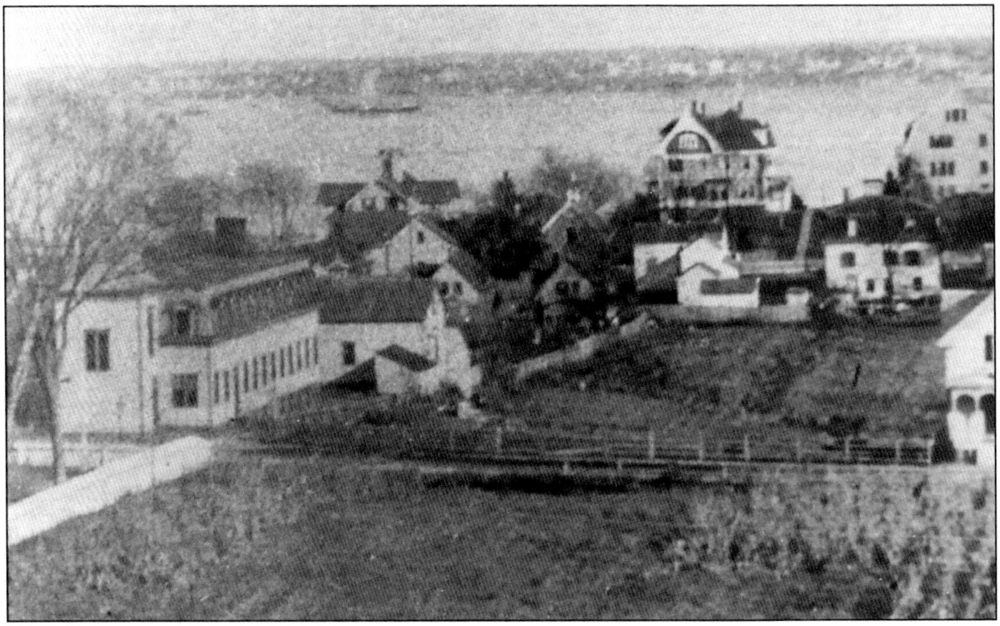

Included in this 1889 photograph of Pawtuxet Cove taken from the roof of the Baptist church is the "new" Bloomer factory (on the left). Bloomer's early factory was destroyed by fire in 1888. In 1889, the old Commercial Street School was still there on its original site. The summer cottages on Pawtuxet Neck in background are those north of the Revolutionary War fort. (William Hall Library Collection)

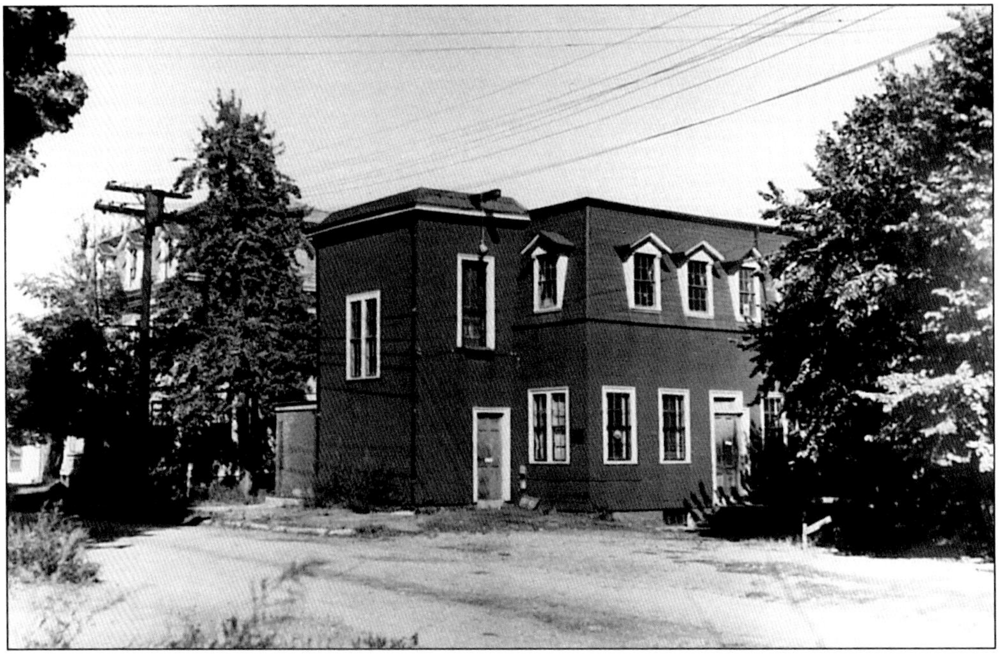

The burning of the original Bloomer's factory in 1888 prompted the organization of the Pawtuxet Volunteer Fire Company #1. Charles G. Bloomer owned and operated C.G. Bloomer and Sons, Aluminum Novelty Works. He employed fifty people, as did the factory on the second floor. Bloomer's factory is shown here *c.* 1950. (William Hall Library Collection.)

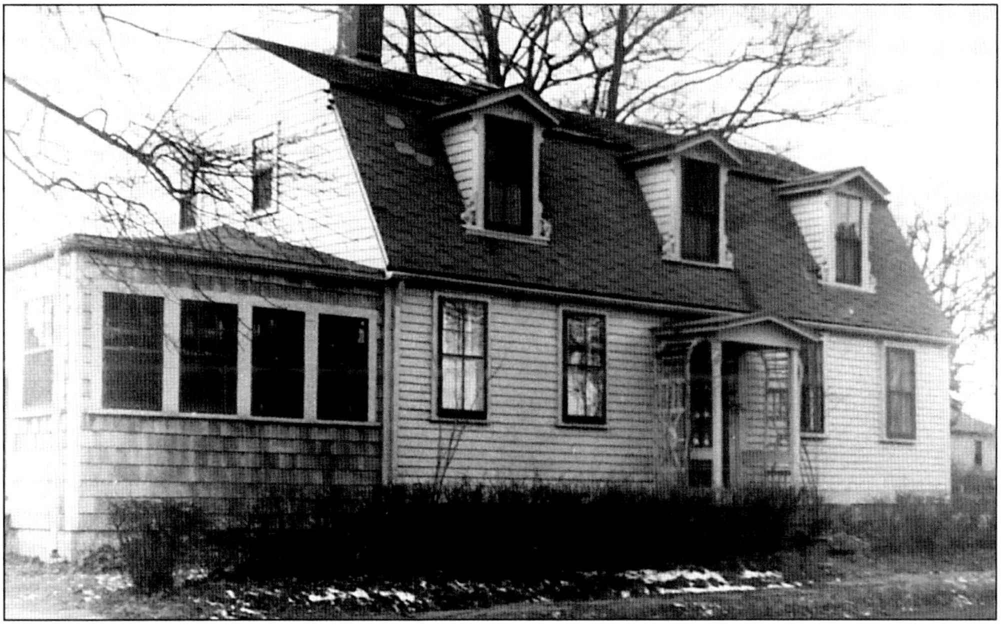

Rufus Greene, a prominent Providence banker, was one of those who saw the possibility of Pawtuxet Neck as a summer colony. He built this enchanting house at 12 Seaview Avenue at the corner of Fort Avenue in 1863. The house remained in the Greene family until 1911. The house was remodeled in the twentieth century and had this appearance in 1936. (Cranston Historical Society Collection.)

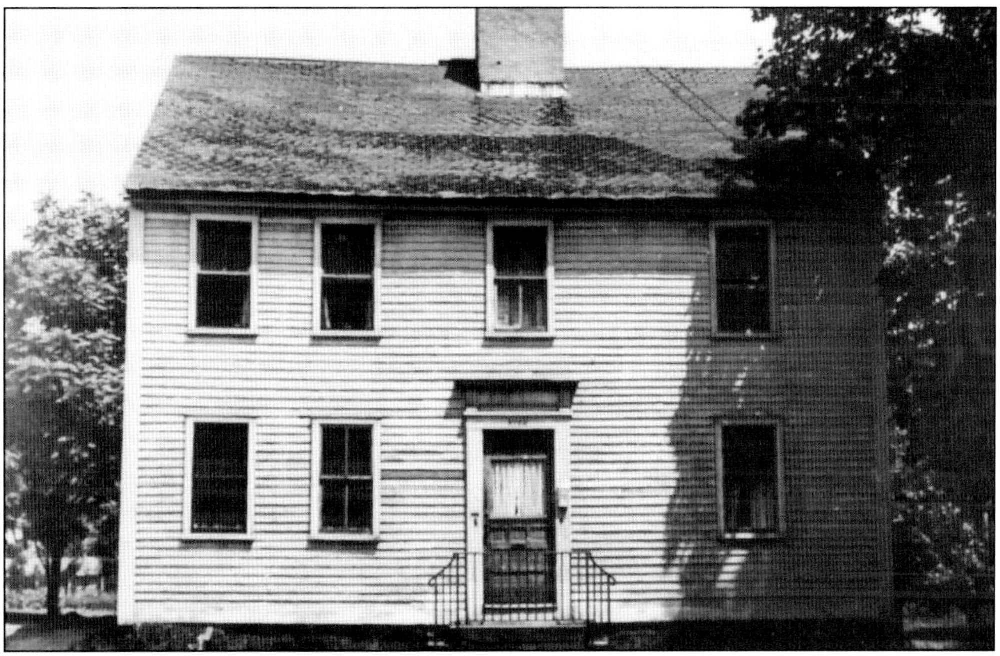

The Elisha Smith house at 2154 Broad Street was built in 1740 and is the oldest surviving building on that street. This photograph was taken in 1935, about twenty-three years before the renovations were done for the Edgewood Credit Union. In recent times, the structure housed a store dealing in antiques. (Cranston Historical Society Collection.)

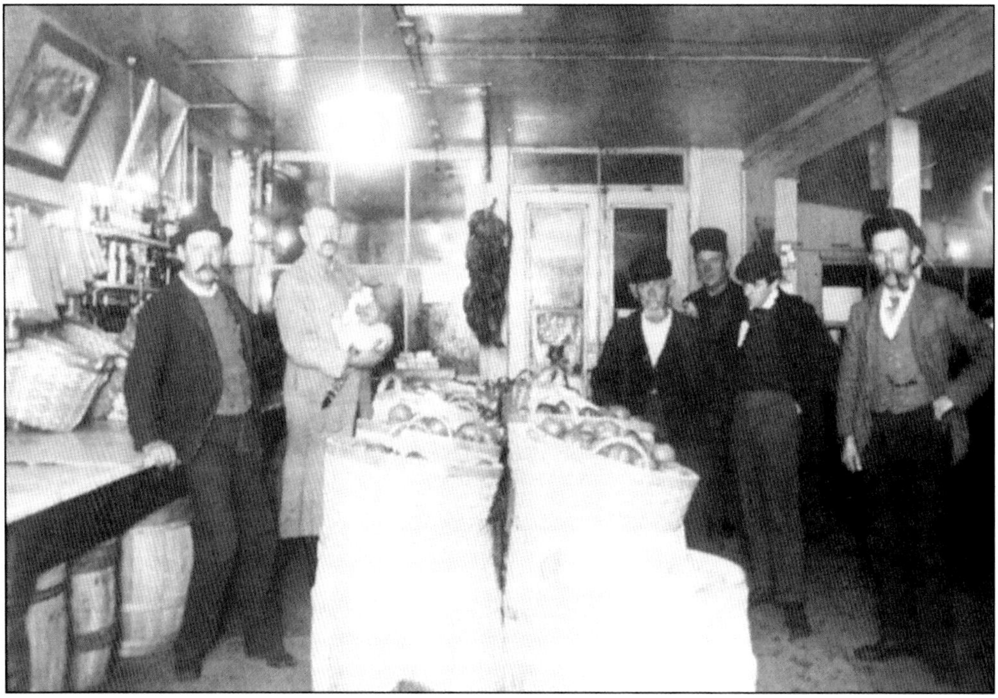

Ben Wilbour's store, the Pawtuxet Public Market, was a great place to browse and visit in 1898 because sooner or later, everyone in the village would come by and share the latest news (gossip?). (Don Cameron Collection.)

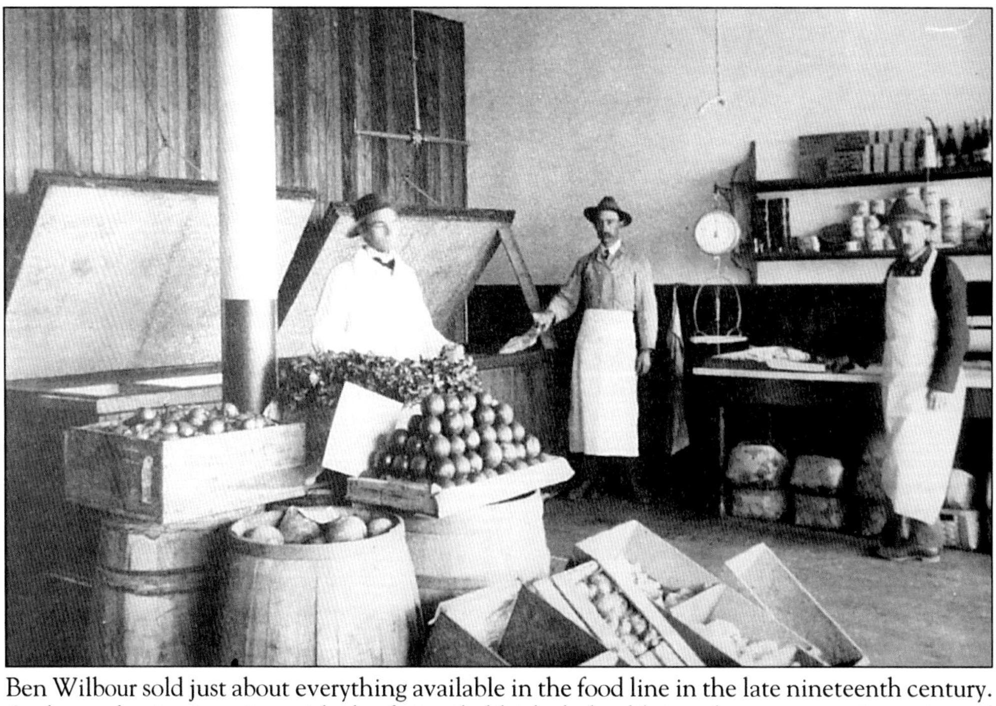

Ben Wilbour sold just about everything available in the food line in the late nineteenth century. A clean, pleasing interior, with the fruit piled high, helped bring the customers in again and again at this Broad Street emporium. (Don Cameron Collection.)

One of the most popular shops in Pawtuxet at the turn of the century was the old barbershop located on the second floor over Ben Wilbour's store. (Don Cameron Collection.)

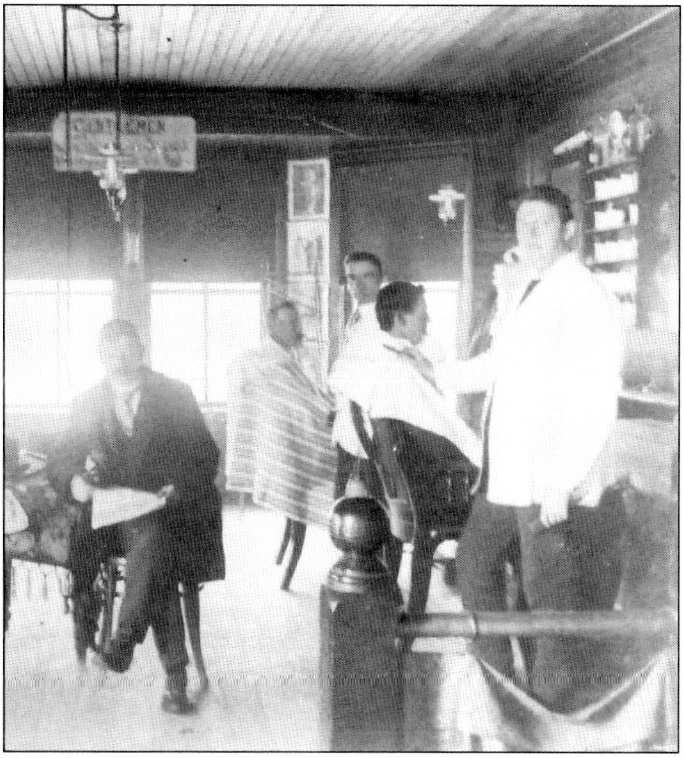

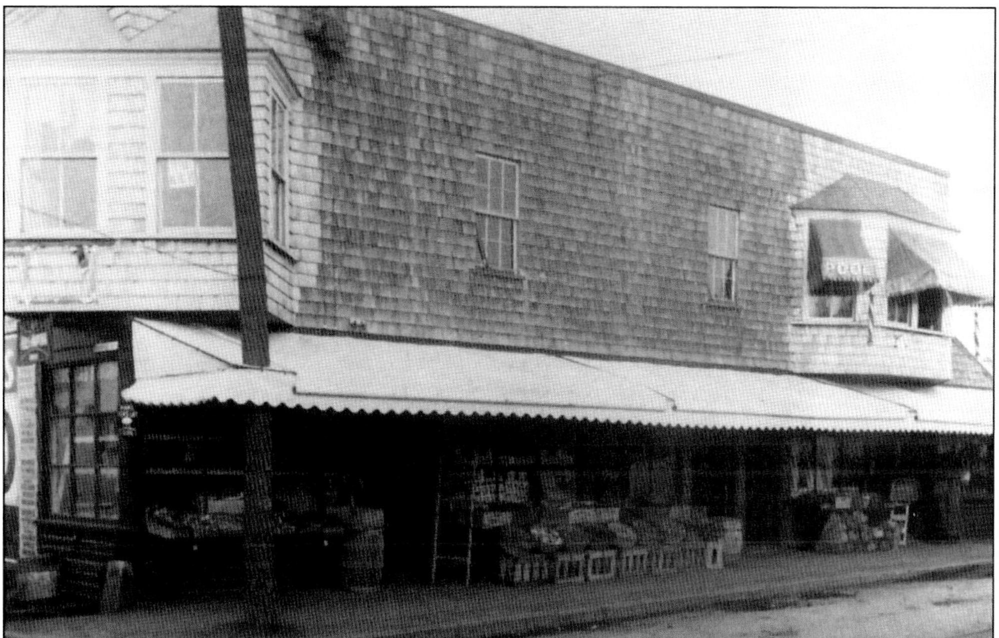

The Pawtuxet Public Market, built in 1875, was on the corner of Broad and Bridge Streets. The section of the building closest to Bridge Street was used as a fish market. Note the poolroom on the second floor above the market. (Cranston Historical Society Collection.)

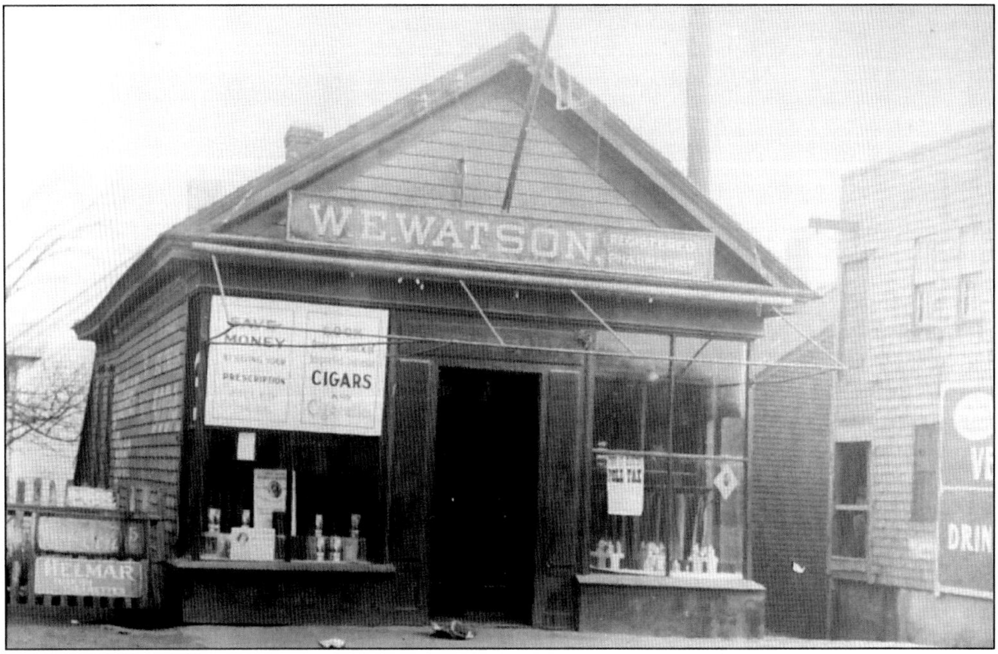

In 1890, Walter E. Watson, the village's first druggist, opened his pharmacy (shown here c. 1895). After many years, the business changed hands, became known as the Pawtuxet Pharmacy, and was purchased by the Cameron family. Today, Cameron's Pharmacy has expanded and is one of the village landmarks. (Henry A.L. Brown Collection.)

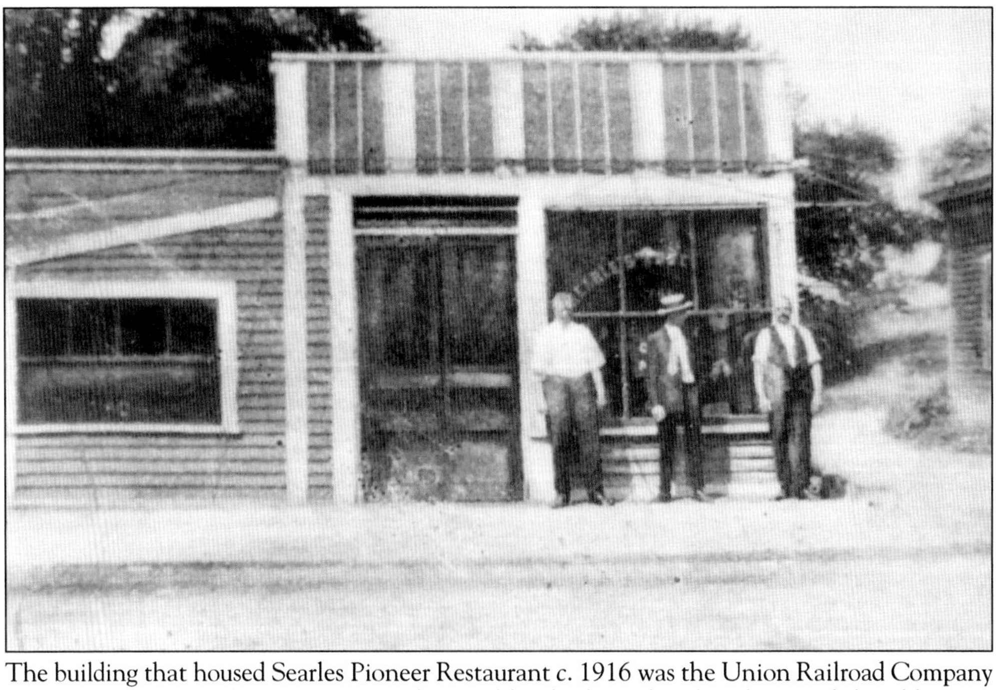

The building that housed Searles Pioneer Restaurant *c.* 1916 was the Union Railroad Company Horse Car Depot in the 1870s. It was damaged by the large fire that destroyed the old Pierce Stafford Mill in 1875. (Henry A.L. Brown Collection.)

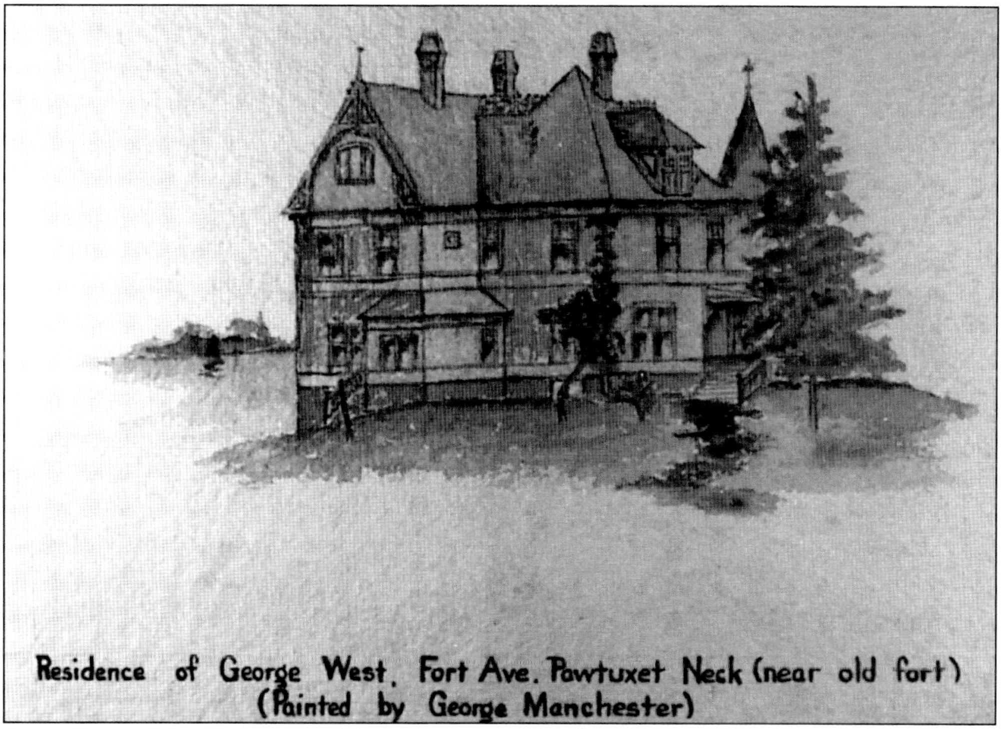

Artist George Manchester's rendering captures much of the elegance of the George West house at 22 Fort Avenue. West built the house c. 1890. It was later owned by Cranston councilman Arthur Ernest Austin. (William Hall Library Collection.)

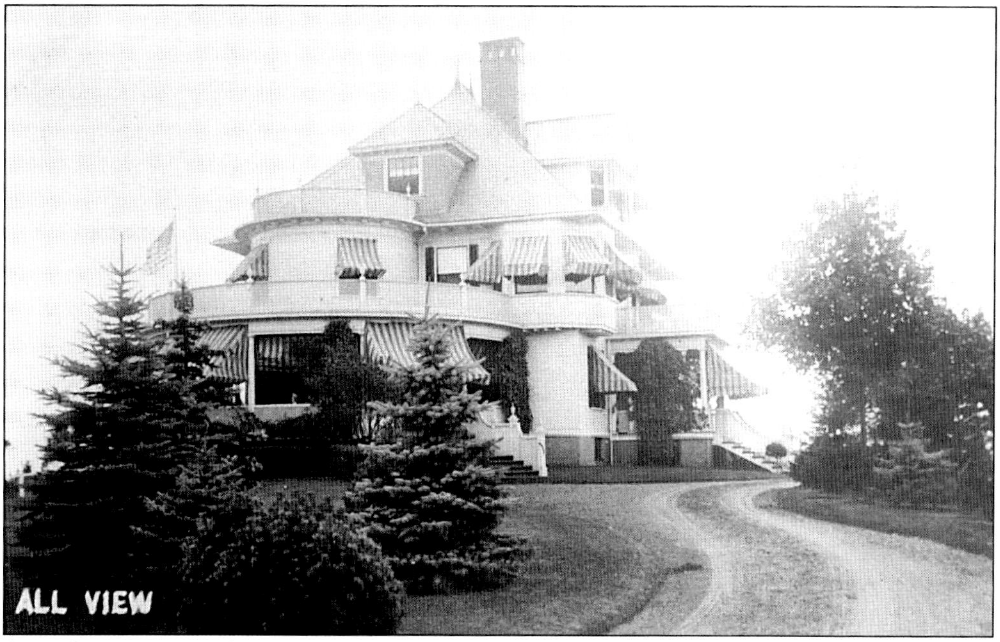

One of Pawtuxet Neck's most imposing homes, the Charles S. Horton residence, is shown here shortly after its renovation in 1909. During the early twentieth century, it was owned by Samuel R. Baker, a well-known local mariner. (William Hall Library Collection.)

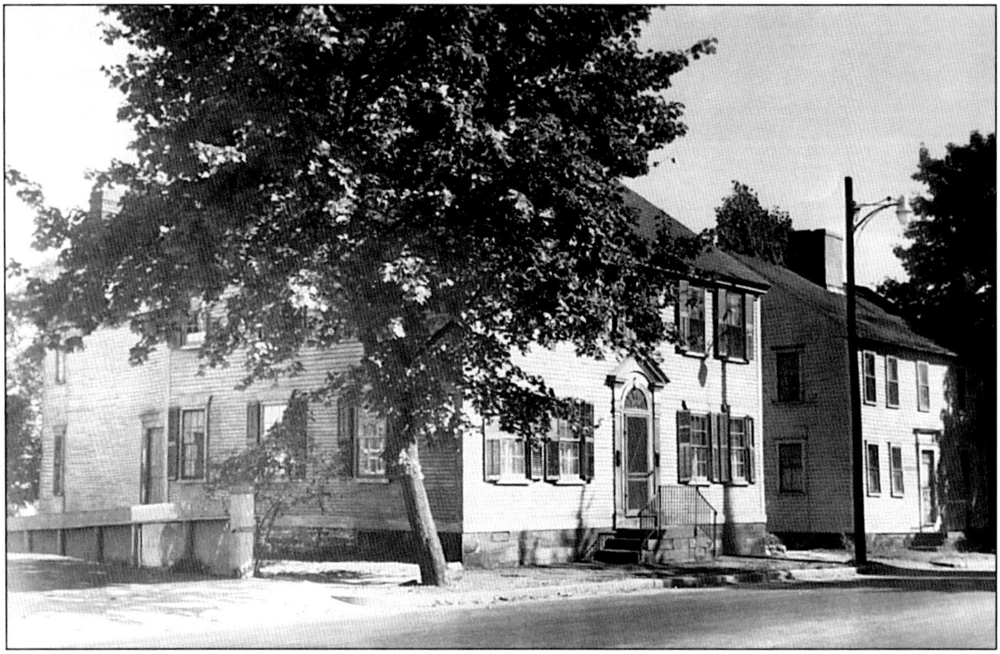

The section of Broad Street across from the Pawtuxet Baptist Church looked like this in 1940. The house on the right, the Elisha Smith house (built in 1740), is still there, but the beautiful home in the foreground has been demolished and now a Cumberland Farms store is on the site. (William Hall Library Collection.)

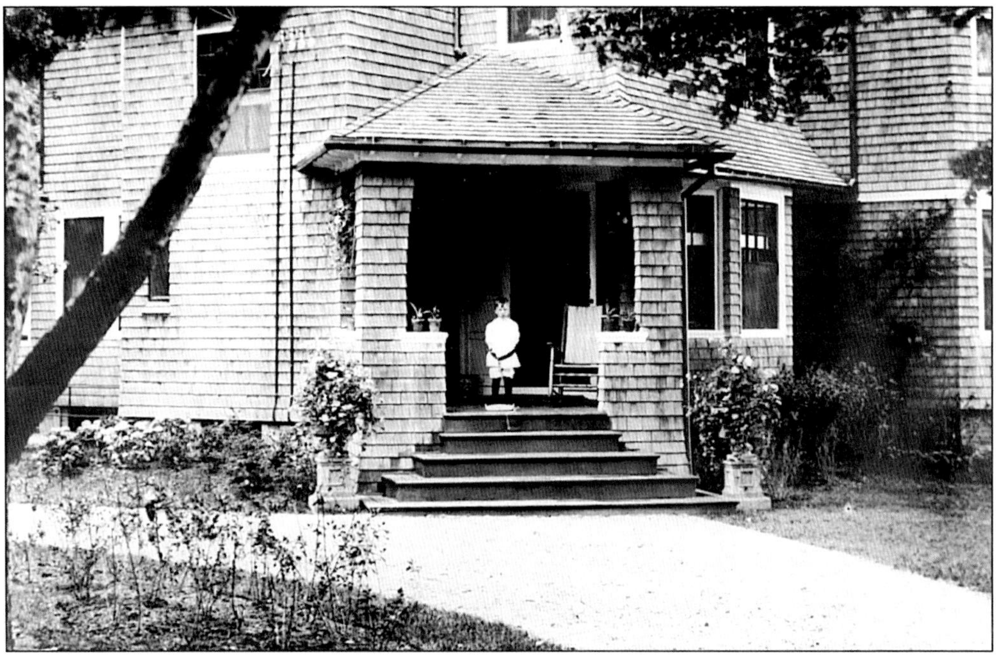

One of the Louttit children is seen here on the steps of the Louttit house at 18 Seaview Avenue. The large, two-and-a-half story dwelling was built *c.* 1867 and was one of the largest on the neck at the time. From 1909 to 1952, it was owned by the William E. Louttit family. (William Hall Library Collection.)

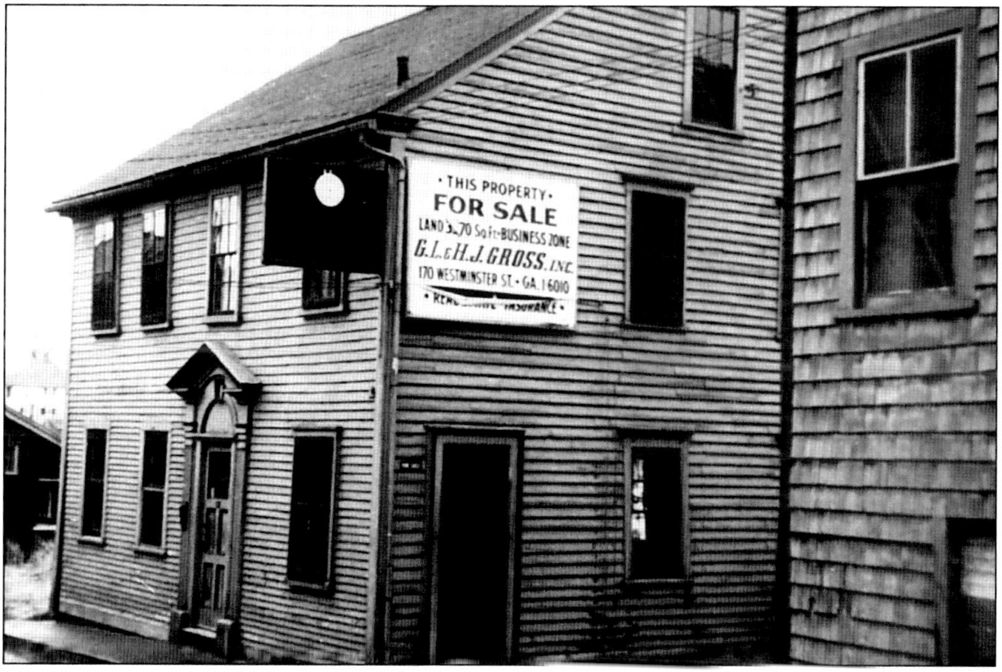

The Remington Arnold house at 12 Bridge Street has been restored and is one of Pawtuxet's most pleasant visual reminders of its rich heritage. Arnold, a successful early trader during the pre-Revolutionary period, built this handsome, two-and-a-half-story, four-bay dwelling *c.* 1740. The house remained in the Arnold family until the 1930s. After that, the ravages of time and neglect took their toll, and in 1958 the house was put up for sale by G.I. and H.J. Gross, Providence realtors. (Cranston Historical Society Collection.)

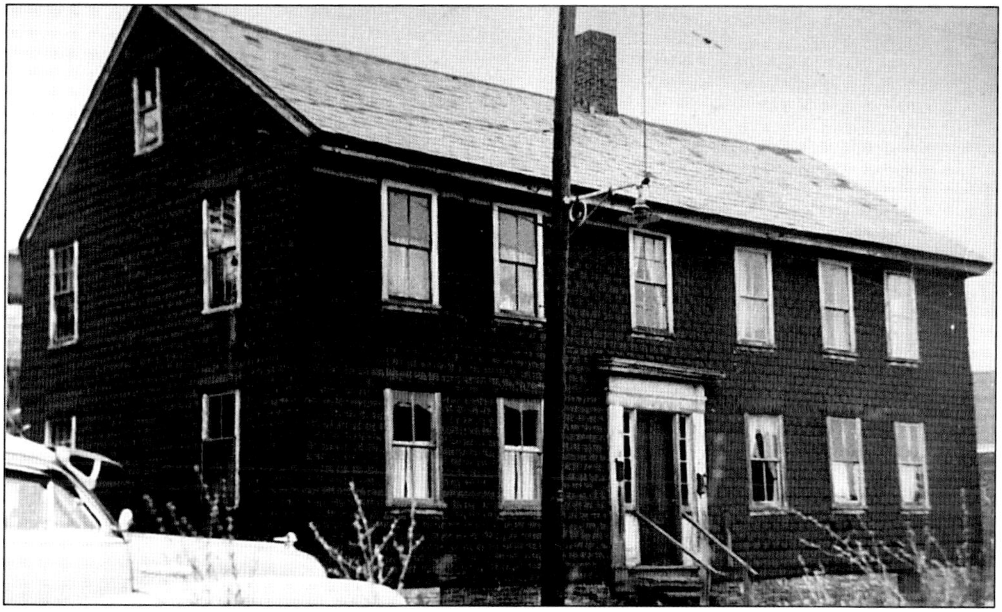

The Anthony Aborn Tavern, built *c.* 1789 between Bridge and Aborn Streets, was one of the village's most famous inns. It was altered considerably by the time of this photograph, *c.* 1952, shortly before it was demolished. (Cranston Historical Society Collection.)

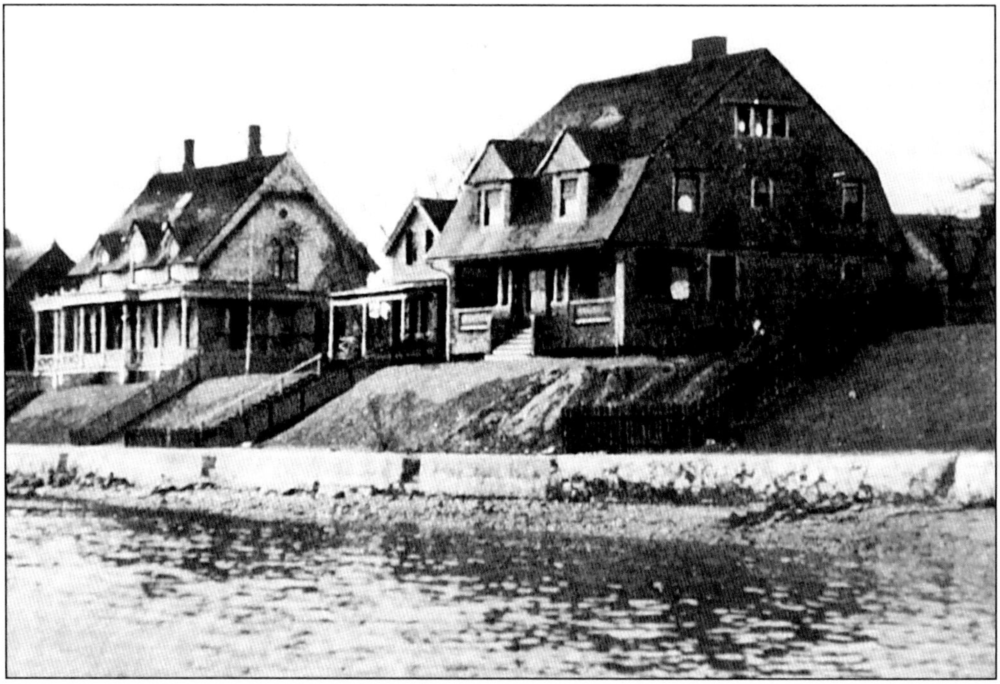

Exquisite Victorian cottages overlook the bay at Pawtuxet Neck in 1910. The houses are on Seaview Avenue. The one on the right was the home of William E. Louttit, the president and treasurer of Louttit Home Hand Laundry in Providence. (William Hall Library Collection.)

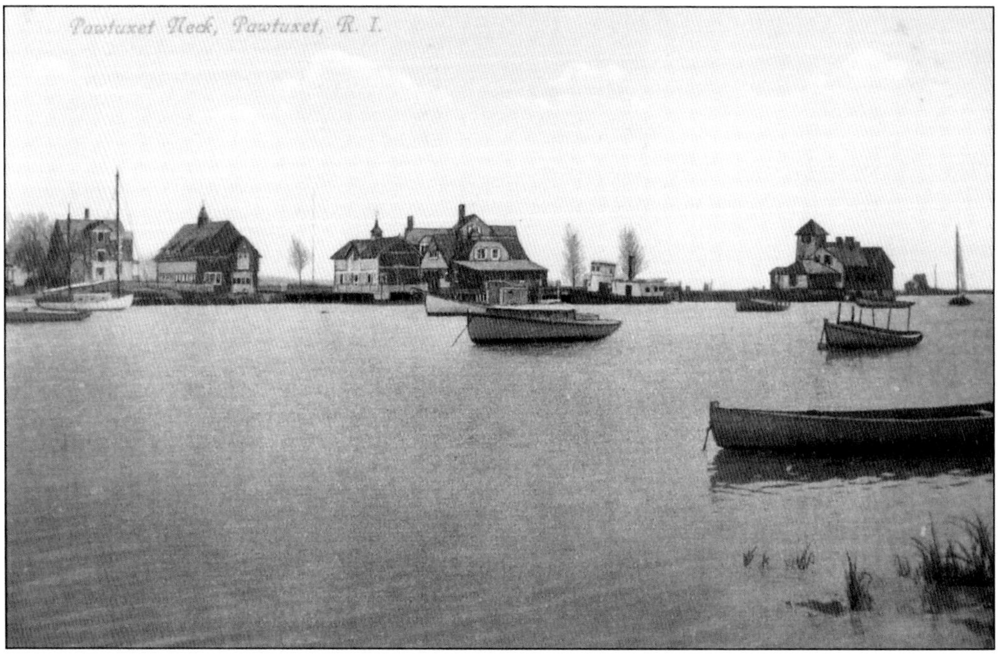

Robert Pettis was also famous for his other restaurant, the Oyster Room, in Providence in the late nineteenth century. In 1906, his oyster boats were in front of his attractive home on Pawtuxet Neck (visible in the center of the photograph), which has since been demolished. (Henry A.L. Brown Collection.)

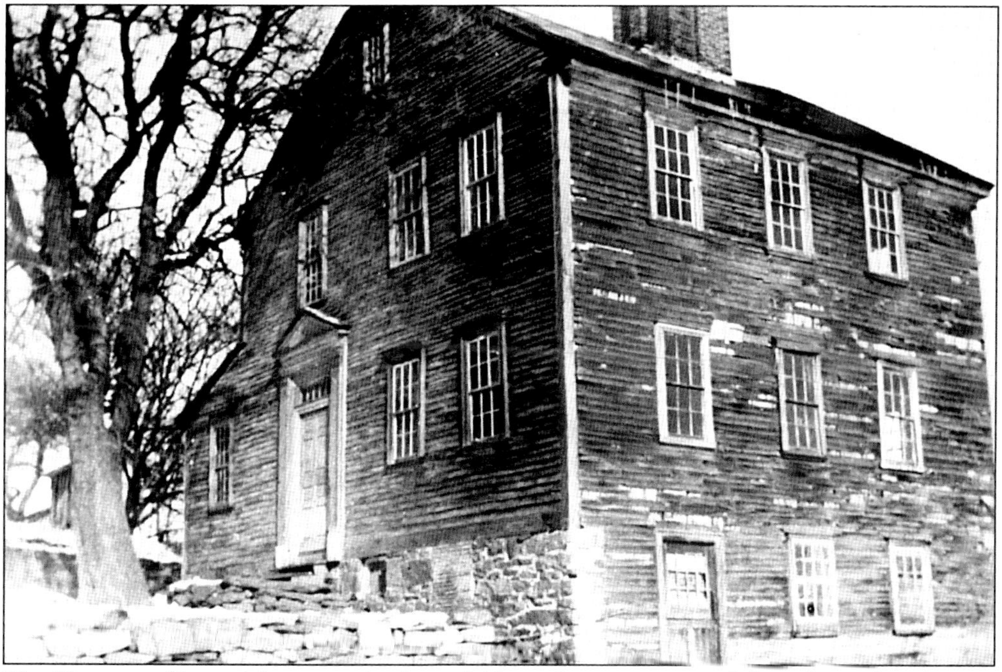

The Thornton (Battey) house at the foot of Aborn Street was one of the village's best-known old houses. Like some of the other old Pawtuxet houses on Aborn and Bridge Streets, the Battey house, in sad repair, was torn down to create the parking lot behind Cameron's Pharmacy. Elizabeth Betty Budlong Briggs had this photograph of the old house shortly before it was torn down. (Cranston Historical Society Collection.)

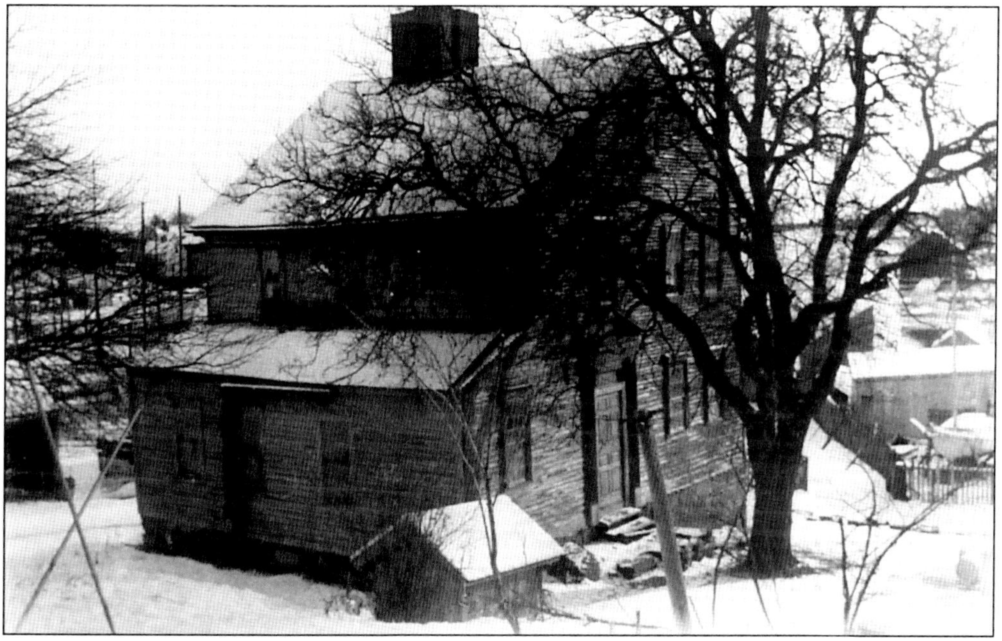

The Thornton (Battey) house appears here in 1925. In the early years (*c.* 1800), the house belonged to Solomon Thornton. During the nineteenth century, the home passed to the Battey family. (Cranston Historical Society Collection.)

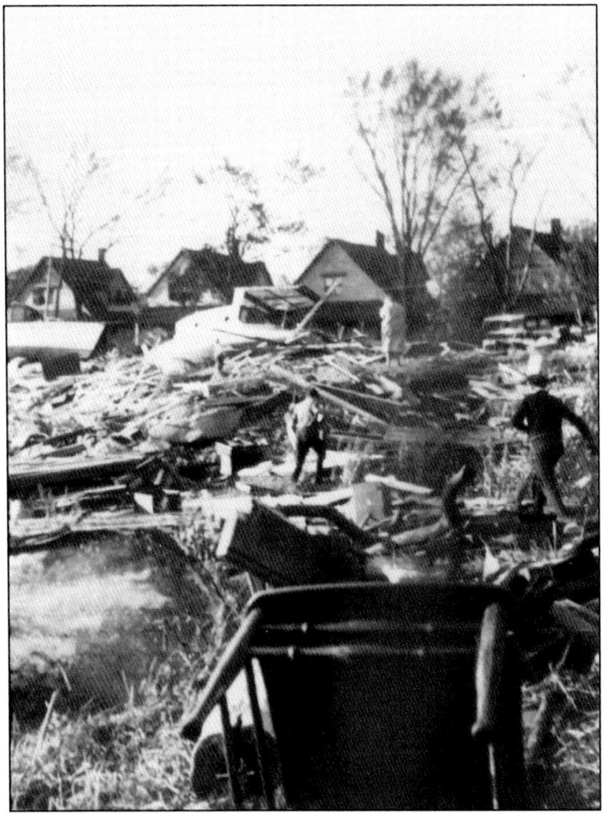

The Hurricane of 1938 inflicted heavy damage on Pawtuxet. The houses depicted here are the rental cottages built by Charles G. Bloomer *c.* 1887. Some of these were moved to Sheldon Street at the head of the cove from other locations in the 1920s. (Henry A.L. Brown Collection.)

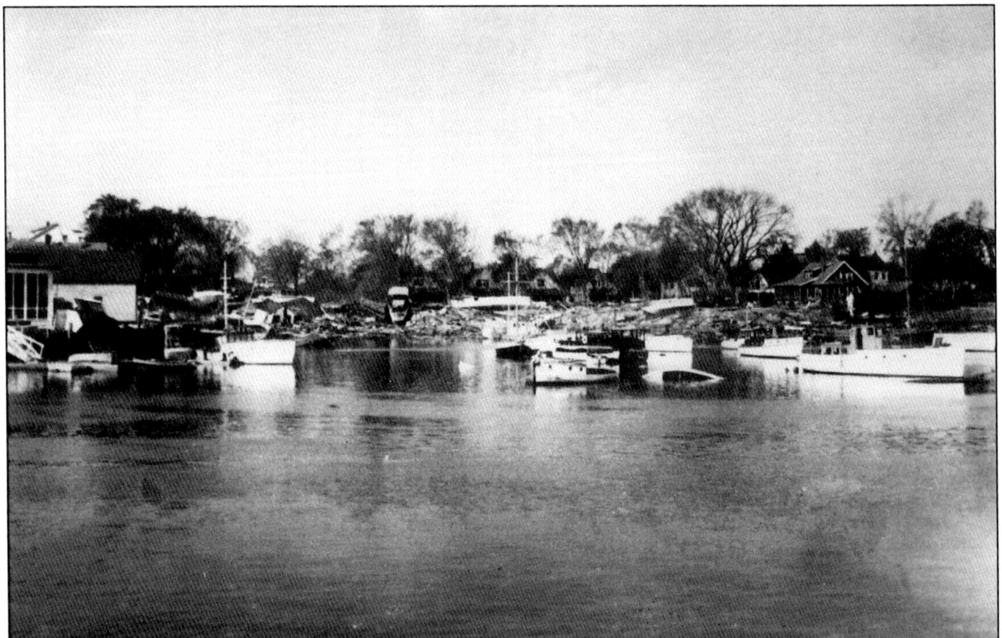

The Hurricane of 1938 wreaked a great deal of havoc along Pawtuxet Cove. Very few boats remained after the fury of the storm passed. (Henry A.L. Brown Collection.)

The Anthony Aborn Tavern and doorway are shown as they looked in 1916, probably before electricity was added to the building. The tavern, once located at the foot of Bridge Street, was erected c. 1740 and became a public tavern in 1798. During the nineteenth century, it was converted into a tenement. The building was demolished in 1954. (Cranston Historical Society Collection.)

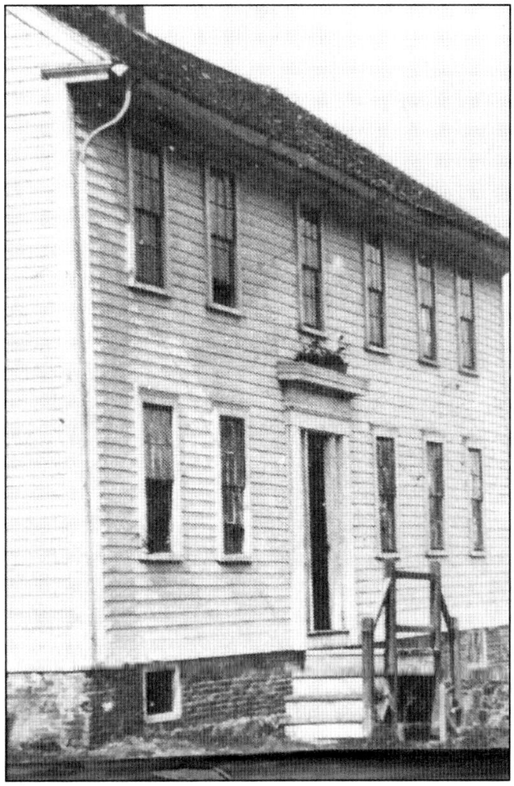

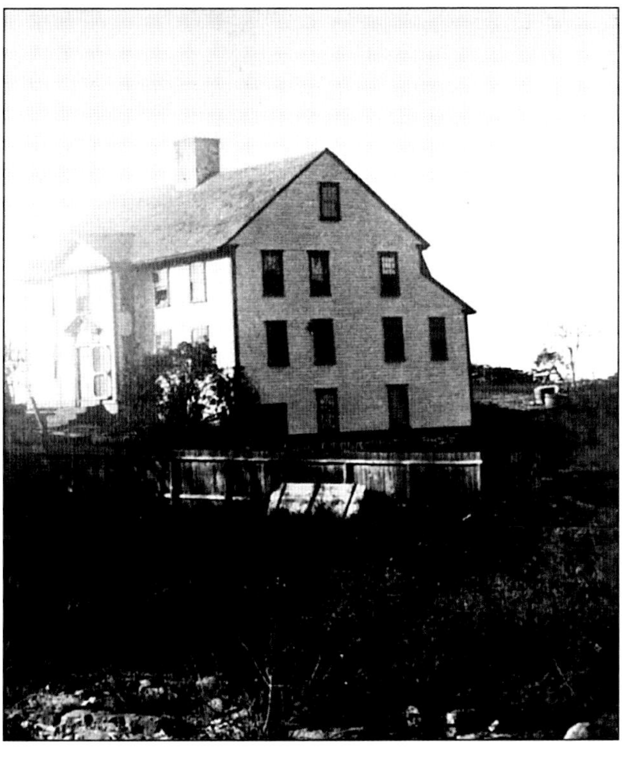

At one time the Providence Water Authority owned this old house along the river on the north bank in Cranston. In 1890, when this photograph was taken, Providence still depended heavily on the Pawtuxet River for water. (Cranston Historical Society Collection.)

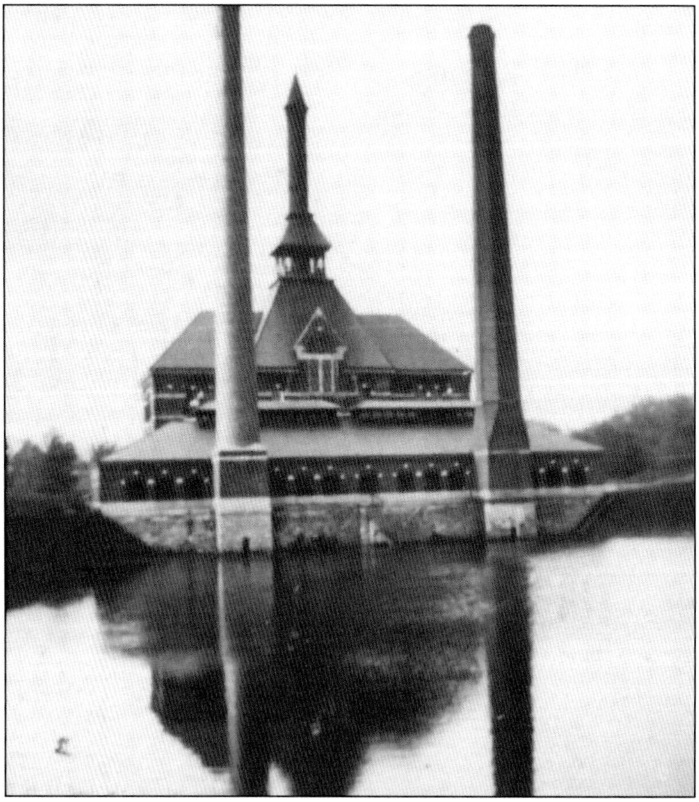

Before the building of the Scituate Reservoir (1915–1929), Providence depended very heavily on water pumped from the Pawtuxet River at the Ponagansett Pumping Station (shown here in 1892), which was located just outside Pawtuxet Village. (Henry A.L. Brown Collection.)

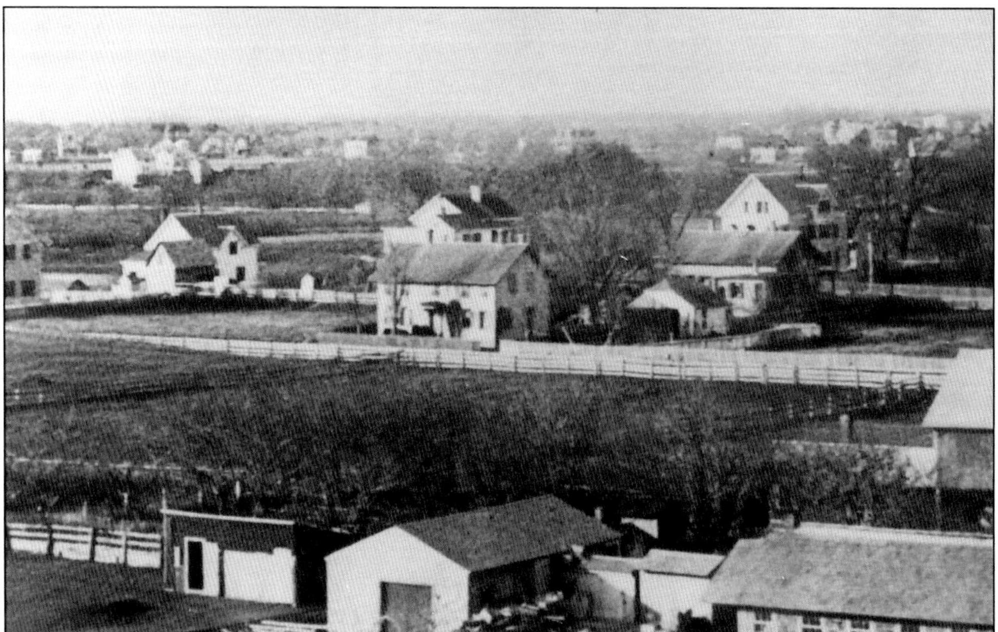

Fortunately a number of photographs taken from the roof of the Pawtuxet Baptist Church in 1889 have been preserved. This fenced-in road led to Rhodes-on-the-Pawtuxet. (William Hall Library Collection.)

William Wilson Little smiles happily in front of his Socony Gas Station in 1936. At that time, Little sold gas under the sign of Pegasus, the flying horse of Greek mythology. For a number of years, when his was the only garage in Pawtuxet, city ordinances forbade the selling of gas after sunset. (Henry A.L. Brown Collection.)

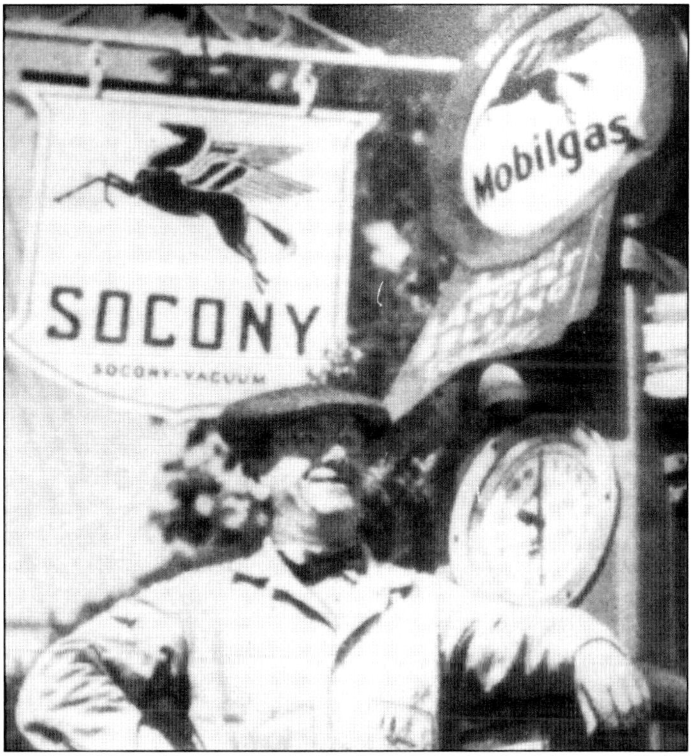

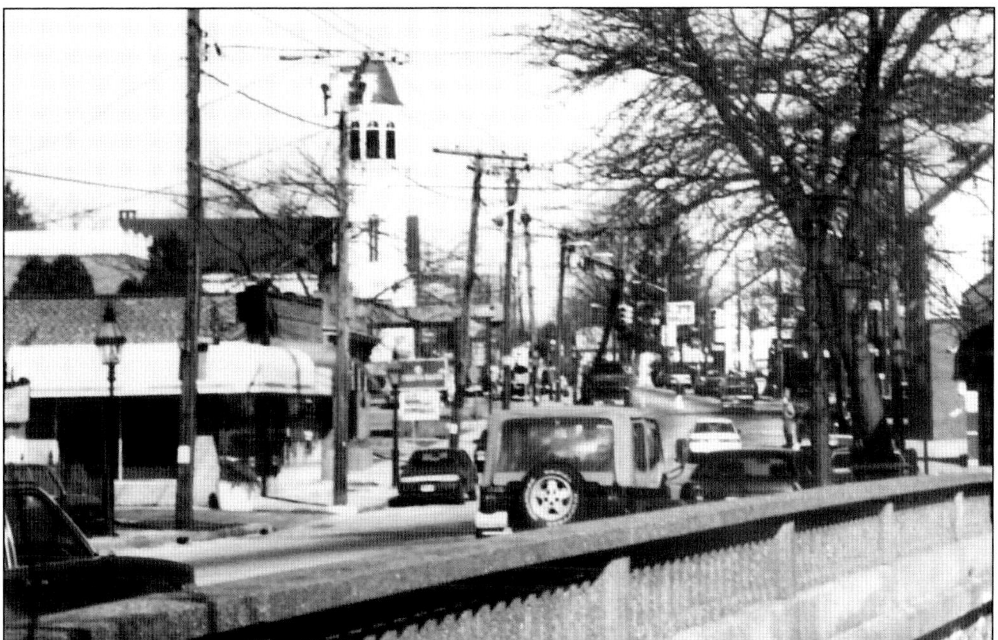

The number of automobiles has increased drastically since the time of World War Two. There are a number of gas stations in and around the village now to handle the never-ending demand. This late-twentieth-century view of Broad Street gives us some idea of how the automobile has replaced the horse and the trolley. (Don D'Amato Collection.)

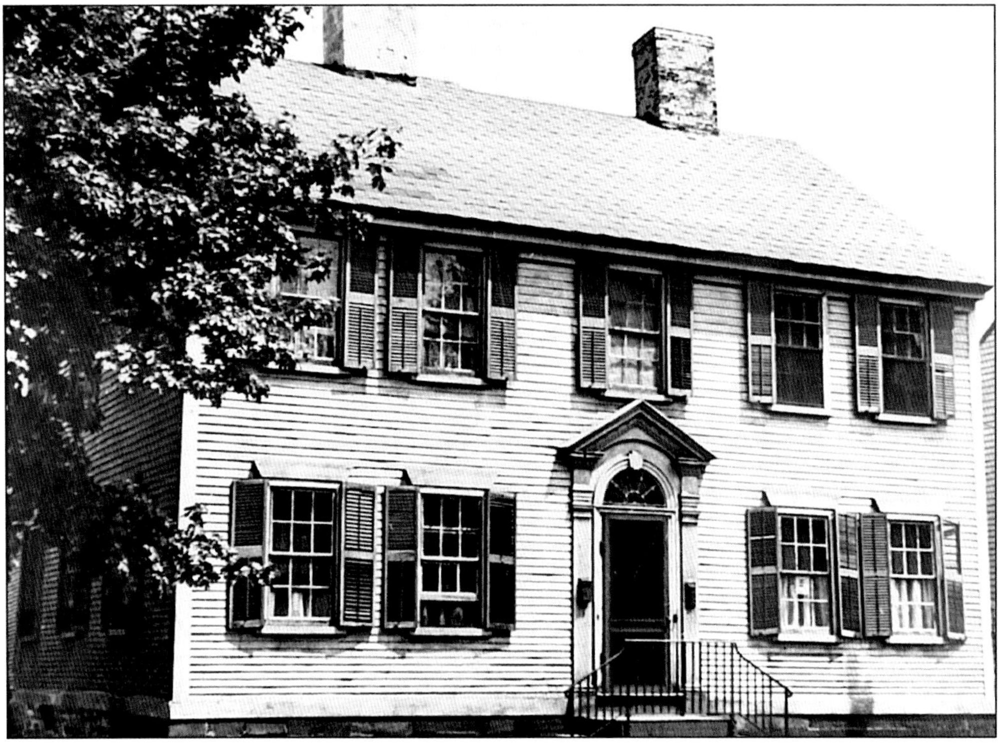

The Remington Smith house at 2150 Broad Street (shown here) was demolished between 1957 and 1961. The Pawtuxet Deli is on the site at the present time. (Cranston Historical Society Collection.)

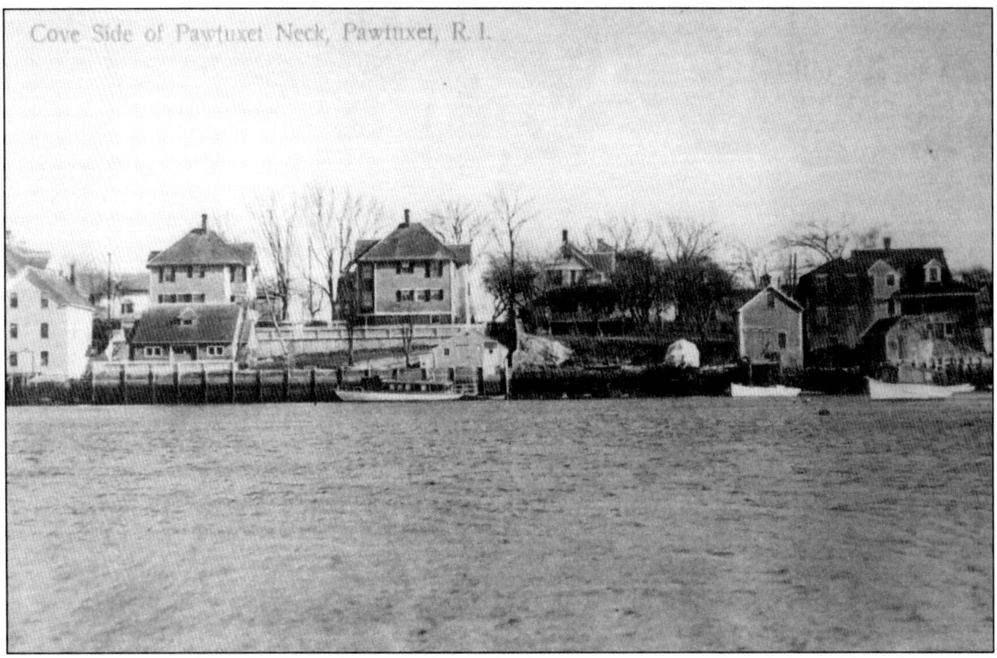

These stately and serene houses seemed to be guarding Pawtuxet Neck on the cove side in 1906. (Henry A. L Brown Collection.)

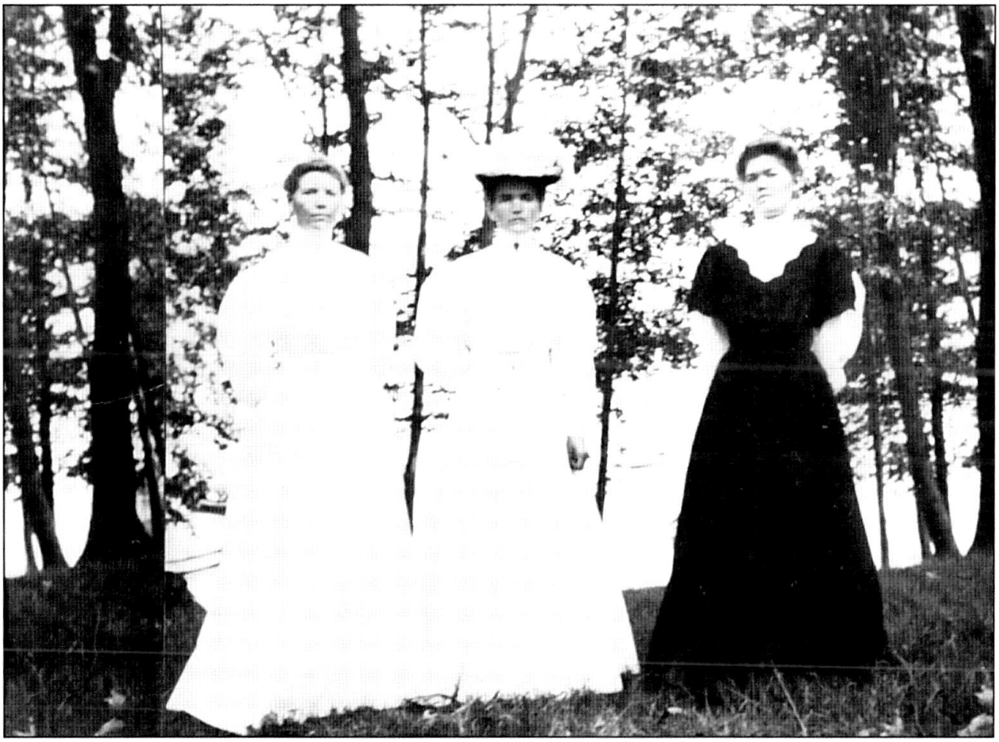

Three of the ladies of the Taft family enjoy a picnic at Spring Garden in 1906. The Tafts were among the most prominent families in Pawtuxet and Cranston at the turn of the century. The charming Taft house at Stillhouse Cove has been demolished. (Henry A.L. Brown Collection.)

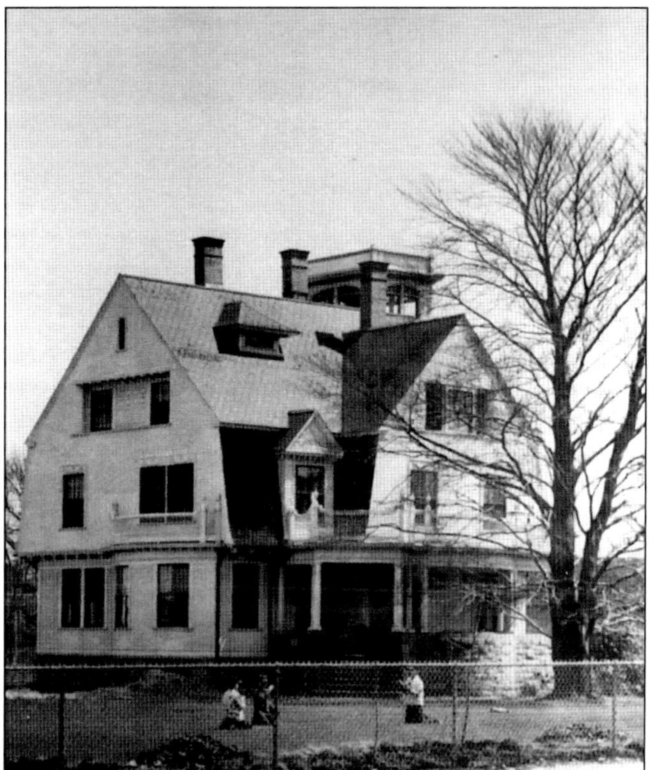

The Hulda F. Chase Smith house at 2124 Broad Street was occupied by Dr. Ben Van Housen in 1892. It still stands on the corner of Ocean and Broad Streets. (William Hall Library Collection.)

Acknowledgments

This history of Pawtuxet Village has only been possible because of the assistance and generosity of the many who have contributed their photographs and information. Henry and Don are very grateful for the help and support received from Robert Hunt Rhodes, Frank Pettis, Ray Peterson, Hazel Wade Kennedy, Richard Harnedy, Edward Lawrence, Don Cameron, Jack and Bill Lindsay, Madeline Toy, the William Hall Library, the Cranston Historical Society, the Pawtuxet Volunteer Fire Company #1, the Trinity Church, and the Warwick Historical Society. In addition, thanks to T.D. Brown Studios for developing the photographs and, of course, a very special thanks to Jean D'Amato for her editing, proofreading, patience, and persistence.

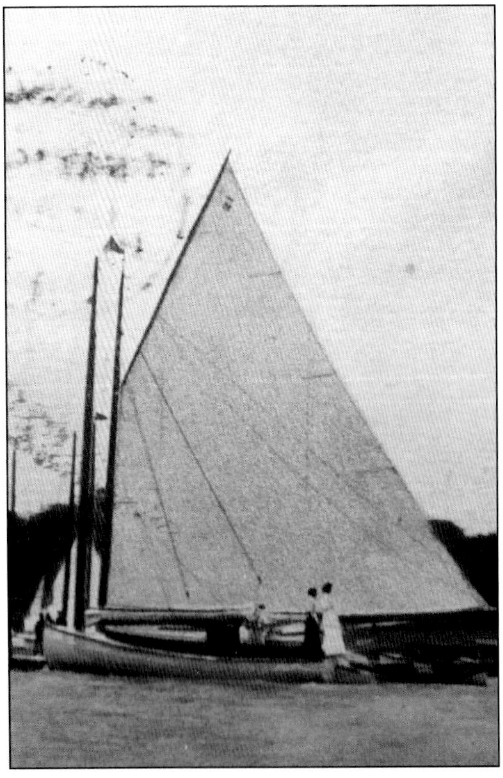

Ladies prepare to board a catboat at the Rhode Island Yacht Club on July 4, 1910. Catboats were very popular in Narragansett Bay in the early twentieth century. (Henry A.L. Brown Collection.)